INJURIOUS LAW

In the 1950s Britain joined the nuclear age, detonating 21 nuclear bomb experiments in Australia and the Pacific. In *Injurious Law,* Catherine Trundle crosses countries and traverses decades to explore the lingering, metamorphizing impacts of radiation exposure and militarism. Through a compelling portrait of the lives of test veterans seeking compensation and healthcare, Trundle reveals how injury law, and the political and medical processes upon which it depends, generates a troubling paradox for claimants. While offering the possibilities for recognition and redress, the very process of making injury claims generates new and cascading harms. Recasting injury to include its social, moral, and political aftereffects, Trundle exposes the quotidian and often banal practices that make the law injurious. Moving between archives, living rooms, laboratories, courts, parliament, and veteran social gatherings, *Injurious Law* offers a justice-centred lens for understanding legal contestations in the aftermath of radiation exposure and other invisible environmental harms.

Catherine Trundle is a senior lecturer in Health and Society at La Trobe University, Australia. She is a leading expert in health justice and ethics, and the co-editor of *Competing Responsibilities: The Ethics and Politics of Contemporary Life,* and *Detachment: Essays on the Limits of Relational Thinking.*

LAW IN CONTEXT

Since 1970, the Law in Context series has been at the forefront of a movement to broaden the study of law. The series is a vehicle for the publication of innovative monographs and texts that treat law and legal phenomena critically in their cultural, social, political, technological, environmental and economic contexts. A contextual approach involves treating legal subjects broadly, using materials from other humanities and social sciences, and from any other discipline that helps to explain the operation in practice of the particular legal field or legal phenomena under investigation. It is intended that this orientation is at once more stimulating and more revealing than the bare exposition of legal rules. The series includes original research monographs, coursebooks and textbooks that foreground contextual approaches and methods. The series includes and welcomes books on the study of law in all its contexts, including domestic legal systems, European and international law, transnational and global legal processes, and comparative law.

Books in the Series

Acosta: *The National versus the Foreigner in South America: 200 Years of Migration and Citizenship Law*
Alaattinoğlu: *Grievance Formation, Rights and Remedies*
Ali: *Modern Challenges to Islamic Law*
Alyagon Darr: *Plausible Crime Stories: The Legal History of Sexual Offences in Mandate Palestine*
Anderson, Schum & Twining: *Analysis of Evidence, 2nd Edition*
Ashworth: *Sentencing and Criminal Justice, 6th Edition*
Barton & Douglas: *Law and Parenthood*
Baxi, McCrudden & Paliwala: *Law's Ethical, Global and Theoretical Contexts: Essays in Honour of William Twining*
Beecher-Monas: *Evaluating Scientific Evidence: An Interdisciplinary Framework for Intellectual Due Process*
Bell: *French Legal Cultures*
Bercusson: *European Labour Law, 2nd Edition*
Birkinshaw: *European Public Law*
Birkinshaw: *Freedom of Information: The Law, the Practice and the Ideal, 4th Edition*
Blick: *Electrified Democracy: The Internet and the United Kingdom Parliament in History*
Broderick & Ferri: *International and European Disability Law and Policy: Text, Cases and Materials*
Brownsword & Goodwin: *Law and the Technologies of the Twenty-First Century: Text and Materials*
Cakal: *Law and Torture: Widening the Apertures, from the Doctrinal to the Critical*
Cane & Goudkamp: *Atiyah's Accidents, Compensation and the Law, 9th Edition*
Clarke: *Principles of Property Law*
Clarke & Kohler: *Property Law: Commentary and Materials*
Collins: *The Law of Contract, 4th Edition*
Collins, Ewing & McColgan: *Labour Law, 3rd Edition*
Corrias, *Law and Inhumanity: Dehumanization, Silent Claims and Atrocity Crimes*
Cowan: *Housing Law and Policy*
Cranston: *Making Commercial Law Through Practice 1830–1970*
Cranston: *Legal Foundations of the Welfare State*
Darian-Smith: *Laws and Societies in Global Contexts: Contemporary Approaches*
Dauvergne: *Making People Illegal: What Globalisation Means for Immigration and Law*
David: *Kinship, Law and Politics: An Anatomy of Belonging*
Davies: *Perspectives on Labour Law, 2nd Edition*
Dembour: *Who Believes in Human Rights?: Reflections on the European Convention*
de Sousa Santos: *Toward a New Legal Common Sense: Law, Globalization, and Emancipation*
Diduck: *Law's Families*

Douglas-Scott: *Brexit, Union, and Disunion: The Evolution of British Constitutional Unsettlement*

Dowdle: *Transnational Law: A Framework for Analysis*

Dupret: *Positive Law from the Muslim World: Jurisprudence, History, Practices*

Dutta: *A Jurisprudence of Conversations: Law, Life and Feminism in Post-colonial India*

Emon: *Jurisdictional Exceptionalisms: Islamic Law, International Law, and Parental Child Abduction*

Estella: *Legal Foundations of EU Economic Governance*

Fortin: *Children's Rights and the Developing Law, 3rd Edition*

Garnsey: *The Justice of Visual Art: Creative State-Building in Times of Political Transition*

Garton, Probert & Bean: *Moffat's Trusts Law: Text and Materials, 7th Edition*

Ghai & Woodman: *Practising Self-Government: A Comparative Study of Autonomous Regions*

Glover-Thomas: *Reconstructing Mental Health Law and Policy*

Gobert & Punch: *Rethinking Corporate Crime*

Goldman: *Globalisation and the Western Legal Tradition: Recurring Patterns of Law and Authority*

Goodrich, Kimmel & Meyler: *Performing Law: Actors, Affects, Spaces*

Graber: *The Technosystem of Free Speech: Enriching Fundamental Rights in a Digital Society*

Haack: *Evidence Matters: Science, Proof, and Truth in the Law*

Harlow & Rawlings: *Law and Administration, 4th Edition*

Harris: *An Introduction to Law, 8th Edition*

Harris, Campbell & Halson: *Remedies in Contract and Tort, 2nd Edition*

Harvey: *Seeking Asylum in the UK: Problems and Prospects*

Herring: *Law and the Relational Self*

Hervey & McHale: *European Union Health Law: Themes and Implications*

Hervey & McHale: *Health Law and the European Union*

Holder & Lee: *Environmental Protection, Law and Policy: Text and Materials, 2nd Edition*

Hommes: *The Convention and the Kingdom: How the Netherlands Received the European Convention on Human Rights*

Jackson & Summers: *The Internationalisation of Criminal Evidence: Beyond the Common Law and Civil Law Traditions*

Jeutner: *The Reasonable Person: A Legal Biography*

Kennedy: *Inducing Intimacy: Deception, Consent and the Law*

Kostakopoulou: *The Future Governance of Citizenship*

Kreiczer-Levy: *Destabilized Property: Property Law in the Sharing Economy*

Kubal: *Immigration and Refugee Law in Russia: Socio-Legal Perspectives*

Lewis: *Choice and the Legal Order: Rising above Politics*

Likosky: *Law, Infrastructure and Human Rights*

Likosky: *Transnational Legal Processes: Globalisation and Power Disparities*
Lixinski: *Legalized Identities: Cultural Heritage Law and the Shaping of Transitional Justice*
Loughnan: *Self, Others and the State: Relations of Criminal Responsibility*
Lunney: *A History of Australian Tort Law 1901–1945: England's Obedient Servant?*
Maughan & Webb: *Lawyering Skills and the Legal Process, 2nd Edition*
McGaughey: *Principles of Enterprise Law*
McGlynn: *Families and the European Union: Law, Politics and Pluralism*
Mertens: *A Philosophical Introduction to Human Rights*
Miller: *An Introduction to German Law and Legal Culture: Text and Materials*
Moffat: *Trusts Law: Text and Materials*
Monti: *EC Competition Law*
Morgan: *Contract Law Minimalism: A Formalist Restatement of Commercial Contract Law*
Morgan & Yeung: *An Introduction to Law and Regulation: Text and Materials*
Nash: *British Islam and English Law: A Classical Pluralist Perspective*
Ng: *Political Censorship in British Hong Kong: Freedom of Expression and the Law (1842–1997)*
Nicola & Davies: *EU Law Stories: Contextual and Critical Histories of European Jurisprudence*
Norrie: *Crime, Reason and History: A Critical Introduction to Criminal Law, 3rd Edition*
Norrie: *Rethinking Criminal Justice: Punishment, Abolition And Moral Psychology*
O'Dair: *Legal Ethics: Text and Materials*
Oliver: *Common Values and the Public–Private Divide*
Oliver & Drewry: *The Law and Parliament*
Palmer & Roberts: *Dispute Processes: ADR and the Primary Forms of Decision-Making, 1st Edition*
Palmer & Roberts: *Dispute Processes: ADR and the Primary Forms of Decision-Making, 3rd Edition*
Petersen: *Practices of Restitution: Law and Aesthetics in Modern Germany*
Picciotto: *International Business Taxation*
Pieraccini: *Regulating the Sea: A Socio-Legal Analysis of English Marine Protected Areas*
Probert: *The Changing Legal Regulation of Cohabitation, 1600–2010: From Fornicators to Family, 1600–2010*
Qiao: *The Authoritarian Commons: Neighborhood Democratization in Urban China*
Radi: *Rules and Practices of International Investment Law and Arbitration*
Reed: *Internet Law: Text and Materials*
Richardson: *Law, Process and Custody*
Roberts & Palmer: *Dispute Processes: ADR and the Primary Forms of Decision-Making, 2nd Edition*

Rowbottom: *Democracy Distorted: Wealth, Influence and Democratic Politics*
Sauter: *Public Services in EU Law*
Scott & Black: *Cranston's Consumers and the Law*
Seneviratne: *Ombudsmen: Public Services and Administrative Justice*
Seppänen: *Ideological Conflict and the Rule of Law in Contemporary China: Useful Paradoxes*
Siems: *Comparative Law,* 3rd *Edition*
Stapleton: *Product Liability*
Stewart: *Gender, Law and Justice in a Global Market*
Tamanaha: *Law as a Means to an End: Threat to the Rule of Law*
Taylor: *Fortin's Children's Rights and the Developing Law,* 4th *Edition*
Trundle: *Injurious Law: Nuclear Exposure and the Harms of Redress*
Tuori: *Properties of Law: Modern Law and After*
Turpin & Tomkins: *British Government and the Constitution: Text and Materials,* 7th *Edition*
Twining: *General Jurisprudence: Understanding Law from a Global Perspective*
Twining: *Globalisation and Legal Theory*
Twining: *Human Rights, Southern Voices: Francis Deng, Abdullahi An-Na'im, Yash Ghai and Upendra Baxi*
Twining: *Jurist in Context: A Memoir*
Twining: *Karl Llewellyn and the Realist Movement,* 2nd *Edition*
Twining: *Rethinking Evidence: Exploratory Essays,* 2nd *Edition*
Twining & Miers: *How to Do Things with Rules,* 5th *Edition*
Varney: *Disability, Human Rights and Contract Law*
Wan: *Film and Constitutional Controversy: Visualizing Hong Kong Identity in the Age of 'One Country, Two Systems'*
Ward: *A Critical Introduction to European Law,* 3rd *Edition*
Ward: *Law, Text, Terror*
Ward: *Shakespeare and Legal Imagination*
Watt: *The Making Sense of Politics, Media, and Law: Rhetorical Performance as Invention, Creation, Production*
Wells & Quick: *Lacey, Wells and Quick: Reconstructing Criminal Law: Text and Materials,* 4th *Edition*
Woodhead: *Caring for Cultural Heritage: An Integrated Approach to Legal and Ethical Initiatives in the United Kingdom*
Yeung and Ranchordás: *An Introduction to Law and Regulation: Text and Materials,* 2nd *edition*
Young: *Turpin and Tomkins' British Government and the Constitution: Text and Materials,* 8th *Edition*
Zander: *Cases and Materials on the English Legal System,* 10th *Edition*
Zander: *The Law-Making Process,* 6th *Edition*

International Journal of Law in Context: A Global Forum for Interdisciplinary Legal Studies

The *International Journal of Law in Context* is the companion journal to the Law in Context book series and provides a forum for interdisciplinary legal studies and offers intellectual space for ground-breaking critical research. It publishes contextual work about law and its relationship with other disciplines including but not limited to science, literature, humanities, philosophy, sociology, psychology, ethics, history and geography. More information about the journal and how to submit an article can be found at http://journals.cambridge.org/ijc

INJURIOUS LAW

Nuclear Exposure and the Harms of Redress

Catherine Trundle

La Trobe University

CAMBRIDGE
UNIVERSITY PRESS

CAMBRIDGE
UNIVERSITY PRESS

Shaftesbury Road, Cambridge CB2 8EA, United Kingdom

One Liberty Plaza, 20th Floor, New York, NY 10006, USA

477 Williamstown Road, Port Melbourne, VIC 3207, Australia

314–321, 3rd Floor, Plot 3, Splendor Forum, Jasola District Centre, New Delhi – 110025, India

Cambridge University Press is part of Cambridge University Press & Assessment, a department of the University of Cambridge.

We share the University's mission to contribute to society through the pursuit of education, learning and research at the highest international levels of excellence.

www.cambridge.org
Information on this title: www.cambridge.org/9781009721509

DOI: 10.1017/9781009721547

When citing this work, please include a reference to the DOI 10.1017/9781009721547

First published 2026

Cover image: 'Chain Reaction', Catherine Trundle.

A catalogue record for this publication is available from the British Library

A Cataloging-in-Publication data record for this book is available from the Library of Congress

ISBN 978-1-009-72150-9 Hardback

Contents

Acknowledgements

I owe a deep debt of gratitude to those who participated in this study, especially the veterans and their family members. Thank you for sharing so generously of your time, experiences, and memories; for welcoming me into your homes and talking with me for hours; for sending me follow-up documents in the post or calling to give me an update; and for including me in your daily work of claim-making. Thank you for your patience, insights, and good humour as you shared your lives.

The research for this study was generously supported by a Royal Society of New Zealand Fast Start Marsden Grant. I am grateful to have received this funding at such a pivotal stage upon returning to New Zealand after my doctoral studies in the UK. I am also thankful to my clever and deeply caring colleagues of over a decade at Te Herenga Waka Victoria University of Wellington, Brigitte Bönisch-Brednich, Jeff Sissons, Eli Elinoff, Grant Otsuki, Caroline Bennett, Lorena Gibson, Kevin Dew, and Elizabeth Stanley. And I am grateful to current colleagues at La Trobe for such collegial support, especially Robyn Dwyer, Caroline de Moel, Ruth MacKenzie-Stewart, Jodi Oakman, Megan Bugden, Rwth Stuckey, Deb Gleeson, Victoria Weale, Jess Gill, Susan Chong, Fernanda Nava Buenfil, Laura Petridis, Jo Marcucci, Sabrina Gupta, Melissa Graham, Sora Lee, Belinda Crockett, Timothy Jones, Elizabeth George, Péta Phelan, Matt Ruby, and Scott Alterator.

Thank you to the medicolegal reading and writing group run by Harris Solomon and Sarah Pinto for thoughtful and engaged feedback on Chapter 5. I also appreciate the encouragement and support I received for early stages of this work while on sabbatical at the University of Michigan from Elizabeth Roberts, Eric Plemons, Jessica

Robbins, and Sarah Besky. I am grateful for fruitful and insightful conversations at a range of academic fora from anthropologists of militarism, especially Zoë Wool, Ken MacLeish, Nomi Stone, and Sahil Can Açiksöz. Tarapuhi Vaeau also generously offered deep insights during an article writing collaboration on Māori test veterans. Thank you to long-term collaborators, Suzanna Trnka, Nayanika Mathur, and Joanna Cook, who each engaged in early chapter drafts, invited me to give talks, collaborated in conference organization, and supported my development as a scholar immensely, with much good food and good cheer along the way.

In New Zealand the medical anthropology community is an enormously supportive and critically engaged group, and I am grateful for the feedback I received in diverse fora from Nayan Shearon Appleton, Courtney Addison, Julie Park, Ruth Fitzgerald, Susan Wardell, and Sam Taylor-Alexander. To the medical anthropologists and science and technology scholars of Melbourne, thank you all for welcoming me into such a vibrant intellectual community, especially Emma Kowal, Tim Neale, Narelle Warren, Andrea Whittaker, Lenore Manderson, Jack Taylor, Natalie Araújo, Ana Éclair, and Lewis Johnstone, as well as Sonja Van Wichelen in Sydney.

Two close friends and collaborators also intervened at moments when I had all but abandoned the book, when the writing journey felt too circuitous, and when the pressures of Australasian academia for short and immediate outputs felt too strong a headwind. Tarryn Phillips and Rachel Douglas-Jones both insisted the project needed to come to fruition, and for their faith and good-natured cajoling, I am immensely grateful.

Thank you to Molly Turrell, Sumaira Khan, and Heidi Stabb, who supported proof reading at the end stages of the manuscript. Thank you to my poetry mentor, Claire Gaskin, for the precious lessons on life and writing. And thank you to Tobias Ginsberg, Gemma Smith, Matt Gallaway, and Suman Bhatt at Cambridge University Press for their careful work overseeing the book's review and production. The four anonymous reviewers also offered thoughtful and incisive feedback.

Thank you to my family for all the support and care. Book writing can require an intolerable amount of solitude and focus, and my family of writers, especially my mother and father, have always understood the collective patience required. Friends, too, gave much needed care and distraction, especially Jake Preval, Dharamjot Kaur Khalsa, Amy Faram, Sue Jessep, and Kate Yesberg.

To my son, Christian, thank you for patiently waiting during the pauses after you asked your questions when I was immersed in writing. And Volker Schlue, thank you for putting up with my furiously loud typing at unreasonable hours, for the cups of afternoon tea, East Frisian style, and for always, unfailingly encouraging me to finish this book.

Abbreviations

AMA	American Medical Association
AWE	Atomic Weapons Establishment (UK)
AWRE	Atomic Weapons Research Establishment (Predecessor to the AWE)
AWTSC	Atomic Weapons Tests Safety Committee (Australia)
BNTVA	British Nuclear Test Veterans Association
CO	Colonial Office (UK)
DNA	Deoxyribonucleic acid
ECtHR	European Court of Human Rights
FOI	Freedom of Information
GZ	Ground Zero
HMNZS	Her Majesty's New Zealand Ship (naval vessel)
HMS	Her Majesty's Ship (UK naval vessel)
ICRP	International Commission on Radiological Protection
LNT	The Linear No Threshold Dose Response
MoD	Ministry of Defence (UK)
MP	Member of Parliament
NRPB	National Radiological Protection Board (UK)
NZNTVA	New Zealand Nuclear Test Veterans' Association
PAT	Pension Appeals Tribunal (UK)
PRO	Public Records Office (Now The National Archives, UK)
QC	Queen's Counsel (Senior barrister in the British legal system under Queen Elizabeth II)
RAAF	Royal Australian Air Force
Rad	Radiation absorbed dose
RAF	Royal Air Force (UK)
RSA	Royal New Zealand Returned and Services' Association
TNA	The National Archives (UK)
VANZ	Veterans' Affairs New Zealand

Introduction

The Injurious Nature of Law

BETTY OFFERED TO LEND ME THE ALBUM OF BROWNING newspaper clippings. No, I insisted, I would simply photograph them. Throughout the interview the album sat on the coffee table atop a pile of radiation dose records and war disablement pension letters. She repeatedly picked up and set down the album, holding it gently with both hands. In this pile lay material evidence documenting the harms she believed her husband had suffered during the British nuclear bomb testing programme in the 1950s. That she was willing to entrust them to me revealed her deep determination to bring the British Ministry of Defence to account.

Betty was a small woman in her seventies with bushy silver hair. She had met me at the train station, leaning on her walking cane and waving with her free hand. Settled in her warm lounge, she chose her words with precision. Silences punctuated her account with increasing gravity as our conversation progressed. Her husband, Henry, always assured her that the safety protocols at the bomb tests had kept him safe. But Betty began to privately wonder about the effects of radiation exposure after she suffered from multiple miscarriages. Even when Henry developed cancer, she explained, he still believed that the Royal British Air Force had kept servicemen safe.

It was years after his death that Betty requested his radiation dose record and learned he had been exposed to dangerous levels of gamma radiation. Henry had flown in the compact bomber planes collecting radiation samples from the clouds of numerous nuclear detonations in Australia and the Central Pacific. He had not talked much about the top secret bomb tests in the subsequent decades. Only after Betty spoke with another member of Henry's plane crew did she learn of the risks to which her husband was exposed.

She recounted an eerie moment from her husband's service. After collecting samples inside an atomic detonation cloud, the men landed their plane in the usual way. Normally, the ground scientists would immediately surround the plane to collect the radiation sampling filters. But on this occasion the scientists had all 'run-away'. Multiple alarms were sounding in the hanger, indicating dangerous radiation levels emanating from the plane. While the scientists waited several hours before approaching the plane in protective gear, the flight crew immediately clambered out of the cockpit and down the side of the plane in their thin flight suits and made their way to the decontamination area.

Some weeks later, they received a letter from the Task Force Commander. Betty read it aloud to me in a slow, cool voice. 'I enclose a photograph of the atomic cloud through which you flew at Maralinga. It comes to you with the director's compliments and my congratulations on obtaining a record sample.'

Betty let silence hang between us then gravely shook her head. This was how it was, she explained. Experimental injuries were militarily repackaged into a record-breaking dose of pride, duty, and technoscientific achievement. So strong was this military ethos that, despite a blaring alarm and scurrying scientists, the invisible radionuclides released by nuclear fission remained imperceptible to the men most at risk of harm. Barely keeping her voice even, she declared the whole 'sorry history' as 'morally reprehensible and unforgivable'.

This book is a meditation on the *injurious law* with which claimants like Betty engaged. Over decades, test veterans and their families worked to achieve proof of radiation injuries, recognition of suffering, compensation, an apology, and access to healthcare. I use the term injurious law to denote a double edged and paradoxical experience. The chapters of this book chart how participants experienced the claim-making process as simultaneously hope-filled and harmful. Test veterans who became deeply engaged in the quest for redress experienced this work as offering meaning, purpose, and relational connection. At the same time, claim-making was deeply injurious to their bodies, minds, and social worlds, adding and exacerbating illnesses, hardships, and suffering.

This book thus attends to the enduring question Max Weber (2015 [1919]) posed a century ago. How does one manage the conflicting values embedded within contemporary politics, ethics, and law, and the imagined and unimaginable consequences of action that stem from engaging with them? When injury claim-making is simultaneously the pathway to redress injury and the cause of fresh injuries, then when, from whom, in what social arenas, and at what cost is redress possible?

In this book, I follow the work of law and legal reasoning in and out of courts, into the varied medical, political, and lay systems of knowledge that have the power to render injury visible. Epidemiology, genetics, legislation, collective memory, and the archive all offer possibilities for legal redress. As the following chapters reveal, efficacious engagements with law hinged upon claimants crafting persuasive accounts of nuclear exposure, radiation dose, genetic risk, debility, and illness latency. And all such modalities of proof are shadowed by militarism and its legal exceptionalities. Each chapter thus reflects an ethnographic effort to trace the wounds of war far beyond battlefields and kinetic fighting, into the pull of military preparedness and the long wake of military injury and recovery (Lutz 2002, Stone 2022).

SETTLING AND UNSETTLING THE FACTS OF INJURY

When remembering the British nuclear testing programme, certain events have settled into historical fact. Here are the surest of them: at the conclusion of World War II, Britain set about developing nuclear weapons. The first atomic bomb was detonated in the hull of a naval ship off the western coast of Australia, near the Monte Bello archipelago. It was codenamed Operation Hurricane, and the blast from the explosion tore a crater in the ocean floor 6 meters deep and over 300 meters wide (National Archives of Australia n.d.). From 1956 to 1963, testing shifted to the South Australian outback. At Emu Field and Maralinga, nine atomic bombs were detonated, most mounted on 100 feet towers or explored directly on the surface of the desert.

Then, between 1957 and 1958, trying to keep pace with US and USSR nuclear experiments, Britain developed the more powerful hydrogen bomb through atmospheric tests in the Pacific. They chose for their testing site the small atolls of Kiritimati (Christmas) and Malden Islands in the Republic of Kiribati, then a British colonial territory. Detonated at high altitude, thousands of troops witnessed the giant fireballs from the islands or from naval ships. In total, Britain detonated twelve bombs in Australia and nine in the Pacific, and carried out hundreds more 'minor trials' to test weapon components containing uranium and plutonium (Arnold and Smith 2006, see Appendix 1, Crawford 1989a, 1989b).

It took an immense amount of labour to build the infrastructure necessary to execute these experiments, with up to 22,000 British armed forces personnel and civilians, 551 New Zealand naval men, over 16,000 Australian armed forces personnel and civilians, and over 200 Fijian troops deployed to the testing sites to prepare the needed infrastructure, and execute and record the bomb tests.[1] Most worked on mundane and unspectacular infrastructural tasks essential to a military site but unrelated to the nuclear experiments, such as loading and unloading planes and barges, clearing and levelling land, maintaining the power generators, constructing the storehouses or the parish church, or crushing coral rock into aggregate for road building. Indigenous communities in both Australia and Kiribati were either 'removed' to make way for these experiments or 'relocated' to the testing sites to provide labour.[2]

This book explores nuclear test veterans' claim-making in the unsettled gaps between these historical facts. At the heart of injury claims are two questions, to which test veterans and the state give very different answers.

Were armed forces personnel exposed to dangerous radiation at the testing sites, which for many has manifested years later in radiation-related illnesses, suffering, and premature death? The British Ministry

[1] No exact records exist of numbers, and these are official estimates.

[2] For historical accounts of this nuclear testing programme, see Bowler (2022, 2025), Crawford (1989a, 1998b), Maclellan (2017), Michel (2003), Priestley (2013), Tynan (2016, 2022), and Wright (2007).

of Defence has always contended that its nuclear programme was conducted safely: except for a few known exceptions, the servicemen were exposed to negligible, harmless levels of radiation (MoD 2017). The government argued that the vast numbers of servicemen present at Maralinga and Kiritimati Island were required to build and maintain the site and execute the measurements and sampling tests required to gain knowledge of the bomb (see Moonie 2002, MoD 2012). State officials and politicians wielded documents containing gamma radiation records and military safety protocols, epidemiological studies, and the expert options of radiobiologists to support their claims (see Appendix 2).

Many nuclear test veterans, by contrast, remembered a less-ordered, much riskier military operation that bears little resemblance to its official archival record. They used their own genetic studies, supportive nuclear physicists, legal experts, embodied illness experiences, and archival documents to recount another history. They contend that, for much of the testing programme, the government demonstrated a negligent indifference to protecting the health of service personnel, despite knowledge of the potential biological harms of radiation. Many suspect even darker motivations: that the British government purposely exposed them to radiation, and that their health status and unfolding illnesses have secretly been of interest to the government for what they might scientifically reveal about the effects of radiation on human biology.

A second unsettled question: have governments done enough to care for nuclear test veterans as they have aged, developed illnesses, expressed concerns about their health and the health of their descendants, and sought support? This question speaks not only to rights instantiated in common law to safety, due process, and redress but also to norms of 'military citizenship' (Trundle 2012), to covenants between soldiers and the state, and the unique support services and entitlements military personnel expect to receive in recompense for the risks and sacrifices of service. In response to test veterans' claims, government representatives cite the numerous inquiries, government-sponsored health studies, government expert panels, medallic recognition, military disablement pension schemes, and meetings with test veteran groups over four decades to demonstrate their attentiveness towards the men and their concerns. Test veterans mobilize different narratives, documents, experiences, and evidence to offer an account of governmental neglect, denial, indifference, and even a concerted cover-up, all of which have caused them profound stress, suffering, and compounding illnesses.

Drawing upon archival documents, legal decisions, interviews, and participant observation, this book emerges at the confluence of three intellectual currents: socio-legal studies, the history of science and medicine, and the anthropology of nuclearity.[3] It focuses upon a recent period of test veteran claim-making, from the 1980s to the 2010s, when injury claims grew to a peak of activity in diverse legal arenas. By focusing on this unique period, I am able to spotlight those who pioneered injury claim-making, the emergent challenges test veterans faced, and their shifting tactics of response. The contributions veterans of historical nuclear tests can make to global debates about nuclear injuries and their ongoing impacts are significant. As the world grapples again with rising nuclear tensions, and emergent debates about 'clean' nuclear energy in a time of climate change, the stories presented in this book offer a cautionary tale about the injuries that permutate across time, within families, within militarism, within medicine, and within law.

INJURY AND INJURIOUS LAW

As the anthropologist Michael Jackson contends, well-being is not 'a settled state but ... a field of struggle' (2011: ix). Injuries too are sites of struggle, often over what biomedicine and law are capable of recognizing. As McCann and colleagues argue (2018: 2), 'the subtle, formative, interactive processes through which injuries are perceived, categorized, associated with particular cultural norms and practices, and – sometimes through the invocation of law – contested, resisted, or accepted by the injury victim and the broader public ... tend to produce, reproduce, and even magnify inequality and injustice in society'.

Test veterans are not alone in struggling to make tortious claims for environmental exposures, mirroring the challenges faced by other

[3] Gabrielle Hecht (2012) defines 'nuclearity' as the processes by which places, persons, and objects acquire the status of 'being nuclear', or indeed, fail to achieve such a status.

industrial and workplace claimants. These include those suffering from asbestosis and mesothelioma due to asbestos exposure (Felstiner and Dingwall 1988, Green 2017, Schuck 1992), lung cancer from diverse workplace chemical compounds (Steele and Wikeley 1997), coal workers' pneumoconiosis, or 'black lung' disease (Shriver and Bodenhamer 2018), cancers from Agent Orange dioxin exposure (Scott 1992), and leukaemia linked to toxic waste (Brown and Mikkelsen 1997). Like radiation exposure, such environmental exposures are complex to prove when the causative period or periods of exposure are unclear, when a lag exists between exposure, disease, and legal response, and when multiple possible actors across a working life might be blamed for negligence. Many environmental exposures, moreover, do not produce a 'signature disease'. These uncertainties particularly impact claims for cancers, which 'can be caused by several different agents, working synergistically, additionally or multiplicatively' (Green 2017: 29).

In this book, I treat injuries and their causes holistically, as reflecting the wounding and coactive effects of an array of harmful exposures, historical circumstances, technologies, environments, and political systems. For Saxton and Stuesse (2018: 70), worker injuries are best understood within 'injurious cultures' that 'layer in the bodies and communities of workers, interacting synergistically with or exacerbating other illnesses or health disparities, and evolving over the life course of the worker' (see also Saxton 2021). Manderson and Smith-Morris's concept of 'chronicity' (2010: 18) elucidates this life course approach. Attention to chronicity, they show, documents the shifting inequities of illness, and the ways in which injurious conditions become socially and politically permissible. 'Increasingly, chronic, long-term conditions are not naturally occurring ones, but are those for which the political will and economic resources are simply not brought to bear for a given community' (2010: 18).

Questions of injury require not only wider structural frames that account for social and political forces but also intimate and existential frames of analysis. Medico-legal conceptualizations of injury have foregrounded physical and to a lesser extent, psychological injuries (Saxton and Stuesse 2018). But what of injuries accrued to and through ethical domains of life? What of moral injury?[4] Considering the moral dimensions of injury acknowledges how well-being is tied to existential questions such as truth-seeking, to meaning making, and to a sense that one's life matters to others and has purpose.

The increasingly recognized diagnostic category of moral injury envisages certain event exposures that assault a person's core values and cause existential crisis and distress.[5] While the diagnostic category was pioneered within military medicine and healthcare, as MacLeish shows (2018, 2022), the diverse and often ambiguous ethical situations military personnel experience in service and its aftermath problematize any simple idea of ethical assault and moral wounding. In a similar vein, I reveal how the claim-making process generates ethical and existential conflicts that become bound up within injuries. Like Ralph (2014), I treat injuries and systems of redress and recovery as containing both ethical potency and peril. Out of injury emerge not only stuckness and ongoing harms but also forms of social critique, methods of hope, and the means to transform the future and attend to the wrongs of the past.[6]

In conceiving of injury across different scales of time, this book offers insights into what health scholars term the 'secondary' impacts of injury. Secondary health conditions, secondary mental injuries, secondary stress, secondary psychological injury, and secondary traumatic stress are medical categories denoting the emergence of biopsychosocial illnesses and debility that result from the impacts of a prior injury.[7] Also recognized in this sphere of research are 'secondary victims', whose health suffers from 'caregiver strain' and 'caregiver suffering'.[8] Increasingly, scholars recognize that compensation systems, medico-legal assessments, and

4 Contested but increasingly recognized, moral injury has been pioneered within military medicine, but is increasingly extended to a wider array of settings of moral injury. See Litz et al. (2009), Shay (2014), and Williamson et al. (2021).

5 See also Omri Elisha (2011) for a discussion of 'spiritual injury'.

6 For a different example of how injury is used to transform the future, one that focuses on confluence rather than conflict, see Tine Gammeltoft's (2008) study of prenatal testing in Vietnam, which reveals the affects and embodiment of the state within prenatal genetic screening and decisions that result from such tests.

7 See for example Cameron et al. (2006), Sareen et al. (2013), and Kendall-Tackett and Beck (2022).

8 See for example, Case (2004), Handsley (1995), and Whitlock et al. (2018).

claim-making practices themselves contribute to or cause significant and secondary impacts to both the injured and their families.[9]

Studies of secondary injury impacts reveal in a wide range of settings how negative experiences with injury claim-making systems result in significantly elevated rates of stress, anxiety, emotional instability, depression, long-term disability, reduced social functioning, extended injury recovery time, trauma, and financial precarity.[10] Such studies lend empirical weight to the underlying principle of a therapeutic jurisprudence approach, which recognizes that law itself and its adversarial practices have the capacity to cause and exacerbate biopsychosocial harm.[11] Equally, they offer grist to feminist critiques of tort law which argue that the implicit and dominant cultural norms of injury law fundamentally fail to reflect or enact relational ideas of care and responsibility for injury victims and their carers (Handsley 1995).[12]

In contrast to the medical language of primary and secondary illness, in this book I offer a participant-centred and experience-near account. I trace the connections test veterans themselves draw across time and within their personal and community illness narratives, as they built understandings of radiation injury and harm. Original injury or

9 See for example Kirsh and McKee (2003), Orchard et al. (2020), Lippel (2007), and O'Donnell et al. (2015).

10 See for example Barr et al. (2016), Collie et al. (2021), Grant and Parker (2020), Kim (2013), Sareen et al. (2013), Ureta et al. (2020), and Wall et al. (2008).

11 See for example Wexler (2008, 2020), Wexler and Winick (2008), Ison (1986), and Stobb (2020).

12 We understand far less about why and how such experiences of engaging with medico-legal systems lead to such negative impacts on well-being. To what are claimants exposed, repeatedly, that leads to such harm? Some studies offer psychological answers that limit explanation to the internal and individual claimant's psyche, showing, for example, how internalized stigma and a sense of powerlessness contribute to secondary mental injuries (Lippel 2007) or how perceptions of procedural unfairness and procedural injustice (Orchard et al. 2020) lead to mental illness. Other studies take a more systemic viewpoint. For example, MacEachen and colleagues (2010) describe the health impact of a '"toxic dose" of system problems' on injured workers. Focusing on how work institutions engaged with claims, they chart how workplace policies and dysfunctional workplace practices failed to address conflict, power imbalances, and communication in adequate ways, causing stress and lengthening the negative impacts of workers injuries. Yet explanations that centre on organizational cultural and procedures – the meso level – fail to address how wider economic and political structures also make an impact.

exposure 'events' were narratively enfolded within the cascade of transforming and accumulating harms that participants experienced. For test veterans, many of the same bureaucratic systems, military logics, and medico-legal norms that enabled radiation harm in the past endured to refuse them care in the present. And these same forces refused to proactively address their risks of future and intergenerational illness.

Attention to the widest temporal dimensions of 'historical injury', Castillejo-Cuellar argues, reveals an 'accumulative phenomenon ... a kind of existential palimpsest in which layers of collective suffering entwine' (2013: 19). Injuries from nuclear exposure stretch history and time in ways that demand an intergenerational ethic of risk and responsibility (Kinsella 2020). Radiation exposure may endure within both genes and environments, revealing the 'temporal inadequacy' (Adam 1998: 193) in current approaches to injury, and our ongoing struggles to reckon with radiation, be it conceptually, legally, politically, environmentally, and in the intimacies of the everyday.

Centrally, the concept of *injurious law* explored throughout this book captures claimants' experiences of the double binds and irreconcilable impacts of injury claim-making. The medico-legal avenues that claimants learned to navigate in the wake of nuclear exposure were powerful pathways for uncovering nuclear harm and pursuing health justice. At the same time, these very avenues compounded claimants' sense of injury and created fresh harms to well-being. This approach centres the 'incongruent obligations' (Fortun 2001: 54) that claimants of environmental exposure must navigate. Indeed, managing the paradox of harm within redress was, I show, central to the labour of injury claim-making.

The book thus seeks to understand how claimants approached pursuing justice over decades when the doggedness required to make such claims strained their health and intimate family relationships and generated a powerful sense of exacerbated injury. And it asks *why* medico-legal injury claims can take such a harmful toll on claimants, yet still hold their hopes, desires, and attention, and offer them meaning and purpose. What structural conditions exist in the claim-making process – be they political, epistemic, or social – that compound the injuries for which law promises to offer fair redress? Such an approach aims to avoid what Bagelman and Wiebe describe as the 'axiomatic neatness' that too often underpins narratives of environmental injustice and harm, which discount contradiction and tend towards 'narrow narratives of victimhood' (2017: 78, see also Laidlaw 2023).

Scholars have critically theorized the double binds of injury and response in a range of ways. Lauren Berlant (2011), for example, offers the notion of *cruel optimism* to describe the condition of desiring something that becomes an impediment to flourishing and to attaining the thing desired. Such a concept shows how quests for redress can constitute an absence of redress into their core, trapping claimants in a harmful bind of desire and denial. In a similar vein, Wendy Brown proposes the notion of *wounded attachments*, a contemporary political subjectivity that forecloses its own freedom by crafting identity out of woundedness and exclusion, diminishing the possibilities for power and action. From this vantage point, a claim-based identity can become 'invested in its own subjection' (1993: 403).

Rather than theorize the paradoxes of law in ways that ultimately reduce them to harmful foreclosures – to the loss of agency and justice – I opt here for a more granular analytic undertaking. This means taking participants' ongoing, varied engagement with claim-making in good faith, remaining curious as to why they have stuck with the law for so long despite its harms. This entails paying less attention to the question of winning or losing as judged through law, and attending more to the multiple and often contradictory outcomes test veterans experience from engaging with claims. This allows claimants room to be complex and contradictory beings themselves. It allows us to pay attention to their shifting attachments to the law over time, as they move between diverse tactics, be it silence and seeming passivity, retreating and resignation, and rising once more to fight (cf. Billias et al. 2023).

INJURIOUS ADVERSARIES

This book attends to test veterans' own understandings of their adversary: the state. But what is 'the state' and how does one study it ethnographically? Recent scholarship critiques Weberian portraits of the state that reify a rationalist and monolithic system within which ideologies and motivations cohere. Rather, scholars show, the state is produced in diverse sites, institutions, and actions in ways that reveal a myriad of competing objectives, ethics, and values. Recent studies thus centre, as Didier Fassin (2015: 4) describes, the diverse 'persons who constitute the state and … the historical reasons that account for its development'. Such studies challenge visions of the state and its systems of law as a 'cold monster' of rationality and instead reveal the range of affects, ethics, motivations, and pressures that coexist and emerge within state and legal arenas (e.g. Bear 2007, Mathur 2016, Navaro-Yashin 2007).

But how should the ethnographer respond when her interlocutors insist that the state is a cold monster, when they frame encounters with the state as governed by cruel indifference, when their claims for redress come to depend at their very core on such a portrayal? Rather than problematizing the coldly monstrous state, I have opted to make it an object of ethnographic attention. What exactly makes the state coalesce into a cold and monstrous entity in the eyes of claimants, and what diverse actions, ethical stances, and attitudes do they regard as especially monstrous? Rather than shun such portrayals, we learn much by focusing our attention on the everyday encounters that lie behind them. And we are only able to understand such portrayals if we take seriously the emotional charge that builds within participants' engagements with the state and accusations of state monstrosity.[13] This approach reveals the range of ways that state harm manifested in law, and as participants understood, these harmful legalities were not always cold, and not beholden to a single version of rationality.

If my use of a monstrous metaphor appears hyperbolic, then consider the assertions of Shirley in 2018. A test veteran's widow, Shirley discovered an archival document detailing the instruments that scientists positioned in the cockpit of the plane her late husband flew through a mushroom cloud on Kiritimati Island. Film badges to measure radiation exposure were affixed purposefully only inches from her husband's head, arms, and testicles, and recorded radiation doses far in excess of safe limits. 'It's absolutely wicked. It's evil', she responded publicly. 'It makes me furious to think it was done on purpose, that my Eric mattered

[13] Anthropologist and ethnographer Sarah Horton describes such an approach as a form of 'moral engagement from empathic listening' (2016: 186).

so little to them.' Such unequivocal condemnation was commonplace. I heard many references from participants to the evil and wicked nature of the state. Rather than invoking the logic of detached rationality, they understood the state as suffuse with moral obligations, as ideally capable of care, but so often capable of moral failure. Injury claims in the wake of radiation exposure do not simply produce a condemnatory rhetoric. They bind claimants to the state through desired notions of citizenship and state responsibility (Petryna 2002).

To foreground the monstrous state inevitably ignored its complexity. I do not attempt to demystify or interrogate every description participants make of 'the powers that be'. Rather, the question I return to is this: what actions and utterances made test veterans perceive the state as a source of harm? What chains of events and lines of reasoning led them there? What did the state look and feel like to them in legal settings? And, in understanding this, what might test veterans teach us about the injurious paradoxes of redress that animate historical injury claims?

MAKING, FORSAKING, AND REMAKING RELATIONS

Ethnographic labour is as unpredictable as it is rewarding. Throughout, the researcher necessarily remains open to shifting questions, possibilities, and focus. Ethnography requires a commitment to understanding people 'on their own terms and in their own words' (Trundle et al. 2024: 2), and according to their own priorities. It seeks to contextualize people's lives within the wider social and cultural worlds that shape them and which they in turn shape. Ethnography requires relationality, a 'dwelling with' people on their own turf and through their own systems of meaning. It is, moreover, a mode of paying attention and writing descriptively that evokes those worlds and the particular people in them, as vividly and as humanely as possible (Wardell 2025). To study legal practices through an ethnographic lens is to understand how law plays out from the 'ground up', in everyday decisions, in embodied experience, in the mundane challenges of sustaining a life, and in the dynamic human agency of ordinary moments.

This research began in New Zealand in 2009, in the living rooms of men in their seventies and eighties, who wanted to tell me in great detail about their lives, their service, their bodily decline, their decades of fighting 'the system', and their fears for the future. These men directed me towards London, to law courts and meetings with solicitors and scientists, and then to days pouring over photos and maps and radiation graphs in national archives. This led me to the homes of retired men and widows across the UK, and to pubs and cafes where these test veterans gathered. I followed along in both New Zealand and the UK as they hunted out information about the causes of their ill-health, accompanying them to conferences on low-level radiation and to test veteran meetings. I spent hours with them in their home offices or garages sifting through their voluminous personal archives of once-classified military telegrams from the 1950s, denied pension claims, letters from ministers, and faded medical and military records.

Thirty-six months of longitudinal ethnographic fieldwork spanned three time phases: between 2009 and 2014, then between 2016 and 2018, and again in 2021. I conducted seventy-eight formal, audio-recorded interviews and hundreds of informal interviews and follow-up conversations jotted down on notepads with test veterans and their families, medical researchers, legal professionals, archival experts, and nuclear activists. Formal interviews were minimally structured and participant-led, lasting between one and three hours. I interviewed 10 per cent of all New Zealand test veterans. I conducted participant observation in over fifty social gatherings and events, conducted court room observations over seven days, and collected and analysed over 3,000 pages of archival documents, case law, parliamentary debates, legislation, and governmental reports produced between 1950 and 2023. Test veterans often send me letters with newspaper clippings, photocopied archival documents, and handwritten recollections of service over months and sometimes years.

I travelled the length of the North and South Islands of New Zealand to speak with interlocutors.[14] Soon after I began, I realized I could not tell

[14] I have used pseudonyms throughout this book, except in one instance when I was given both written and recorded oral consent to reveal the participants identity, and in three instances when I quoted participants from the public record and where I have known explicitly that participants had robust control over the public accounts and representation of their words, for example, in autobiography, or in media interviews

the New Zealand story without understanding something of the British veterans who were their friends, collaborators, and fellow claimants, and I took five trips to the UK for fieldwork. I soon realized that the stories and experiences I found in the UK did not always lead me back to New Zealand, but were interesting in their own right. One year in, I let go of my urge to hold the fieldsite together as a connected whole, and started to look not only for links but also disconnections and contrasts between the two countries, and to think about how their shared and divergent histories, governmental approaches, and veteran support systems generated diverse approaches to redress.

I considered, for completeness, extending the field to test veterans from Australia and Fiji.[15] But the data I had generated, the relationships that I formed in the first two years, the ties I worked to sustain with interlocutors, the intensity of working with sick, sometimes dying men and their families, felt deeply occupying. Widening the field would have meant narrowing, neglecting it in other places. Ultimately the field makes demands on us, as much as we make demands upon our fieldsites. *People* make claims on us. In the end I was answerable to these claims and accepted the richness that I had been graciously offered, as well its inevitable flipside, a reoccurring sense of incompleteness.

My fieldsite not only tacked across geographic boundaries but also sought to interrogate and connect diverse modes of knowledge. Test veterans' claims relied upon legal, genetic, epidemiological, bureaucratic, and embodied ways of knowing. Like my participants, engaging claims required developing a flexible and wide expertise. I have thus

with journalists they deeply trusted. In some instances, where aspects of participant stories may be known publicly, I have also assigned different pseudonyms to different parts of an interview to help prevent identification for sensitive stories. In some places, I have left out or slightly altered identifying features of their lives that do not affect the fidelity of accounts of claim-making.

15 I was most concerned that such decisions excluded Indigenous perspectives. Consequently, I worked with a Māori collaborator to consider a Māori test veterans' claim before the Waitangi Tribunal (Bryers-Brown and Trundle 2017), and in interviews and the analysis of documentary data I dedicated time to exploring the test architects' engagements with Indigenous peoples at and around the testing sites. For important work that focuses specifically on Indigenous experiences of injury and claim-making, see Alexis-Martin (2021), Maclellan (2017), Mathis (2024), Mattingley (2016) and Urwin (2025).

dwelt within diverse bodies of knowledge, learning to see the gaps and assumptions that claim-making produces, and regularly having to prove to others that I could intellectually manoeuvre within relevant debates.

This was thus a project in which I followed the flow of information, relationships, and claims that I encountered over a decade in order to understand the painstaking work required of test veterans seeking redress. I also sometimes moved against the current of these flows, strategically widening the scope of the research to new actors and settings when I had a hunch that the questions I was asking and the answers I was receiving had reached some kind of epistemic limit. I attempted to understand 'both sides' of the dispute, to compare the proof-making processes of claimants as well as their perceived adversaries. I spoke with government ministers, Defence Force historians, and sceptical scientists. This was illuminating, in part because in the first years I felt blocked by the legal sensitivities of a *sub judice* case, as well as the potential for further legal action. For many government officials, speaking with me – with my suspect sympathies for claimants – was a risky endeavour.

Trying to tunnel into the intricacies of this dispute, I felt the immediate tug to pick a side, or be assigned one by others. Building trust and the rich social relationships that are fundamental to ethnographic research positions the researcher in ways that are both essential and complex when examining acrimonious disputes. Building visible ties with certain actors negates easy access to others. This has resulted in a book centred on the question of what it means to seek redress 'against' the state and its institutions. Yet this was not simply a result of methodological fate. I found the test veterans' claims, struggles, and experiences compelling, and I chose to dwell on their side of the ledger.

Despite this, my methodology at times marked me as an outsider of both groups. By the standards of some scientists, government officials, and military figures I demonstrated a reckless intimacy with the test veterans' social world, too interested in collecting 'unreliable data' about their narratives and emotions, too far from the objective principles of scientific inquiry when I bought rounds of beer with veterans at a military club or sat drinking cups of tea with them in the Supreme Court tearooms. I refused to separate data from the process of gathering it, or the relations I studied from the relations I became imbricated within, what Hastrup called 'living our part' in the social worlds we study (2004: 465).

But to test veterans I was also sometimes untrustworthy. I took far too long to write, betraying the temporal urgency of their bodily decline, and their desire for a final act of redress and recognition. I went off periodically to ask the views of governmental people who they deemed untrustworthy and corrupt, who they had subtly told me to avoid. They oscillated between two poles. They sometimes wanted me to keep my distance to ensure that my 'expert' findings could convey a detached scientific 'objectivity' and thus be politically and legally efficacious. At other times, they needed me to assert my loyalty, to not be yet another person to add to their long list of those who had talked sympathetically, then let them down. These tensions helped me see the ethical and the political dimensions of scientific, biomedical, legal, archival, embodied, and everyday knowledge-making practices, of which I was a part.

Test veterans felt that every study ever produced about them – their bodies, their suffering, and their histories – has been an opportunity to end the conversation as to what happened and what forms of redress must ensue. This was a hope that I felt destined to betray, with my conception of truth-making that infolded objects into their processes of objectification. I could thus never produce the object that I sought to unpack. It is also no small irony that it took me over a decade to conduct my research and produce my book, which meant I was slower than the most glacial governmental report or the indifferent bureaucratic processes that both test veterans and I critique in this book. This experience made me acutely aware that ethnographers are in ways no less implicated in the promise-making, the disappointments, and the movement of time animating participants' lives than other agents of the medico-legal process.

With the bulk of the fieldwork completed by 2018, I then returned to the project in 2021 but more intermittently and with less intensity, following up with participants, following medical and political developments, and dwelling in the voluminous piles of documents I had not managed to yet touch. Time is a valuable currency for the ethnographer, setting us apart from other more expedient and less relational research methodologies. Ethnographers often report with vagueness their actual fieldwork time within the long durée of their projects (Trundle and Phillips 2023). But the gaps 'away' from the field are worth accounting for, not just for the sake of honesty and specificity but also for what they tell us about the work of being an ethnographer, the work of enacting our commitments, and sense of failed commitments, to communities over time (Günel et al. 2020).

Sometimes, fieldwork mirrors life in ways that are too painfully raw to anticipate or respond to ethnographically. In 2014, I adopted a newborn through the foster system. I occupied myself with caring for him, understanding his emergent disabilities, and found myself simultaneously confronted by the slow, unending complexity of the state fostercare system and biomedical practices of disability diagnosis. Then, in 2018, my husband developed leukaemia, and after a year of hospital care, he died. After years of engaging closely with my interlocutors' accounts of the joys, challenges, and worries of caring for disabled kin, stories about diagnoses of blood cancers, stories of grief and loss, stories of bureaucratic refusal, I found myself capable only of attending to the immediacy of such themes in my own life. I withdrew from the field, focused my strength on meeting the care needs before me, and two years later, returned gently to my research. I tell this as a way to encourage ethnographers to demystify the disjointed temporality of research, and to caution against the heroic ideal of uninterrupted social intimacy that guides the important turn towards collaborative methods (Yates-Doerr 2020). For a method that prides itself on reflexive writing styles that disclose the researchers' situatedness within the field, ethnographers are often silent about the ways we exit research, leave and re-engage the field, and the effects this has on us, our participants, our data, and our ideas.

The transforming contours of my engagements with the field, the emerging intimacies and distances that resulted, disrupted some relations but also offered a longer view, and new points of personal commonality and connection with participants. Despite and because of this, I remain optimistic that this book witnesses the injurious impacts of medico-legal systems upon participants, and reveals their tenacious commitments to the paradoxes of injury claim-making. I have attempted, as Hastrup phrases it, to 'get it right' by 'being *in touch* with reality – not by standing outside it looking for evidence' (2004: 469 emphasis in original). A significant portion of the participants I engaged with for this research have now died. This book is an attempt at ongoing witness in the wake of this community's loss, a small act of reciprocity and gratitude for the conversations we had that I cannot ever fully repay.

A WAY THROUGH LIVES

Across its chapters, *Injurious Law* explores nuclear test veterans' experiences of traversing medical, legal, and political institutions in their quest for health justice. Chapter 1 attends to the historical context of British bomb testing through an exploration of contrasting accounts of nuclear risk. It juxtaposes archival and official narratives of military risk management with test veterans' own memories of hazardous events. This reveals the jarring mismatch that test veterans experienced when encountering official records detailing moments their younger selves experienced first-hand. I explore how radiation measurement technologies, material infrastructures, and a military culture of hierarchical trust negated the perception of risk, yet still left room for servicemen to experience doubt and fear. This chapter also places the harms to service personnel in the wider colonial context of racialized hierarchies and the theft of lands, revealing how stories of Indigenous injury became uncertain undercurrents within test veterans' own narratives.

Chapter 2 turns to the second betrayal. This chapter scales down into the personal accounts of test veterans' post-service lives, when emergent illnesses eluded explanation and social recognition, and many felt private shame and debility stalled their lives. I show how unsettled memories and unsettled illnesses coalesced with the slow-moving invisibility of radiation in ways that negatively impacted their families and their well-being. Claim-making thus began as prefigurative struggles driven by delegitimating encounters with medical actors, and the accumulating acts of sharing service memories in veteran spaces. This chapter charts how in these practices test veterans and their family members first became claim-makers, a collectivity that produced the possibilities for political and legal action.

Chapter 3 asks what is counted and who comes to count in the enactment of epidemiological knowledge. It explores the presence and absence of injury in statistics, blood, chromosomes, memory, and radiation records, and asks how those exposed to toxic environmental harm experience and evaluate epidemiological accounts of their health. The chapter also examines how scientists who use epidemiological reasoning in toxic exposure studies understand and enact the ethics of their practice. It charts how test veterans grappled with the troubling evidentiary burdens of exposure upon which claim-making depends. In attempting to contest accounts of 'safe' radiation exposure embedded within government records, test veterans condemned some epidemiological studies and praised others. 'Good' numbers, emergent if they were temporally responsive, appropriately connected and detached from study subjects, separable from the state's influence, epistemically humble, future focused, and contextualized within the practices of their production. 'Bad' numbers, by contrast, were those that perpetuated and exacerbated the injuries they denied.

Chapter 4 centres on the restitutive and injurious properties of documentary practices. Test veterans sought out state documents in order to locate evidence of radiation exposure and its evidentiary omission. I track three legal disputes originating in the UK before the Pension Appeals Tribunal, the British Information Commissioner, and the European Court of Human Rights, in which test veterans sought to hold the state to account for failing to document injury and risk. Despite a lack of success in securing redress, and a sense of compounding harm and injury endured across these claims, their claims nonetheless produced paper trails of the state's moral failure and its lack of restitutive care. These legal disputes moreover, brought to light the existence and contours of a secretive archive, clarified democratic avenues for accessing documents held within the state's grip, and legally asserted the positive duties of the state to ensure the right of claimants to access health records.

Chapter 5 dwells on the legal reasoning that governed New Zealand military disablement pensions. It charts how test veterans experienced law as an arbitrary logic, one that remained simultaneously open and closed to them. Law, many felt, was a force capable of dividing their community according to the vicissitudes of luck. This chapter also engages with the labour of pension Appeal Board members who tried to fit veteran accounts of injury within legislative notions of reasonable evidence and plausible causation. Sitting face-to-face in Appeal Board meetings, veterans and those adjudicating their claims attempted to embody the state's legal and moral responsibilities to offer benevolent and exceptional military entitlements to veterans. Test veterans reveal how thresholds of proof and exposure become negotiable and unstable objects of law and medicine that shift dynamically throughout the proof-making process. As this chapter shows, flexible proof-making systems that aim to overcome unfair evidentiary burdens of exposure can, for claimants, ultimately reinscribe a sense of injustice and harm due to their seemingly arbitrary, opaque, and inconsistent judgements.

Turning from low-tier legal settings to the highest courts of law, Chapter 6 traverses a test veteran group action against the British Ministry of Defence. The chapter moves through the High Court of England and Wales, the Court of Appeal, to a final ruling in the UK Supreme Court. I focus on how the law constructs knowledge in relation to injury and time. According to the legal principle of limitation, test veterans needed to offer the courts life histories proving ignorance of nuclear risk. The MoD's legal counsel argued that an individual's obligations to anticipate and understand injury were unrelated to the pragmatic enactment of such knowledge. Test veterans sat in witness stands and recontextualized their knowledge of injury in ways that animated state, medical, and legal actors as powerfully capable of stymying veterans' thoughts, actions, and opportunities to understand nuclear risk. This chapter explores how injury law led claimants to experience a series of unjust legal reversals and ironies. First, the actions and duties of claimants, rather than those accused of injuring them, became the primary subject of moral and legal judgement. Second, claimants' long-running quests for knowledge and answers about their health became the very legal rationale to deny them justice. And third, such legal processes imposed strict time limits on claimants' actions. At the same time, however, claimants waited decades for justice and appeals stretched over years, failing to attend to the urgent needs of sick, older claimants, and oft-times even outliving them.

To conclude, I turn to Tessa, a widow, and her uneasy reflections on the claim-making process. Recognizing the double-edged nature of seeking justice, its enlivening and injurious potential, she asks that we take seriously the enduring challenges of injury claims, that we continue to interrogate how and why contemporary institutions turn justice making into pathways for ongoing harm.

CHAPTER 1

Reconstructing Risk

PETER WAS NINETEEN YEARS OLD WHEN HE VOLUNTEERED TO serve in the British Royal Air Force at Maralinga. I interviewed him in his late seventies. To begin, he wanted me to really picture the place.

> There's a village in Maralinga, about 20 miles from where the test site was. You know, aluminium buildings in the sun, looking like a diamond if you look from the air, all sparkling in the desert. Man-made marvel, atomic town. Everyone in the paper saying, they've built this town up there, everything is great. It was built only 20 miles away from where they were dropping the bombs, and of course with all the dust storms you were getting in that area.
>
> We used to get up in the morning in Maralinga, we were in these tin huts, and everything would be coated in dust! There'd been a dust storm. And everything in the tin hut you were in, everything was covered in dust. And I mean, the fission of material from the tests was all about us. But then, they say, 'there's no way, there's no hazard from dust storms at Maralinga'. They tried to play all that down.[1]

A year later I met up with Joseph, a British veteran in his eighties. Before the interview began he asked me if I had seen 'that document', about not taking blood tests. By the time I interviewed him, other

[1] Dust has a particularly invasive elemental quality when irradiated, as well as a liminal, dangerous perceived quality. Like sand, it 'complicates attempts to define it as hard or soft, rough or sticky, granular or wavelike' and, in its capacity to get inside of buildings, clothes, and bodies, it troubles the boundaries between inside and outside (Engelmann 2022: 159).

veterans had shown me this document many times. He went to get it for me anyhow. I read the faded photocopy of a photocopy in his garden while he watched me carefully for the resigned outrage I had learned test veterans checked for. Regardless of how familiar the information became, they wanted to know I was still emotionally affected and morally unnerved, that amongst all the stories of harm I was hearing, I had not become desensitised to the full weight of the government's betrayal.

I held in my hands the minutes of a meeting at the Atomic Energy Research Establishment on the 15th of July 1958 'To discuss radiological safety precautions at Christmas Island'. An Air Commander objects to blood sampling being carried out on individual servicemen, arguing that 'if the person was examined and found to be normal before posting to Christmas Island and who later developed leukaemia, it might be difficult to refute the allegations that this is due to radiations received at Christmas Island'.

'So you see', Joseph said, making sure I had connected the dots. 'They told us there was nothing to worry about. But they knew of the risks. They knew even then.'[2]

Back in New Zealand, I interviewed Ben, who served on Kiritimati Island. He began by wanting to describe what occurred after the bomb tests.

> We didn't at the start realize the significance of washing the ship down as soon as possible afterwards. Because the damn stuff kept getting in everywhere. And three or four years later, they were still getting radiation readings off those ships. Different places around the deck, like your birthing lines, the wire ropes, and your hoses – the ideal place for radiation to get washed into it.

He explained the basic necessities of service.

> Salt water, it was the only fresh water you had. You had to make water yourself, or collect it off the awnings. But we didn't realize at the time that

[2] By the 1950s, radiobiology and nuclear science had determined the deleterious health effects of both high and low levels of radiation, although the causative relationship between different low exposure levels and types, and their exact biological effects were (and continue to be) debated (Laucht 2016).

> the awnings were contaminated. We drank it and washed ourselves in that water from the awnings. And on two or three occasions we were told to operate, sail somewhere in the ocean around Christmas Island after the bombs. And it was the worst possible position they put us in in terms of the winds and fallout. We sailed straight into it, radioactive rain, straight into it, and we didn't know at the time.

Blood, dust, and water. The risks of nuclear injury constituted threats that invaded test veterans' bodies through the most quotidian, elemental, and unavoidable of acts: breathing, drinking, and washing.[3] This chapter introduces the nuclear tests and the sites of nuclear experimentation, Maralinga and Kiritimati Island, revealing how Britain justified the contamination of colonized lands and their peoples. I seek to historicize the stakes and challenges that test veterans have faced when seeking redress for latent and slow-moving illnesses, and uncertain and invisible exposure. By tracing these challenges back to the test themselves, I explore the everyday encounters with risk that continued to occupy veterans' memories and their engagements archives. In remembering the tests, participants reflected on how the test planners and military superiors rendered exposure risk invisible, manageable, or calculable. Despite this, test veterans' embodied encounters with the bomb and with contaminated space and landscapes endured through memory, becoming an experiential bedrock for later claims of toxic harm.

LOCATING LANDS AND DISLOCATING PEOPLES

By the conclusion of World War II, both the US and the USSR possessed the scientific knowledge to develop atomic weaponry. Their subsequent nuclear bomb testing programmes launched the Cold War nuclear arms race, threatening to sideline Britain geopolitically.[4] Before the end of the

[3] See Neale et al. (2022) for a discussion on how the political adjoins the elemental through socio-technical practices in diverse settings.

[4] Lord Cherwell, Churchill's scientific advisor, warned that Britain would soon 'rank with other European nations who have to make do with conventional weaponry' (in Arnold and Smith 2006: 5). The dropping of atomic bombs on Japan had turned nuclear weaponry into what Hecht calls 'modernization spectacles' (2014: 206), spectacular events that signified modernist ideals of 'progress'. 'We must do it, it's the price

War, British scientists were contributing vital scientific breakthroughs to the early development of nuclear physics and to the scientific work at the Los Alamos laboratory and testing site.[5] With the McMahon Act (1946), however, the US refused further scientific cooperation with its allies.[6] Britain set about at pace designing and developing its own nuclear programme. The first problem was finding a location to test large-scale bombs. Britain was too densely populated, and so the government surveyed its Empire for a suitably remote site.[7]

we pay to sit at the top table', Winston Churchill said in 1954 of the nuclear testing programme (Hennessy 2002: 52).

[5] During the war, for example, a team of scientists at the Cambridge Cavendish Laboratory gained access to the only stock of heavy water in the world. Heavy water contains a hydrogen isotope double the mass of ordinary hydrogen. It acts to moderate a nuclear reaction, slowing down the neutrons (Clark 1961: 99). The Cavendish team theorized that a slower reaction would allow unrefined uranium to produce a new and deadly human-made compound. This was named plutonium (Stannard 1973: 309–310). The risks of war, however, moved atomic research and its gathering potential away from Britain. After the fall of France in 1940, Germany increased its aerial bombardment of England. British leaders began to strategize ways to protect weapons development from an unthinkable invasion. They agreed to share research with their North American allies (Clark 1961: 159–161). Many Cambridge scientists moved to work on atomic research in laboratories of Canada. As cooperation increased, Winston Churchill and President Roosevelt agreed to share their developing atomic technology, to not use any atomic bomb without the other's consent, and to not share information with any other parties. In 1943, the two countries formalized this agreement with the Quebec Agreement. By now most wartime British atomic scientists were working on building an atomic weapon at Los Alamos in New Mexico under Oppenheimer's command (Laucht 2012, Powaski 1987).

[6] After the war, under a newly elected President Truman, the Atomic Energy Act 1946 (US), also known as the McMahon Act, made it illegal to share any classified material about nuclear technology with other countries, including the allies of the US (Young 2007: 5). British politicians became concerned about the country's decreasing global influence and defence capabilities in a shifting geopolitical arena. By 1949, the Soviet Union was testing atomic bombs in Kazakhstan. The Cold War edged closer to home, the sense of risk more palpable with the communist coup in Czechoslovakia and the Soviet blockade of Berlin in 1948 (Hennessy 2002: 245–272).

[7] As Elizabeth Tynan (2016: 6) notes of the choice of Australia for the testing site: 'This story is not as simple as the oppression of a former colony by a fading imperial power. ... Australia entered into the agreement with considerable ambitions of its own. The Menzies government had its reasons, not all of them sycophantic. One incentive was to maximise the value of the country's newly discovered and extensive uranium resources. Uranium was the raw material for both atomic weaponry and atomic energy, but few countries in the world possessed it in such large and accessible

Maralinga was then and remains today Aṉangu land.[8] The Chief Scientist of the Australian Department of Supply, William Alan S. Butement, first proposed the name Maralinga for the selected test site, an arid, remote area in the centre of South Australia. Maralinga means thunder, but not in the languages of the Aṉangu peoples. Butement took the word from the once-spoken Garik language of an Aboriginal people thousands of miles away in the Northern Territory (Tynan 2016: 1). The Aṉangu people were forced off their lands in South Australia in the immediate years preceding the construction of the British-run nuclear test site. Many families were relocated 400 kilometres south, to the Lutheran Mission at Yalata. The Australian government did not hand the land back nor allow them to return until 1985, three decades later.[9] In readying the site for nuclear tests, Australian officials considered the testing ground to be vast, desolate, and only sparsely populated by Indigenous peoples (Arnold and Smith 2006: 278).[10] Yet

quantities. Second, the Australian Government believed that if nuclear war loomed, assisting Britain with its nuclear program would help guarantee Australia's own protection by Britain at least, and possibly the US as well. A third reason was that in the 1950s, Australia toyed with the idea of both civilian nuclear power and its own nuclear weaponry.'

8 The Aṉangu include peoples of the Pitjantjatjara and Yankunytjatjara language groups. The Aboriginal communities of this region are today commonly referred to as the Maralinga Tjarutja, the name of the body corporate representing Traditional Owners. This name acknowledges the history of nuclear testing as well as the care and custodianship that the Traditional Owners provide their radiation affected Country.

9 For thirty years after the tests, Traditional Owners were forbidden by law from returning to the testing sites and surrounding lands. In 1968, a clean-up failed to address contamination and may have in fact made the problem worse by dispersing radioactive materials. Environmental testing in the 1980s showed continuing unsafe levels of plutonium, uranium, and beryllium, as well as plutonium waste pits in different parts of the land (Commonwealth 1985c: 27).

10 Walter MacDougall, a missionary turned native patrol officer for the British Atomic Weapons Research Establishment in 1947, was responsible for 'Aboriginal welfare' at and near the atomic testing sites of Maralinga and Emu Field. In 1955, he was charged with keeping Indigenous communities out of the testing sites. Chief Scientist of the Atomic Weapons Research Establishment, Butement complained in 1956 that 'He is apparently placing the affairs of a handful of natives above those of the British Commonwealth of nations' (in Mattingley 2016: 53). MacDougall's job was to map the settlements and movements of First Nation people within the Yankunytjatjara territory. His numerous reports from 1953 to 1955 contained headcounts of communities, and maps of the places they travelled seasonally in order to hunt dingo pups, or

after the tests, reports calculated that up to 1,200 Aboriginal people remained in the region during the tests (Mathis 2024).

William Penney, Britain's head scientist of the operation,[11] proposed a military exclusion zone. He believed the zone needed to extend around 100 miles downwind of the testing site to prevent harm to human health.[12] Despite the exclusion zone, in practice the military dedicated

collect dingo scalps, and to camp near sources of water. It is difficult to square this assurance with the varied details in his reports and notes. He recorded instances where a local man travelled sixty-five miles south of Emu Field. He details how the 'nearest family territory still occupied' was only eighty-six kilometres from Emu Field and the line he drew on his map marking the limits of occupation was at one point only sixty-three miles away from the test site. His notes are shadowed with the uncertainty of his methods and task. 'I am not aware of any occupants of the Ngalea Tribal area. There are persistent rumours of aborigines occupying that area. I have not been able to contact anyone who has actually seen Natives there' (in Commonwealth 1985a: 170). On the eve of the tests, MacDougall assured his superiors of the safe, distant location of Indigenous communities from the test site. He wrote: 'There is no fear of Jangkuntjara natives moving out of pastoral areas, nor is there any possibility of natives based on Missions or Stations in South Australia moving south of the reserve' (in Commonwealth 1985a: 172). This language of certainty and its portrait of an empty land turned Country into resource and erased the traces and tracks of Indigenous world-making.

11 William Penney was the director of the Atomic Weapons Research Establishment across the 1950s. He was a noted mathematician and physicist and a professor in mathematics in Oxford. He worked under Oppenheimer at Los Alamos to build the first atomic bombs (Arnold 1992). The atomic historian Lorna Arnold, who worked closely with the Atomic Energy Agency where Penney had once been director, and who offered historical accounts from a perspective highly sympathetic to the British government, argued that he cared deeply about the safety of Aboriginal people near the Australian testing sites, and that 'he was deeply distressed when some thirty years later at hearings of an Australian Royal Commission the conduct of the tests was criticized with the suggestion that Aboriginals might have been harmed' (Arnold 1992: 447).

12 Before the Australian government offered it final approval of the testing programme, Australian physicist and chairman of the Atomic Weapons Tests Safety Committee (AWTSC) Professor Leslie Martin wrote to the Australian Prime Minister, Robert Menzies, explaining that 'On the basis of the information made available by Sir William Penney, we are able to assure you that the isolation of the site of the trials precludes any possible damage to habitation or living beings by the "shock" wave, thermal radiation, gamma rays and neutrons. . . . It is possible for us to assure you that the time of firing will be chosen so that any risk to health due to radioactive contamination to our cities, or in fact of human beings, is impossible' (in Commonwealth 1985a: 173). This trust stemmed from conversations and correspondence with William Penney. As the Australian Royal Commission into the test programme noted, all members of the AWTSC were vetted and approved by Britain. 'The atmosphere of

few resources to patrol or prevent Aboriginal people from crossing through the area (Commonwealth 1985a). The testing sites were close to traditional hunting and ceremonial grounds, which were increasingly irradiated as the testing programme progressed.

Pollution and lingering toxicities have long been intrinsic to the colonial project (Fisher et al. 2021, Liboiron 2021). Colonial power operates not simply by claiming dominion through legally denying Indigenous connections to their customary lands. Rather, the violent fiction of *terra nullius* is made real by the elemental, toxic work of making land unsafe for human bodies, in rendering land uninhabitable for the communities whose lifeworlds, ancestral ties, and well-being are intertwined with it.

William Penney's method of calculating risk at Maralinga reflected limits of experience, imagination, and observation. Initial radiation fallout models were quantified based on the ways that European settlers engaged with the landscape. This anticipated people protected by sturdy houses, and bodies shielded from their environment by clothes and shoes. They did not anticipate people cooking, touching, eating, or resting their bodies and skin against plants and earth in the way that Aboriginal communities did (Commonwealth 1985c: 16).[13] The scientific model mistranslated cultural ways of being into politically acceptable and expedient forms of risk (Boholm 2003: 174).[14]

mutual trust between the watchers and the watched was altogether unsatisfactory and dangerous. The watchers who, after all, had the power to prevent the tests should have been considerably harder to convince and should have required much more than assurances from the British before granting approval' (Commonwealth 1985c: 11).

13 The Royal Commission on nuclear testing noted that in the later Buffalo tests at Maralinga, the tests were regularly carried out when the scientists knew the detonations would not meet safety requirements and that fallout would exceed the limits set by the AWTSC. The Commission concluded that 'Overall, the attempts to ensure Aboriginal safety during the Buffalo series demonstrate ignorance, incompetence and cynicism on the part of those responsible for that safety. The inescapable conclusion is that if Aborigines were not injured or killed as a result of the explosions, this was a matter of luck rather than adequate organization, management and resources allocated to ensuring safety' (Commonwealth 1985c: 20).

14 Given that the nuclear testing programme left Maralinga contaminated with dangerous levels of radiation (Commonwealth 1985c), the Royal Commission recommended the land be decontaminated and the traditional owners compensated. In 1993, the British government paid £20 million to the Australian government to decontaminate

Minimal measures were taken to monitor Aboriginal peoples' movements across the exclusion zone. When aircraft arrived or took off at the test site, they were told to scan the environs for any campfires or tracks. With a bare eye, aircrew could only do so for about a mile before such patterns in the deserts would vanish from view. No pilots ever reported seeing any signs of Aboriginal camps. Land patrols would also occasionally venture out, but never further than around twenty miles (Commonwealth 1985a: 171).[15]

Calculations of risk blur optical and institutional fields of vision. What the eye could not see, the priorities of military risk obscured further. The test architects refused to scale the search in ways that might have rendered Aboriginal people visible to both the naked eye and the bureaucratic record. The anthropologist Jane Guyer encourages us to think of scale not as a cognitive map but rather as a repertoire for performance (2004: 60). Scale prompts action, and conversely, inaction.

Scale can also prompt refusal. When Britain set out to develop the capacity to test a much larger hydrogen bomb, the Australian government rejected hosting such tests.[16] They feared nuclear fallout across settler cities, as well as public backlash. Britain once again looked to its Empire for 'suitable' land. They determined they would need land somewhere remote and ideally uninhabited, but accessible by harbour and an airstrip.

Astride the equator in the Pacific Ocean exist two island states. Tuvalu and the Republic of Kiribati consist of a wide sweep of coral atolls and reef islands lying across five million kilometres of ocean. At its far eastern tip lies Kiritimati Island, 3,680 kilometres away from Banaba Island to the furthest

the land. A year later, the Australian government paid $13.5 million in compensation to the Maralinga Tjarutja people (Ford 2023).

15 In his evidence at the Royal Commission, Morrison, the project security officer at Maralinga in charge of the security plan reflected on the assurances of the native patrol officer, Walter MacDougall, who had argued the site of the safety zone was empty of Aboriginal peoples. Morrison said, 'In a vast area like that it would be impossible to guarantee any protection for natives. They could be sitting behind a salt bush and you would never know: even low-flying aircraft would not pick them up. So, in that sense, he would be a foolish man to guarantee that he could ensure us that there were no natives in the area' (in Commonwealth 1985a: 172–173).

16 When the Australian government first agreed to bomb-testing on its soil, they imposed a fifty kiloton limit to prevent the spread of radiation from contaminating cities. In this we can see how the safety of white urban settler bodies counted above Indigenous peoples and Country (Jacobs 2013: 168).

west. At the beginning of the twentieth century, Banaba was already being mined into a labyrinth of sharp pinnacles to extract phosphate, used to fertilize the farms of New Zealand and Australia (Teaiwa 2014). At the other end of this arc of islands, Kiritimati Island became the site of British atomic testing.

In 1886, German and British governments agreed to carve up western and central parts of the Pacific into two 'spheres of influence'. The Gilbert and Ellice Islands, as they were then known, became Britain's concern. By 1892, German officials had convinced Britain of the need for greater control in the region to secure the 'supply' of local labourers to German plantations in Samoa. The islands collectively became a British Protectorate in 1892 and then, from 1916, a British colony. Christmas Island, as Britain named it, lying at the far north tip of the Line Islands, was the last to be formally incorporated into this colony in 1919 (McIntyre 2012).

In the late 1940s, as independence struggles succeeded to free India, Burma, and Ceylon from British rule, the British Colonial Office conducted the Smaller Territories Enquiry. They concluded that its twenty-six smaller colonial territories, including the Gilbert and Ellice Islands, were unsuitable for independence. This was due, the inquiry argued, to a lack of educated elites, the remote and scattered location of the islands, and a lack of 'viable' economic resources and activities (McIntyre 2012). The cultural metrics by which the report imagined nationhood, by which it understood a capacity for sovereignty, were British class hierarchies and market-based economic logics.

During the African decolonial struggles of the 1950s, British Prime Minister Macmillan initiated an 'Audit of Empire', which also assessed that the Gilbert and Ellice Islands were ill suited for independence. In 1957, a report as part of this audit, *Future Constitutional Development in the Colonies*, reached this conclusion: upon independence, the Gilbert and Ellice Islands 'would relapse into primitive savagery unless another civilized country assumed the administration'.[17] The report was released the same year that nuclear testing on Christmas and Malden Islands began.

[17] GEN 174/012. Colonial Office Print, May 1957, pp. 73–75. CAB 134/1551, CPC (57) 27.

In both reports, danger and opportunity interlocked to strengthen empire and reveal a fear of empire's retreat. The perceived threat of 'chaos' that peoples labelled 'primitive' posed to colonial order coincided neatly with the strategic advantage of turning Indigenous lands into a toxic experimental site. Asserting that local peoples were not evolutionarily 'ready' to govern themselves – as a risk unto themselves – justified the classification of their lands and seas as governable, and under the virtue of productivity, as a site to enact experimental value.[18] Colonial extraction was not a material subtraction, but rather an addition. 'What they possessed was open space that could be contaminated without political recourse' (Jacobs 2013: 160).

TRUST, YOUTH, SECRETS

Peter recounted to me how, 'at 19, I volunteered. Because I was in the Air Force and I had not long come out of apprentice training school, so they said, you know, you're due to go abroad somewhere'. He explained the process.

> They let you have three choices of where you'd like to go. And I put down three choices, and I'd heard, there was a guy there I was talking to, he'd been to Maralinga. Because the tests were an official secret, he wouldn't tell me anything about it, Maralinga. He said, Maralinga is in Australia, you know, a couple hours flight down to Adelaide. So I put that as one of the three choices.

Stories of fateful choices such as these indexed the absence of choice, the impact of secrecy, and the naivety of youth, all of which they later came to understand as leveraged for militarism's advantage.

At the age of nineteen years, Ben became an able seaman in the New Zealand Navy. Now in his mid seventies, with a thatch of white hair and a resting grin, I met him at his tidy suburban house. His lounge was cold. He was being careful with the heating bill. But he knew how to make

[18] As Emma Kowal notes (2015: 94), time and temporal scales of comparison represent 'one mechanism through which Indigenous-modern dichotomies are created and maintained and an enduring trope of difference in the settler-colonial imaginary'.

a cup of coffee strong and scalding hot. He began to recount his first year of service.

> We left New Zealand on the ship, and only then we were told that there was going to be nuclear tests carried out at Christmas Island, and that we were going to be a weather reporting ship. The head scientist came on board, and we cleared lower deck. And he spoke to us about weather reporting and the need for accuracy, and how they would give us some protective clothing. And he assured us it was safe because he demonstrated it was safe by being there during previous tests.

Ben sat back in his armchair. 'He died some years later. And he was riddled with cancer.' He paused for a brief, respectful moment. Then he went to the kitchen table to gather the information manual they were given once aboard the ship. A thin blue booklet's cover bore the emblem of Operation Grapple, a cormorant bird clutching a large four-pointed grapnel hook, representing the four arms of the taskforce: the three branches of service and the civilian scientist group. Ben began to read aloud the forward from the British Minister of Supply. The tests were 'essential to the defence of the country and the prevention of global war. They represent . . . the minimum necessary to ensure that our weapons shall be powerful and effective, and a real deterrent to a potential aggressor'. Ben's voice both rose and slowed in emphasis at the next paragraph. 'No effort has been spared in the organization of the tests to ensure the safety of personnel involved and to obviate danger to persons and property.'

Ben lowered the booklet to his lap and removed his reading glasses. 'And so you see', he said with a sigh, sensing no need to explain what could be seen in such a passage.

British test veteran Joseph suffered from multiple health conditions, and his adult child was born with a congenital disability: 'When I was coming up to twenty-three [years old], within two months of getting married I was [told] by the Air Force that I was going to Christmas Island. At the time we didn't realize this was part of the [nuclear] experiment. Because we were all youngsters, and we didn't know.'

Once stationed on the island, Joseph recalled, the experiments themselves remained opaque. 'They didn't actually call them bombs, they just called them devices, they weren't referred to as bombs.' Normally, he explained, when working in the hangers loading and unloading the supply planes, 'You can see everything that was going on.' However, when it came to the planes used to drop the bombs, secrecy shrouded procedures. 'So when they actually loaded the aircraft up, they went behind screens ... there was a hanger here, they pushed the aircraft in, the screens were put up, so you couldn't see anything. You couldn't see what the bomb looked like.'

'Did you worry about radiation?', I asked Joseph.

'You trusted what you were told ... [the officers and scientists told us] it wasn't harmful. I didn't even really understand what a gene did back then or how it all worked with radiation.' As many test veterans emphasized, nuclear injury was possible because of an institutional culture, a faith in authority that made militarism function smoothly. Test veterans conceptualized nuclear injury as stemming from the exploitation of this deeply socialized mechanism of trust.

British test veteran Peter recounted how his superiors normalized the experimental environs and the traces of bomb blasts. 'When you arrived in Maralinga, the Ranger comes over and made a point of taking you out to the main test sites and letting you see the actual craters and standing on the craters and walk down in them. This Colonel used to come out with us, and stand there. And I just wonder whatever happened to that guy.'

When authority figures clambered into craters or demonstrated to seamen that the deployment was safe 'by being there during previous tests', they used their own bodies as evidentiary tools, living exemplars of scientific safety models. In this way radiation injury could cut across hierarchy and those tasked with facilitating trust were also the victims of it.

INJURY AND AFFECT

Service at the testing sites oscillated between dealing with boredom and dealing with terror, between passing time and enraptured presence. Ben explained, 'to operate the weather reporting apparatus, it was quite simple. It was just balloons with helium, and we tracked it with a radar set'. When off duty, 'our recreation was to go ashore, drinking beer, and that was about that. We played rugby but it became a bore, because we got to the stage we were beating everyone, especially the Poms [British], and nobody wanted to play games with us'. Detonation days were different.

> During the bombs, we all had to be on the upper deck and we had to sit down and with our back facing the bows. You had to put your hands over eyes and the bomb went off and the first thing you'd feel was this intense light and then heat like when you walk past an oven door that's just been opened. And when you put your hands over your eyes, during the blast you actually see the bones in your hand.

With an effort he added, 'It was awesome.'

As I got up to leave from our interview, Ben insisted he read me one more passage from the Operation Grapple information booklet he received once aboard the naval ship sailing to Kiritimati Island. Standing now, he spoke theatrically. The Task Force Commander Air Vice-Marshal Oulton hoped this '*little booklet will give greater interest and enjoyment in the job which you are going to do for the next few months and will serve as a pleasant souvenir of what must surely be one of the most interesting episodes of your lives*'. Ben laughed while shaking his head.

The idea of touristic pleasures was present in other official records. I sat with Paul reading and drinking a sweet hot blackcurrant drink he kept in the back of his fridge for his grandkids. The winter sun receded from his compact lounge as it rose towards midday. The week before I'd spent a day photographing records from the National Archives in Wellington, and as promised, I brought over printouts to discuss. He was disappointed, I hadn't discovered any 'new, secret files', but still he picked over each document, holding them at a distance for us both to read together.

We work through the New Zealand frigate HMNZS Pukaki's Report of Proceedings from 1957. This was one of two New Zealand naval ships that attended the tests. The Report of Proceedings offered a Captain's log of activities, including for each nuclear test. We read together:

> At 0826 the second weapon was detonated off the S.E. corner of CHRISTMAS ISLAND. PUKAKI was stationed thirty-five miles to the N.

> E. and had excellent views; and the ship company being dressed in full anti-flash gear as a precautionary measure. This being a larger weapon, the effects were correspondingly more impressive, the flash penetrating closed eyelids and most people feeling at the same time a distinct warmth on their backs.

I was struck by the Commanding Officer's up-beat tone. Paul was also amused. 'Excellent views', he scoffed, wriggling his feet in his slippers. 'Like we were on a cruise ship of something.' I pointed to the word 'Impressive'.

'Everyone will have told you, how we saw the bones in our hands, eyes closed. I know everyone's told you, but just think about that for a minute.' He held up one hand, the fingers gnarled a little from arthritis. 'Seeing your own skeleton. Almost, like you were dead.' He put the document down, and with feigned chipperness, he repeated, 'Excellent view!'

British test veteran, Harvey, recounted how he and his friends spent their time off at Maralinga. They often spent a day 'just driving about in Land Rovers and making a hole in the ground and having a barbeque'. He worried now that the digging and unsettling of the dry earth and the fire and cooking of food against the earth had exposed them to radiation. 'No-one told us that the ground was contaminated.' He reflected on the invisibility of risk in the material infrastructure of the site and its surroundings. 'If there had been hazard signs everywhere then we would have been much, much more careful. But there was nothing.'

Another test veteran, Graeme, a stores assistant in the New Zealand Navy, was sent to Kiritimati Island when he was eighteen years old. He had heard about my research and contacted me. 'I was on the main deck of the Rotoiti ship when the bombs went off', he recalled on the phone. In the interview, I asked him what he remembered. He paused, and his eyes dampened.

'Terrifying. I just don't quite remember them. They later sent me to psychiatrists and everything, and as I said to them, I just don't want to remember them, because if I do, if I even talk about them too much, you finish up with virtually nightmares about it.'

Alarmed, I tried to shift the subject, but Graeme continued:

> Because I think it was 13 or 15 seconds after the bomb blasts that you turn around to look at it. And you were issued with black glasses and these ones you could look at the sun and all you saw was an orange ball. And when you looked at this from a distance, between 25 and 30 miles away, you could see, it was like looking into a furnace. And that's through these glasses, it was quite terrifying.

Graeme took a sip of his tea and stilled himself. I tried to change the topic again, but he returned to it. 'And there was a couple of our chaps, were sent back home. One was a cook, he's a darn good cook too. He couldn't cope with it.'

Despite the official record showing no fallout into the marine environment, Graeme remembered worrying signs that suggested otherwise.

> And, after that we'd go out and try and catch sharks, and we'd put the Geiger counter over the sharks. Now they said there's no fallout because it was clear like that, no clouds at all. However three or four days later, we pulled in a shark and put the Giger counter on it and ge ge ge ge. We were getting a reading.

Despite official assurances of safety, the actions ordered by the ship officers conveyed a preoccupation with possible risk. After the tests, the ship was carefully washed down.

'And they were pretty methodical. And the seamen would go through, there were a designated group that would go right through the ship, with Giger counters. And they went right through the ship to make sure there was no readings there. And if there was, they never told us.'

I tried to change the topic again, away from the tests themselves. His face lightened.

'Oh, it was quite pleasant. We were in the tropics. We'd go ashore at Christmas Island, and you'd go swimming there. When we were anchored out off Christmas Island you could actually see the bottom about three miles deep. It was beautiful. You could see barracuda and fish swimming down, way down.'

Alex, a British test veteran stationed on Kiritimati Island, also sensed risk in the contrasting protections his own body received compared with the scientists. He recounted how he worked for hours clearing away debris that had fallen around Ground Zero directly after two bomb blasts. He was provided with a thin film gown. His work included picking up 'pieces of metal, and rubbish' dislodged and strewn around by the blast. Alex reflected,

> I didn't even have a pair of gloves. I wasn't even given a pair of tongs to lift the stuff up . . . we were picking up with our bare hands . . . I was on my own and you know nobody told me anything about radiation, and let's be honest, you can't see it, you can't smell it, you can't feel it, so you just did as you were told.

After Alex completed collecting the debris, he 'piled it all into the vehicle and then drove back to the decontamination area'.

> I had to park [the truck] in a certain area and then walk to the decontamination. Well, when I went into the decontamination there were these civilians [AWRE scientists] that came out all dressed in protective gear with the respirators and everything on and they drove my truck away. Now I'd just come out from Ground Zero with just my everyday clothes and they were all dressed up like this just to pick up my truck with.

Alex recalled that medical personnel on Kiritimati Island conducted blood tests on servicemen. 'They never said [what they were for]. They used to just line us up and do things, and that was it. We were never informed.' The blood tests were also repeated after the bomb tests, he recounted.

THE SCIENCE AND POLITICS OF RADIATION INJURY

A crucial question in debates about radiation exposure is this: at what dose threshold does radiation become harmful to the body? The International Commission on Radiological Protection (ICRP) sets safety standards for industrial and medical exposure levels, and its risk models are widely adopted by governments internationally.

The Linear No Threshold Dose Response (LNT) model has been the most broadly used 'gold standard' means of assessing radiation risk (Calabrese et al. 2022, Pennington and Siegel 2019). This model asserts that the risk and degree of individual biological harm occurring will increase in direct proportion to the rate of individual radiation dose, with doses above 100 mGy proven to cause tumour growth.[19] But, according to this model, there is no threshold below which radiation can definitively be classified as safe or harmless.

Industry safety thresholds (the maximum dose a nuclear worker can receive in a year, for example) are thus in large part devised in terms of what regulators regard as socially and politically practicable and acceptable. It has become a 'scientifically defensible approximation' (McEwan 2004: 18) within the uncertainties of radiobiology. At the same time, across the twentieth century the ICRP steadily lowered radiation dose thresholds, including both permissible daily dose rates and annual doses rates. This reflects increased medical caution towards radiation harm, as well as increased public concern and engagement with radiation safety standards.

Scientists devised this linear model based on the results of large population studies on groups exposed to moderate to high doses of gamma rays. These results have been used to extrapolate the effects of low-dose radiation. However, as radiation scientist Andrew McEwan shows, 'a strictly linear dose response should not be expected in all circumstances' (2004:19). Experimental studies show that radiation at very low doses is less predictable than at higher doses. However, according to the ICRP, a similar risk approach should be applied to all forms of low-dose radiation exposure. 'The central assumption of a linear dose–response relationship for the induction of cancer and heritable effects, according to which an increment in dose induces a proportional increment in risk even at low doses, continues to provide the basis for the summation of doses from external sources of radiation and from intakes of radionuclides' (ICRP 2007: 13).

Scientists have in recent decades begun to better understand how low-dose internal emitters, the minute radioactive particles that enter the body through inhalation or ingestion, act differently from high-dose

[19] This refers to low-LET radiation, that is, gamma rays and x-rays. LET stands for linear energy transfer, or 'the rate of energy deposition along a track of an ionising particle' (McEwan 2004: 18). For high LET radiation, such as Alpha particles, the dose will be lower to cause the same degree of biological effect.

radiation. Non-linear risk models are required, and scientists argue over exactly how much risk internal emitters pose to human health.[20] In this debate, biomarkers remain elusive. Tiny, internalized particles are difficult to render visible through medical tests and imaging (Yamaguchi et al. 2022). In navigating dose exposure models, test veterans are also caught in the sceptical inertia of nuclear economics. The costs of lowering thresholds for risk are infrastructurally high. They have the potential, at great expense, to expand workplace safety protocols, risk assessment models, and the wider responsibility of the nuclear industry to workers.

Questions of necessary risk or 'reasonable exposure' (Kumaki 2020) have become intrinsic to questions of nuclear harm. They reflect what Cram (2016: 521–522) describes as 'the fundamental paradox of nuclear safety', in which 'some level of exposure is unavoidable when working with nuclear materials' and thus 'injury is an operational necessity of nuclear industry'. Rates of risky exposure are assessed 'relative to the imagined benefits of radiation. Indeed, this notion of necessary wounding informs the most basic metrics for nuclear safety. Occupational dose rates are calculated using a specific definition of "reasonable" harm.'[21] And as Hecht (2013) and Jobin (2021a) show, notion of reasonable exposure can shift, leading to the dilution and even elimination of responsibility in times of nuclear exceptionality, such as post disaster.

Radiation risk thus emerges as a political-driven calculus between perceived social benefits and their costs (Cable et al. 2008). Within such a calculus, nuclear injuries are not only accepted but also actively denied. Kuchinskaya calls this 'the production of invisibility' (2014: 6) in the wake of nuclear exposure. This highlights the social and political practices of negation, silencing and denial that mimic the imperceivable and invisible presence of radiation (Jobin 2021a, Johnston and Barker 2008).

[20] For examples of this debate see footnote 22.

[21] For example, the ICRP recommendations are used to set radiological exposure standards in most countries, including Britain, Australia, and New Zealand. In their 1977 standards for acceptable industrial dose rates, they specified that for any dose rates set must be justified and kept below an upmost threshold of 50 mSv in a single year, and that 'all exposures must be kept as low as reasonably achievable, economic and social factors being taken into account' (in Commonwealth 1985c: 13). For a member of the public, 1 mSv was and is considered acceptable per year.

The temporality of radiation risk lasts from 'nanoseconds to millennia' (Adam 1998: 193). In the immediate aftermath, there are certain radiocarcinogenic risks close to a nuclear explosion. Exposure to relatively short-lived radioisotopes is among them. Iodine-131 has a half-life of only eight days, but is produced in significant quantities during an atomic explosion. The human thyroid hungrily absorbs iodine, so Iodine-131 can lead to thyroid cancer (Braverman et al. 2014). Strontium-90 has a half-life of twenty-nine years. Scientists called it the 'bone seeker'. It causes leukaemia because the body absorbs and deposits it into bones like it does calcium, and it then proceeds to irradiate the nearby bone marrow (EPA n.d.). The link between exposure to these particles and cancer is uncontroversial. But other radionuclides are also potentially carcinogenic.

As the epidemiologist Steve Wing argues, 'that problems of measurement are secondary to the more fundamental problem of knowing what to measure' (2000: 32). The British Ministry of Defence's approach to personnel safety at the tests sought to understand, measure, and assess the risk of certain forms of radiation. Gamma rays are pure energy, traveling at the speed of light. At high doses their stochastic effects are immediate. The MoD's rejection of tests veterans' claims of irradiation has held consistent assumptions about the mechanisms of radiocarcinogenesis, or how radiation causes cancer. They have assumed that high-dose gamma radiation was the most significant risk to human health. Gamma doses at the bomb testing sites, as measured by film badges, were low or nil.

By contrast, radioactive particles (fallout) contain both energy and mass. Such particles can endure in the environment, and travel through soil, water, and wind. Unlike the highly penetrative gamma rays, alpha particles are heavy and slow moving and cannot penetrate the skin. But they can be inhaled or ingested, and they can enter the cornea of an eye. And they are highly ionizing. As they decay, plutonium isotopes commonly emit alpha particles. A New Zealand geneticist who has studied chromosomal damage explained to me that 'the problem with fallout, with ingested and inhaled radionuclides, is that any dose is potentially harmful. ... With [low level] gamma radiation the DNA repairs itself quite quickly. Not so with radionuclides'.

At stake is how well mainstream models of radiation risk, based largely on acute gamma radiation exposure studies, can account for low-dose internal exposure. Submicron or nanometre radioactive particles below a diameter of 1 μ (one millionth of a meter) are so tiny that if inhaled, they can flow from the lungs to the lymphatic system. Once inside the body, they are too slow moving to escape and can emit radiation to surrounding tissue for decades.[22] This persistent low dose can be more or less harmful due to the particular chemical properties of different types of ionizing particles, and the properties of particular organs and tissue. Plutonium, for example, has an affinity with bone, and can reside there for decades. Test veteran Peter had come to understand it thus: 'what's happening of course, is that once that's lodged in the body, say it's got a half-life of 50 years, for all that time, it's just giving out 50 years of radiation. Any cells immediately adjacent to that particle are killed, and those a little bit further away are damaged. And they can mutate'. In a package of documents that a test veteran, Sam, sent me, he ended his handwritten letter with an underlined sentence, 'Plutonium-239 has a half-life of 24,000 years!' I photocopied the letter, cut out the line, and stuck it above my computer, to remind me of the scalar flexibility this project and topic required of my thinking about harm.

Jeremy sat across from me on a cherry-coloured chesterfield couch. He had invited me for tea at an armed forces club in England. He had worked as a navigator in the RAF at Kiritimati Island. I barely ask a question, as he seemed compelled to explain in as clear, technical detail as possible, the procedures of flying through a mushroom cloud. I sat riveted by his high-octane description.

> At the point that the drop-aircraft dropped the bomb, all the aircraft were turned away from Ground Zero and got off as fast as they possibly could, you know, to avoid the explosion. We had about twenty to fifty aircraft airborne. The purpose being that, the idea was to get as many aircraft off the airfield in case anything might or might not happen in the safety area.

[22] On the debate regarding how dangerous low dose internal exposure is, see for example Braverman et al. (2014), Brenner et al. (2003), Busby (2013, 2022), Dauer et al. (2010), Hahn et al. (1999), and Hande et al. (2003).

And we waited until the blast occurred, and when the bomb detonated, there was a big flash. We all had eyes closed, so then we carried on flying away until we were hit by the shock wave. Even though we were almost a hundred and sixty miles away, the power from that particular bomb really hit us. And the whole aircraft shuddered and shook.

And as soon as that passed, then we were ready to turn around and fly back here to see exactly what has happened. And fortunately, I had a window, and as the aircraft turned I saw the whole thing and it was absolutely incredible a sight. We had the sun above us, we had the sun below us. I saw literally a miniature sun. Yellow and white. We watched it as it sort of eventually started turning colours and then it started to rise. And our function was to monitor the cloud and measure it. Then black rain. Which is very, very unusual, because normally you can fly over the weather.

But when we hit the rain all my radio instruments started to do something, they just, it went off the clock. And then as the rain stopped then the instruments sort of went back to like normal.

But we had flown through the cap. We measured the cap, because that was our function, and we measured the bottom of the cloud, we measured the top of the cloud. We also measured the speed that the cloud rose from the detonation point.

One of the things to bear in mind, a hydrogen bomb would be about the size of a couch approximately, you know, three feet, three feet deep, maybe four or five feet long. But from the point of detonation, it expands from that to a 3.2 mile diameter ball. It doesn't occur just as a bang, it's basically an ongoing eruption. It takes almost a minute for this process to work. It has literally grown and grown and grown and I calculated that it expands outwards from this point in each direction very fast, about ninety-four miles an hour.

Then eventually you get this sort of magnificent sun literally just sitting there. And you know, it was a sight that is absolutely unique. No one else has seen anything quite like it. This was England's largest hydrogen bomb. And what happens is it rises and the air above it is lifted and the air underneath it creates a vacuum and that starts sucking stuff up as the ball starts rising.

Eventually when the cloud starts really falling down, the water in the stem of it, then starts evaporating, then starts coming through the cloud.

> As it comes through the cloud it picks up the nuclear particles within the cloud itself, and then these come down in what is known as black rain. In a lot of cases, a lot of the water droplets, they come down, but the water evaporates so the rain does not hit the ground or the sea around it. But one of the things that does happen is that the microscopic nuclear particles that are pulled up through the cloud are in free fall and that is what causes the fallout.
>
> We had no protective clothing whatsoever. In flying what we would be doing primarily was to have our underwear on, our socks, we had an air ventilation suit, which was kind of a corset or a bodice that had material all over our bodies and once we got in the aircraft we plugged it in and cool air was pumped round. Helmet after that, leather gloves and that was basically it. With the ground group, they had no protective clothing either.

By now Jeremy looked tired and pale. Before the interview began, he alluded to not being well, and an urgency to tell me his story while he still could. He added one final point. 'In the air we were exposed to massive doses of gamma radiation. But the alpha and the beta radiation, the low-level stuff, that was the outside, that was in the fallout area, we didn't get that until we got back on the ground.'

RECORDING RADIATION

In 1956, five New Zealand military officers were sent to Maralinga to join the British Indoctrinee Force. The Force sought to produce observers who could 'see and hear the atomic explosion and go back to their units able to pass on first-hand information of their experience' (in Crawford 2001: 1). The British military perceived the danger of nuclear warfare not only in its destructive effects on life, limb, and property but also to the psychological fitness of those required to fight on under an atomic cloud.

Indoctrination attends to risk through an ideal of exposure, one aimed at desensitizing and mentally strengthening troops. Through indoctrination, the sublime power of the bomb could be tamed and normalized. As Masco reveals (2020: 125), in nuclear preparedness emotions become infrastructural. By imagining and desiring service personnel tough enough to 'carry on' in the face of atomic warfare, indoctrination expanded the risk to which soldiers must prepare. Moreover, it recognized that atomic warfare would not simply entail technological might but also require human affective responses that fulfil its advantage in battle. The experiments at Maralinga not only tested and built a bomb but also transfigured the moral contract of militarism, to include and normalize new atomic risks into the duties of soldiering. Sensorial perception and emotional mastery were essential to such duties (Gusterson 1998, Masco 2004, 2006).

The first test the New Zealand indoctrinees witnessed was a fifteen-kiloton atomic blast mounted atop a tower. Human test dummies, live animals, tanks, and makeshift structures were positioned at varying distances from the tower. The indoctrinees were stationed eight kilometres away from ground zero to witness the tests. On the two days that followed, and dressed in full protective clothing, they travelled to ground zero to inspect the impact of the blast on the environment. They witnessed how a circular area at ground zero had become 'a mass of fused sand and silica' (Crawford 2001: 3).

The next day the Atomic Weapons Establishment (AWE) noted in a report that twenty-four officers and War Office personnel from Australia, New Zealand, and Britain volunteered 'to carry out tests on the protective value of various types of clothing for military activities in the fall-out zone'. One New Zealand indoctrinee, Officer Peat, recounted: 'I don't remember ever being asked if we would like to go into a fallout area or anything like that. It was just part of the duty we had to carry out' (in Crawford 2001: 3).

The experiment contrasted different types of exposure and risk. Men were dressed in different types of protective clothing, from regular Khaki drill to battledress to an atomic protection suit, gloves, and respirator. Some men simply drove through the blast zone. Others marched through the area, while others crawled along the ground. A New Zealand officer who participated in the experiment recounted how he 'marched and crawled along a dirt track for about an hour occasionally being showered with dust from a vehicle which was driven past for that very purpose. I don't think we went closer than 1/2 [a] mile from GZ across the wind' (in Crawford 2001: 5).

After returning to base the men were decontaminated, and their radiation doses recorded. The radiation badges measured gamma and external beta, and the levels they recorded were, according to official records, no higher than what the men would be expected to absorb through background radiation in any given year.

The dosimeter badges used at Maralinga and at Kiritimati Island were Quartz fibre electroscopes and radiation film badges. Badges utilized a small piece of photographic film set in a metal or plastic case. The film was wrapped in light-tight paper, and filters were added above the film to measure different types of radiation. The badge was pinned to serve personnels' clothing, often on the torso (NRC 1989). As the film was exposed to radiation, the silver halide crystals reacted, and when the film was developed, an instrument called a densitometer was used to read the level of darkening and reconstruct exposure dose.

When a nuclear explosion occurs, hazardous radiation is produced in different forms. Film badges measured external gamma rays and high-level beta radiation. Dose reconstruction from film badges did not, however, measure low-level alpha and beta radiation particles, the types that can be ingested and inhaled in minute quantities, such as from crawling through showers of desert dust.

The radiation badges used in the 1950s had other limitations. When beta particles come at the badges at an oblique angle (such as from above or below), they must pass through more of the filter, which can affect the dose recorded. Humidity and heat can also affect the reading, with humidity in particular causing image fade over time (NRC 1989: 21, Ziegler and Chleck 1960). Veterans recounted how the red earth environs of Maralinga could, in the height of summer, reach 40°C. On most days on Kiritimati Island the weather was humid and hot, and the rain could be torrential.

In the decades following the tests, film badge readings of radiation exposure became 'technoscientific witnesses' (Quinlan 2017). They constituted the key form of evidence used by the British Ministry of Defence to demonstrate both their attentiveness to safety concerns and the limited risks to which test veterans were exposed. In doing so, the MoD treated such numbers as untroubled by the contexts of their collection. For test veterans, the entangled effects of environment and social practice that made up such numbers were a vital part – *the* vital part – of their evidence. As Penny Harvey observes, radiation and its risks are commonly encountered as 'a social rather than a physical or chemical relation' (2020: 16).

I sat with Herb in his upstairs home office overlooking an English scene of country lanes and brambles. Few cars pass. He showed me a summary of his military medical records. During his service in Maralinga, he began suffering from painful swelling of the joints and inflammation in the eye. Regular military examinations recorded the debilitating conditions but offered no diagnosis, and later, upon discharge, they offered no entitlement to a military disability pension.

Herb began recalling the treatment of dosimeter badges at Maralinga. Rank and file servicemen often weren't provided with them, he explained, and if they did get them, who knows where they ended up. 'What the British used to do, they used to give the Australian [monitors] radiation field charts, to show what the radiation levels were at the test site, where the bombs went off, [and] they used to give them these film things.'

'But they used to, before they used to give it to them, they used to let them hang around for days before they handed them over.' He studied me for a moment to check if I believed him.

I nodded. 'I've seen that document, by Penney, about leaving the filters around for a few days.'[23]

Herb looked satisfied. 'So they didn't really get an accurate reading from them. So they had faded. They faded daily, so a lot of the radiation dose on those had dissipated. So they were being fed false information, the Australians.'

THE PRESENCE AND ABSENCE OF INDIGENOUS INJURY

Test veterans knew they were not the only ones injured by the tests. Two particular stories of Indigenous harm haunted the fringes of interviews

[23] Many test veterans had shared a copy of a faded and declassified archival letter dated 22 December 1955, in which Penney writes to Sir Fredrick Brundrett of the British Ministry of Defence. Penney reflects on Australian safety officials asking for parts of radiation monitoring filters. In it he suggests that 'On balance, I am recommending that if they ask us we give them a little piece of the filters, but that we wait a few days so that some of the short-lived key isotopes have decades a good deal.'

with test veterans, suggesting the uncomfortable, uncertain narrative work that test veterans engaged in navigating them. Telling these stories involved brief, second-hand accounts that gestured to sources beyond test veterans' ability to know and explain. They pointed to the presence of undercurrent narratives, those stories that 'cannot quite get told', and that 'risk oblivion' under the 'representation pressure' of other dominant stories (Leung 2009: 6).

'You heard things', Bert said, who served at Maralinga, mentioning an Aboriginal family 'Camping in a fresh bomb crater, for the warmth'. I looked up from the notes I was taking. 'Oh', I said gravely, offering him time for elaboration. 'Mm', Bert said with a sad but assertive nod, and waited for me to ask the next question.

'There was an incident', British test veteran Herb said, 'the Milpuddies, you'll have heard of it'. When I asked for him to tell me the detail he said, 'Look that one up', and then began searching for an unrelated set of letters to government he'd mentioned earlier that he wanted to show me.

I did look it up. During the tests, servicemen found an Aboriginal family of four camping in a bomb crater. In 2001, John Hutton, an Australian nuclear test veteran, recounted to a South Australian newspaper that in the test site they came across an Aboriginal man named Charlie Milpuddie, wearing only a light fabric around his waist.

> We ran the counter over him and he was red hot (with radioactivity). . . . A sergeant came out from Maralinga and went to the crater from Marcoo [a ground explosion on October 4, 1956] to get his wife [Edie, who was pregnant and later had a stillborn baby], a boy and a baby girl. They were hot as well. We gave the man and the boy a shower but his wife was pretty shy and only let us wash her hair. We had to shoot two of their dogs because they couldn't be decontaminated. The family were driven to the mission at Yalata.

Hutton recounted that he had been threatened by superiors never to tell anyone of the incident (James 2001). Another serviceman reported seeing an Aboriginal group sheltering in a bunker in the bomb detonation zone shortly before a bomb test. After the detonation, other servicemen recounted seeing the deceased bodies of four Aboriginal people in a fresh crater (James 2001).[24]

I sensed in the brevity, silences, and segues discomfort rather than disinterest. Discomfort perhaps in not knowing enough about these events, in service members' part in keeping secrets about such injuries and deaths for decades, and in the inadvertent role service members' played in producing the dangerous and toxic infrastructures that harmed Aboriginal people while hiding it from public view. Similar questions hung over service at Operation Grapple.

Over 100 I-Kiribati worked as labourers on Kiritimati and Malden Islands supporting the bomb testing programme. 'Everyone sort of stuck to their own group. It was the way it was', Kevin, a British test veteran, explained of the spatial and social separation along national lines on Kiritimati Island. This supports reports of racial separation and even a colour bar on the island (Alexis-Martin et al. 2021). Fijian service personnel were often assigned to work alongside I-Kiribati workers,[25]

[24] Still today, Aboriginal communities recall the evil black mist that swept through the bush after the first bomb blast from Emu Field, and the sticky red dust that settled over their camps and made them ill. The MoD categorized these stories as false, fanciful rumour. For decades, they argued that the Anangu people were confused, that their Dreamtime sent ghosts and spirits into their memories of the past (Tynan 2022). Yami Lester, a Yankunyjatjara Elder, remembered a 'strange black smoke' that was 'shiny and oily' rolling into his family's camp (in Mathis 2024). They fell immediately ill with vomiting, diarrhoea, and skin rashes. Some Elders died. 'I was only a little kid. They were working there, testing the bombs. The first one when they let it go was called Totem 1. We heard it here, loud and clear, and felt the ground shake. We seen the radiation fall out over our camp. It was moving very quietly and very deadly. After that I went blind in the right eye straight away and on the left I had some sight left' (in Ford 2023). The Royal Commission into nuclear tests concluded that 'meteorological, mathematical and statistical modelling indicates that a black mist passing over Wallatinna and Welbourn Hill could have happened. … The Royal Commission believes that Aboriginal people experienced radioactive fallout from Totem 1 in the form of a black mist or cloud at and near Wallatinna. This may have made some people temporarily ill. The Royal Commission does not have sufficient evidence to say whether or not it caused other illnesses or injuries' (Commonwealth 1985c: 17).

[25] Veterans gave me copies of several archival documents to demonstrate this. In a Letter to R. J. Minnit (Acting High Commissioner for the Western Pacific), 20 September 1957, the Colonial Office, London, informed him of plans for Operation Grapple X. 'The Requirements of Grapple X for Gilbertese labour have … been revised … and for the present the 76 labourers on the island and the 40 on their way on the "Tungaru" will suffice to meet the task force's needs.' In September 1957, the Colonial Office in London

who were given hard and dirty labouring work, such as catching and killing birds wounded and blinded by the bomb blasts or emptying the chemical toilets. They were paid less and rarely received protective gear or radiation-monitoring badges (Alexis-Martin et al. 2021, Maclellan 2017).[26] The I-Kiribati village, set amongst barbed wire and palm trees, was also nestled close to fourteen towering grey fuel tanks, capable of each holding 100,000 gallons of flammable fuel and at risk of explosion (AWE 1958).

At 8.30 am, James had the tea brewed.[27] He ushered me in and wanted to get straight to it. He has a grandchild coming to visit mid-morning, and she'd create a howling mess with these files, he explained. I could picture her ricocheting around his tidy garden, out in the Yorkshire sun.

James fanned documents across his kitchen table. But the papers are already watermarked by beverage stains, their corners dog-eared and well-thumbed. Setting them out, James knew each at a glance – by the

sent a letter to R. J. Minnit, the Acting High Commissioner for the Western Pacific (Public Records Office, CO1036/283). They reassured him of the safety plan for Operation Grapple X aimed at 'taking care of the Gilbertese … on firing day'. 'The proposal is to remove the Gilbertese from Christmas Island before the bombing aircraft takes off and to place them in a ship, in the Christmas Anchorage, which has immediate notice for steam. They will remain there in this ship until after the test when they will be returned to their village." The Colonial Office argued that "these arrangements will positively assure the safety of the Gilbertese on the Island.' A similar safety procedure was also noted down in the minutes of a top secret planning meeting for Grapple Y, entitled 'Top Secret/Atomic/U.K. Eyes Only. Minutes of a Conference Task Force Grapple at 11.00 hours on 24th January 1958 to discuss the possible effects of overpressure during Operation Grapple "Y"' as 'Issued on the Authority of the Task Force Commander'. In case of the event of an overpressured explosion, the Gilbertese were to be evacuated before the test. 'The Gilbertese Village complete is being evacuated to HMS Narvik and accommodated below deck before the test because these people and their children can not be relied upon to carry out faultlessly the drill required. They will be brought ashore directly after the test.'

26 As geographer and peace studies scholar Alexis-Martin and colleagues show, 'Kiritimati's Survivor Association has identified 48 survivors who experienced the tests first hand, as well as 800 descendants. Members of the Association report numerous health problems which they attribute to the testing, including blindness, hearing problems, cancers, heart disease and reproductive difficulties. They also report that their children and grandchildren have suffered similar illnesses' (2021: 112).

27 This description of James and my interaction appeared first on the *American Ethnologist* website in a web collection of flash ethnography edited by Carole McGranahan and Nomi Stone (Trundle 2020c).

shape and pattern of the text, the slant of a historical signature, the placement of a grainy diagram.

James handed me the first document. A meeting in London, 19 November 1956. Commander of Operation Grapple, Air Vice-Marshal Oulton, needed to designate a radiation 'Danger Zone' in the Western Pacific.[28] James tabled a map, consisting of two circles drawn out at a radius of 400 nautical miles from Kiritimati and Malden Islands, the chosen location for the nuclear tests. This 'preferred danger zone' was calculated on the assumption that if a nuclear bomb accidentally detonated at ground level, the fallout would at maximum spread that far. This was premised upon a 150-kiloton blast.

'Well, in reality three of the bombs in Operation Grapple were huge. Megaton huge.' James pointed to the margins of the paper where he had scrawled this fact. He was used to arguing with these documents.

James read aloud from the meeting record, in a clipped, officious voice. 'Such an area is patently too large and has been reduced.' Overlaid upon the circles was a smaller, irregular shaped zone drawn with efficient, straight lines. It wove back and forth, vertical then horizontal, excluding all of the nearby inhabited islands. The Washington, Fanning, Jarvis, and Penrhyn Islands were now classified as lying in the 'safe zone'. James offered no commentary, but let the document sit between us for a moment as we gazed at the 'mutability of risk' (McAlinden 2022b: 398) so brazenly narrated within it.

The next record: 27 November 1956. The scientific architects of the British bomb tests met in London to produce a top secret document entitled 'Safety Precautions Planned for Operation Grapple'. They noted that, according to this more limited danger zone, safe levels of radiation 'recommended by the International Commission on Radiological Protection (ICRP) would be necessarily exceeded'. Despite this, they reasoned that 'only very slight health hazard to people would arise and that only to primitive peoples'.[29]

Through all the photocopying of photocopies of archival documents, the word 'primitive' had faded, almost indecipherably, from the page. But James had underlined it, twice, in green ink, and traced back in the

[28] Public Records Office, CO1036/280. [29] Public Records Office, CO1036/280.

vanished letters p and v. His finger was, however, pressed below the word 'only'. He tapped it. He moved onto the next document.

These archival engagements, the acts of sharing them, reading and writing onto them, as well as the silences test veterans let hang over them, gestured to an increasing awareness amongst test veterans that nuclear injuries extended beyond their own communities. They reflected discomforting narrative efforts to reckon with the colonial and racist exclusions of injury, undercurrent narratives that pressed up within test veterans' own histories of harm.

INJURIOUS ENDINGS

The nuclear injuries that test veterans sustained marked the beginning of Britain's entry into the 'nuclear club' of nations. Yet, in a perverse way, injury also resulted from efforts to end nuclear testing. By 1957, the international political consensus supporting nuclear testing began to fray. The UK government engaged in UN disarmament talks, aimed at de-escalating the increasing nuclear arms race between the USSR, the US, and the UK. In the face of an increasingly organized disarmament movement, British leaders were openly expressing a willingness to consider suspending nuclear bomb tests and ceasing production of fissile materials.

The military planners of the British bomb programme recognized the increasing risk of politically imposed restrictions on their work. They accelerated the time frame for the next bomb test on Kiritimati Island, Grapple X. They hoped to build their biggest bomb yet, one with a yield in the megaton range.[30] All this they did in top secret, noting that should the planned tests become public knowledge, 'there was likely to be considerable public outcry against them'. They also anticipated political opposition, and were mindful of the risk that 'if these preparations become known before Parliament adjoined for the summer Recess, the [Labour] Opposition would demand a further debate on nuclear tests'.[31]

[30] A megaton is equivalent to one million tons of TNT.

[31] Ministerial Committee on Atomic Energy, 24 July 1957 (Public Records Office, CAB 134/1328).

The ministerial Committee on Atomic Tests thus noted:

> The longer such tests were delayed, the greater were likely to be the political difficulties in view of the growing pressure of world opinion in favour of a ban. Preparations for the tests should therefore proceed expeditiously with a view of holding them in November this year. Every endeavour should be made to keep these preparations secret for as long as possible.[32]

In March of 1958, the Soviet Union was the first to announce a planned suspension of their nuclear testing programme. The US and UK followed suit, announcing plans for a one-year suspension in August 1958. Less than two weeks later, the Atomic Weapons Establishment began conducting another three bomb tests, under the codename Operation Grapple Z. The first of these was the largest, at 1.21 megaton. They concluded these in quick succession, across the month of September, just before the Conference on the Discontinuance of Nuclear Weapons Tests opened in Geneva in October. Here the Soviets, British, and Americans finally agreed to cease testing while they negotiated the signing a Nuclear Weapons Test Moratorium.

In the end, negotiations for a test ban across 1958 rapidly hastened the rate of nuclear weapons testing, with Britain detonating five nuclear tests in this time, the Soviets conducting thirty-six tests, while the Americans carried out seventy-five tests. These tests were amongst the highest yields detonated. Grapple Y, tested in April 1958, was the largest bomb Britain has ever produced, at three megaton.[33] 'That bomb went wrong', test veteran Joseph told me, his words echoed by many other Operation Grapple veterans. It dropped and detonated

[32] Ministerial Committee on Atomic Energy, 24 July 1957 (Public Records Office, CAB 134/1328).

[33] Between 12 and 18 October 1958, just weeks before the Geneva meeting, the Soviets detonated two 1.5 megaton bombs, and Joe 66, a 2.9 megaton bomb in Novaya Zemlya, an archipelago in the Arctic ocean region of Russia. The largest nuclear bomb ever detonated was the *Tsar Bomba*, tested by the Soviet Union over Novaya Zemlya in October 1961. It was equivalent to fifty megaton of TNT. This was a bomb forty times more powerful than the largest bomb in the current US nuclear arsenal (Wellerstein 2021).

too low, they recounted, and irradiated rain soon fell on the Island, the ships, and personnel.

Military planners and scientists turned growing public opposition to the bomb into a temporary opportunity for increased experimental license. Under the cover of geopolitical uncertainty nuclear technology evades the political (cf. Polleri 2020). The emergent peace movement's impetus to thwart nuclear risk ironically enabled military planners to test even riskier bombs, at a swifter pace, with less oversight, and under a cloak of heavier secrecy than before. In 1958, a moratorium was signed, and thirteen years of nuclear testing came to a temporary end. For three years the boom of bombs ceased above the Australian outback, the Pacific Ocean, the Nevada deserts, and the Soviet tundra and steppes.[34]

In this chapter, I have drawn attention to the ways in which personal and archival memories can coalesce to mark out moments of exposure risk. In dwelling within and retelling memories, test veterans reappraised service experiences to locate both the elemental mechanisms of risky exposure and the military practices that obscured and erased their abilities to apprehend radiation risk. Their stories are of 'long-ago' and 'far-away', revealing how the haunting qualities of colonial pollution concentrate within landscapes geographically, socially, and temporally separable from the political centres of empire where injurious claims must later be heard and tested. Indeed, this distance is what makes colonial pollution politically permissible in the first place. That far-distant sites of pollution are so cleaved from latter sites of justice turns toxins into an unpalpable presence, allowing radiation to become a theoretical, imagined force within legal processes of redress.

[34] The moratorium lasted until 1961, during which time the US and the USSR struggled to agree on terms for a permanent nuclear test ban. In 1961, Russia resumed tests and soon after the US also resumed testing. In 1963, US President Kennedy, the Soviet leader Khrushchev, and the British Prime Minster Macmillan agreed to sign the Partial Nuclear Test Ban Treaty, which banned all nuclear testing except underground. Within six months over 100 countries had signed up, although France and China were notable exceptions. In the decade following the Treaty, the US detonated 35 per cent more nuclear tests that they had in the decade prior (Schwelb 1964).

What then does it take to turn individual memories of long ago and far away into collective claims in the here and now? In the next chapter, I describe how embodied memories worked across time and through the emergence of illnesses, institutional silences, and veteran spaces, building the collective capacity of test veterans to make claims, to see themselves as injury claimants and the state as a liable actor.

CHAPTER 2

The Second Betrayal

THIS CHAPTER EXPLORES THE SECOND BETRAYAL. I USE THIS term to connote the traumas, stresses, debilities, and world-limiting impacts that resulted from the silences and denials that shrouded radiation's aftereffects. These are the injurious processes that occurred in the three decades following radiation exposure, but preceding engagements in more formal mechanisms of claim-making. I refer to the second *betrayal* here, rather than injury, to evoke the affective and moral heft and emerging expectations of state responsibility – and experiences of its lack – that underpinned test veterans and their families' sense of compounding injury.

In the quest for answers about their nuclear exposure and their health, test veterans experienced a range of cultural, political, medical, and legal impasses that prefigured injury claims. The barriers they faced – in understanding their illness and understanding themselves as a collective – were barriers that denied harm, information, explanation, legal rights, narrative, and even history. Within such silences and denials, test veterans and their families were not passive. Rather, they navigated difficult illness and troubling memories, and in the process transformed these experiences into valued claim-making identities and existentially affirming collectivities.

This stage of test veterans' struggles reflects forms of prefigurative legality. Prefigurative legality, as Cohen and Morgan (2023) argue, refers to methods for 'enacting a desired future in the present' that may be tentative, partial, and not clearly or consciously tied to legal goals and structures. Such methods are commonly built through decentralized, small-scale and ground up enactments, prototypes, and practices that do not rely upon formal organizational decision-making (Raekstad and Gradin 2020). Prefigurative legality may thus decentre the law, offer alternatives to law, or involve actions that proceed 'as if' the law was otherwise, that is, as if what one desires from law was already available (Schiller-Merkens 2022). It often seeks to transform reality outside of established systems and beyond purely instrumental and legalistic means (Boggs 1977, Cooper 2020). This chapter foregrounds the temporal dimension of prefigurative legality, asking what the 'pre' contains for claimants. How do claimants understand and narrate the period when they do not yet have sufficient narratives to make sense of injury? What political work occurred in quotidian experiences of emergent illnesses and debility, and the quest for military and medical explanations?

'For a long time, all this, it was static in your mind', explained Robert, a New Zealand test veteran, as we stood on his manicured lawn. 'You couldn't really make head nor tail of it, what was happening to you. Why [illnesses were] happening to us.' Clearing his throat, almost embarrassed by his comment, he quickly shifted our discussion from the aftermath of nuclear bomb testing to his impressive rose garden. He shared tips for how he ensured prolific blossoms, how to avoid black spot, when best to add feed. His old Labrador sat at his feet. She snapped at a passing fly, he leaned down to pat her, and we enjoyed a moment of quiet in the spring sun. Putting this confusing time of his life into coherent words wasn't easy. As an ethnographer I was learning to give it time, to take as long as participants required before we turned the tape recorder on.

The word *static* connotes two values. It first refers to a type of 'noise' or interference. Static noise grates, interrupts, and demands our attention but refuses to yield intelligible meaning. Static also means a state of immobility, stasis, or a lack of change, often one that is undesirable. In this period of the participants' lives many felt caught within elusive illnesses, pain, or disability for which they could not find effective treatments, diagnoses, relief, or recognition, and beyond which they struggled to manoeuvre.

Nuclearity generates a contradiction: both urgent temporalities and temporalities of inertia (Howey 2019). For test veterans, the Cold War rush to nuclear mastery gave way to a slow and unsettled sense of stuck-time that lasted for decades. In the thirty years after the British nuclear bomb tests, many veterans' health began to falter, and memories of the tests refused to recede from the horizon of the everyday. Troubling bodies and troubling memories intruded, even as veterans and their families tried to 'get on' with building post-service lives.

Roy made clear at the start of our interview that he wanted to be named in my book. As a leader of the test veteran community, he felt he needed to 'front up' and be visible. Roy joined the New Zealand Navy as a sixteen-year-old cadet. He trained and qualified as a radio operator, and then at age nineteen was deployed to Kiritimati Island, where he witnessed five nuclear tests. After his return, and two years later, Roy noticed, 'I had painful muscles, joints and in fact I used to . . . play rugby for the communications rugby team and a bit of basketball and softball, that sort of thing . . . then I got to this sort of stage where I gave it up because I noticed that extended movement created even more pain.' Being young, Roy recalled, 'I sort of didn't worry too much about it, I just thought, Oh, I'm just unfit, but oddly enough I hadn't been doing any less than what I'd ever done before. And this carried on, and I became more and more aware of it.' Roy's rising pain was gradual, shifting, and episodic, almost beyond his field of vision. Roy recalled getting sore, frozen shoulders, but, like many men with whom I spoke, he said he 'never went to sick bay, never bothered about that'. Within a military culture that valued masculine strength and stamina, becoming known by one's peers or superiors as a 'sick bay ranger' was a status to actively avoid.

Roy's entire life story was one of sizable talent and ambition, often thwarted by his health. At age twenty-six, Roy had reached the end of his naval contract, and had the option of leaving the Armed Forces. Wanting to 'make a career of it', he reenlisted, working his way up to petty officer. But Roy's unexplained pain continued. 'If I was stuck at a desk, say logging or writing stuff, [I'd] get [a] stiff neck and stiff arm.'

In his late twenties, Roy's illness shifted from the sideline of daily experience to centre stage. 'I noticed then that I was becoming very tired on watch and the major crime in the navy used to be asleep on watch – if you're asleep you can't do your duty – and I realized that something was wrong, this was *seriously* wrong.' Not only was his illness troubling but it also threatened his career and livelihood. He needed to hide it at all costs. Despite all his efforts to stay alert, he experienced a 'tiredness that you can't control'. Still Roy did not seek medical help.

> I made the fatal mistake of not going to the sick bay, but of course naval sick bays in those days were a little different, I mean you sorta went along there and they looked at you and they'd give you a couple of aspirin or something and told you to bugger off and don't be so silly. Bit hard unless they could see it.

Unable to pinpoint a physical location for disease, or visible symptoms of injury, Roy feared that a military doctor might accuse him of malingering.

Roy tried to develop strategies to cope on the job.

> During that period I had to make excuses, I was in charge of a watch in the main wireless office ... in charge of transmitters and receivers, so I would say to the [guys working there], 'Oh, look I'm just going down to the lower transmitter room to re-tune the transmitters', or something like that, and I'd have to go down there and crash for a while.

Roy feared others would soon notice, as his overwhelming fatigue caused him to seek solitude and rest 'almost every night and sometimes during the day'. Eventually the 'fear of being, of thinking, well I may be caught out on this' became difficult to bear, and he decided it was best to leave the Navy.

His strategy of secrecy came at a cost. 'I was 30 . . . I didn't get a medical discharge which is a bit of a problem ... but if I'd said to them what I thought was causing this [radiation exposure], they would've laughed ... I wouldn't, [have got a medical discharge] *no, no, not a show!'* With his pain and fatigue still socially invisible and medically unexplained, Roy re-entered civilian life.

'I originally took a job driving trucks and ... I struggled with that, and that you had to start at six in the morning . . .. And I was continually tired.' Eventually Roy sought medical help and was diagnosed with chronic fatigue syndrome. While it was a relief to have a diagnosis, it was an uncertain, contested label that conferred neither a socially acceptable sick role nor a pathway to healing. Eventually, as work became more difficult to sustain, he was forced to quit.

Over the years, Roy's health problems steadily worsened.

> It got to a stage where I couldn't raise my . . . arms to my mouth to drink tea. I couldn't get out of the chair to walk across the room . . . to change the TV. I couldn't go out to check the mail. . . . So I was in a state where I just wasn't able to do anything, and of course with that comes depression, stress and anxiety, all those things.

Roy's wife had to find work to support their family, which now included a young daughter. '[I] couldn't get down on the floor and play with her, and picking her up [was painful].' Recounting this memory caused Roy's voice to croak; it was the most emotional moment in the interview. Eventually Roy and his family had to move out of their two-storey house to one without stairs to support Roy's limited mobility. Illness is here cast as harmful because it is corrosive of the fundamentals of a good family life. Because of his pain, he ceased to be the breadwinner, could not enact the simple care routines of fatherhood, and was responsible for the loss of a cherished family home.

The mid stage of Roy's life story is one in which radiation and Kiritimati Island had yet to feature significantly. Instead, he learned to live in a body that would not cooperate with the military norms of masculine strength, with medical classificatory systems, or with the regimens of work. At one level this was experienced as an estrangement, the body as uncooperative object. It was also the site of bodily attunement. He learnt to align his desires, hopes, and plans, no matter how circumscribed, with the uncertain limits of debility. This required an embodied attentiveness that became a way of knowing that something was persistently and concretely wrong with him, despite the absence of an adequate medical name or a definable cause. 'The affected, feeling, sensing body is a conduit of knowledge' (Wiebe 2016: 13). Such intimate and private sites of knowledge, as Morimoto (2021) notes, push back against imaginaries of nuclear damage and destruction as always scaled to population, nation, and the global.

As Mattingly points out, simply learning to live as best one can in the presence of disease and debility can be essential to future agency and activist selves, 'the moral ordinary can be more morally subversive than many scholars have presumed' (2014: 26). She asks us to recognize the transformative effects of simply living within the mundanity of illness and debility and its uncertain future tense. Navigating persistent illness alongside everyday emotions like fear, curiosity, despondency, anger, and hope shaped test veterans' determination to both know the truth of their bodies, and the truth of the past.

As Arthur Frank argues, illness can make the past a stubbornly unresolved feature of the present that demands attention. How and why am I sick? While self-narratives attempt to create meaningful coherence out of the flux of unfolding experience, 'Illness intensifies the struggle.' The past intrudes in powerful ways because 'the illness experiences that are being told are unassimilated fragments that refuse to become past, haunting the present' (1995: 60). Test veterans sought an illness narrative that made sense of the self and past while rendering the body legible in the present (Kleinman 1988).

NOT MY HUSBAND

He looked young and handsome. Dashing, I thought, reaching for a word from my grandmothers' generation. Flashing a fearless smile in his crisp uniform. The black and white framed photograph sat in the centre of Kim's mantlepiece in her small flat, next to the colourful pictures of grandchildren he never lived long enough to meet. In her seventies, she had a warm, charming smile and an exuberant way of making people feel instantly at ease in her presence.

As a squadron leader in the RAF, her husband Adam had been sent into the fissioning cloud of a detonated atmospheric test on Christmas Island to collect radiation samples. After his exposure – six minutes flying through the highly irradiated vapours – Adam returned to the UK via Fiji, where he was hospitalized for three days with uncontrolled vomiting.

> He came home and we expected . . . this handsome blond [who had been] out in the Pacific, wonderful you know . . . the most incisive, clever boy. And instead of that we got a different bloke. He was always fairly quiet but full of charm and mischief. But there was no fun and mischief . . . after that. . . . That was not my young husband.

For both Adam and Kim, the change made no sense. In the wake of World War II, the most readily available narrative for understanding the transformation of veterans' personalities was 'shell shock'. But such a diagnosis required the violence trigger of war. Kim described an increasingly withdrawn man who gradually became prone to incoherent ramblings and terrible mood swings.

By 1976, Adam was in his mid forties and faced a bright career in international aviation. Yet, since Kiritimati Island, he had been suffering from a range of chronic health issues, including depression, anxiety, and acute sinusitis. Kim recalled how at this point 'life got really hard, and then one day ... first time ever, he couldn't be near the children you know, he couldn't stand people'. She recounted coming down the stairs to her kitchen late one night to find her husband sitting in the kitchen with his head in his hands. He had been sitting there for hours.

> I said, 'Darling you haven't been to bed, are you alright?' No answer. So I said I will make a cup of tea, British answer to everything. Funny. I went over to the sink to get the kettle and put it on. The wood axe from the shed was propped up against the wall and I glanced at it, and made the tea, gave him his. And he did look up then, And I asked, what is the axe for?

She did not detail the specifics of his later suicide. She described cleaning up clots of blood the size of dinner plates more than once. Towards the end, she reflected, 'I could see it coming. I knew'. Despite all of her efforts, she felt helpless to prevent his death. 'Because there was no hope, Catherine.' Centring her own well-being in the narrative briefly, she added, 'I have seen too much.'

Kim's world shattered. Memory here bears witness to sudden breaks in time. Not only grief, but coming from an upper-class background, Kim has to contemplate a life without the resources from her husband's rising career. 'The life that we had stretching in front of us has turned to dust. ... Fabulous future. Adam just said to me, "Our future is brilliant and totally assured." ... All that gone, everything gone.' She realized her children would be raised in a world of far less material comfort, opportunity, and privilege than her own childhood. They were now all dependent on her own resourcefulness.

Adam's death has a profound impact on one of her children. 'Within twelve, eighteen months of Daddy's death' her child 'just collapsed really' and went on to have difficulties with addiction. For a long time,

Kim focused her energy on her grandchildren, trying to ensure that the devastation of Adams death would not swell further. As a family with meagre incomes and thus limited educational opportunities, joblessness became a commonplace family concern. For Kim, Kiritimati Island had multiple impacts beyond radiation, as trauma and economic precarity travelled intergenerationally.

'Thing is, I manage.' She sat proudly in her armchair. She refused to downplay the challenges, but she underscored her capability of making something enduring, a life that was liveable and even lively in the wake of such distress. Kim spent the remainder of the 1970s and 1980s in the role of matriarch. She occupied herself with getting by financially and trying to hold her family together. There were many joys amongst the hardships. She had little time to investigate the root cause of her husband's death, but she did think about it often, sensing that there was an external reason for such a dramatic change in his personality and well-being. Despite attending to a complex web of familial needs that focused her on the pragmatics of the present, Adam's pain, its lack of knowability, continued to haunt her.

Kim decided to track down Adam's radiation records from the Public Records Office in the early 1990s. In our interview she took out a well-folded photocopy from the inner pocket of her wallet. In wonky typewriter script, it recorded that he had received a radiation dose of 13,000 rad. 'It's like getting 6500 X-rays all at once', she explained. Because Adam was a pilot, he had worn several dosimeter badges from his hip to his head, and, being a high-ranked military figure, he had had his badge dose rates personally recorded. This was in contrast to rank-and-file personnel who reported either not wearing dosimeter badges, or throwing their unnamed badges into a collective bucket. Adam's readings revealed that he received dangerously high levels of radiation, much of it to his head. The MoD then admitted to Kim that this exposure to radiation was indeed unsafe, but they continued to deny any connection to his death.

Kim began to devise a causal explanation. She believed that the level of radiation Adam had received to his brain was lethal to his mental state. She suspects radiation had caused a 'disruptive chemical imbalance' or even a tumour to his brain. When Kim began to press MoD officials about her husband's exposure and death they denied any link between service at

Operation Grapple and his death, and that any psychological and physical sickness must have been present since childhood. This bureaucratic assessment in no way matched the memories of those who knew Adam well. Nor were such illnesses revealed in the comprehensive entry tests for the Air Force and its elite pilot training programme. Still, the MoD parsed action from attribution, enacting only a partial form of moral responsibility. Kim received a RAF house and a military pension without barrier, but on a no-fault basis and without any admission of guilt.

THE INJURIOUS ABSENCE OF NARRATIVE

From a bioethical perspective, Adam's plight is a recognizable one: the right to information is a key principle underpinning the autonomy of a patient. That is, the disclosure of information, and the comprehension of information enable autonomous decision-making in the pursuit of health. On the surface, Kim's lament illustrates this principle. But the story tells a more complex tale of autonomy and disclosure.

Information was not only desired for medical decision-making and action. It was existential. As Kim explained,

> I think if we had known, if the MoD has said to us honestly and immediately, 'look, you have been heavily irradiated, heaviest to the brain, if there are any problems, you know, we will watch you, we will examine you', . . . he might have had enough ammunition from knowing what was causing it to have said . . . 'I am not going bonkers.' . . . And he might have lived.

The MoD's negligence was not simply Adam's exposure to radiation. Put another way, radiation was not the singular cause of death. Rather it was, Kim asserted, that the MoD did not provide him with the information necessary to translate his suffering through a nuclear explanatory frame, a narrative that, despite the physical and psychological pain, might have preserved his sense of self and dignity, a self the existed beyond personal failure, confusion, or madness.

Mattingly defines narrative as 'a discourse featuring human adventures and suffering, one which connects motivations, acts and consequences in causal chains' (1998: 275). Illnesses remaining unclear or contested generate 'emergent narratives' (Mattingly 2000: 181), promising and withholding meaning over years. In test veterans' claim-making, narratives became the means to socially manoeuvre when the body and the state appeared simultaneously to fail the self. As Michael Jackson argues, 'storytelling is a vital human strategy for sustaining a sense of agency in the face of disempowering circumstances' (2002: 15). In contrast to the norms of formal legal testimony, informal practices of narratives have the capacity to '"presence" victims' experiences, accommodate multivocal truths, and provide avenues for epistemic resistance' (Herremans and Destrooper 2023: 521).

Within healthcare, narratives are often reduced to the idea of information. Bioethical principles of informational rights are designed to prevent ongoing and compounding harms to health. Such principles envisage an encounter between actors that necessitates a patient free from the coercive will of another. These principles imagine momentary and voluntary collaborations between information holders (doctors) and decision-makers (patients) that end in treatment plans and the restoration of health. They assume that healthcare information is generated for the pursuit and purposes of health and medicine. They assume that information can be complete and comprehensible. And they assume that the information is separable, can be rendered independent, from the claims for care that might follow (Räikkä 1998). None of these assumptions held in Kim and Adam's case, nor do they hold easily in the hierarchies of militarism.

The information upon which Kim built her understanding of radiation harm was produced not for the purpose of informing or supporting patient healthcare decisions, but for tracking radiological effects on human bodies largely so that it could aid the building of military capacity. Moreover, the information was produced and held by the very actors that Kim would come to believe caused her husband harm. Here test veterans are not alone: radiation injury information is in most circumstances controlled by those accused of harm (Cable et al. 2008). Access to information that might build illness narratives thus reflects real-world struggles over how and why information about nuclearity and its bodily effects are produced, and the politics of how such information is guarded or released.

Medico-legal discussions of the right to health information assume that information flows in one empowering direction, towards the patient. But as Kim made clear, the absence of available radiation records was compounded by the inability of the patient to disclose a history of harm. Kim explained, 'And you see the awful thing is . . . even if it had occurred to me or him that this could be radiation damage that we hadn't known about . . . we actually would not have been able to tell the psychiatrist because of the thirty-year secrecy act.' Despite being ill on his return, Adam received no medical checks. He did not speak of his service to his family. Like many test veterans, he believed himself bound by the Official Secrets Act 1939 ((UK) 2 & 3 Geo 6). As witnesses to a covert government operation, he and other test veterans recounted superiors cautioning them that they were legally forbidden from disclosing details of the tests, even to their wives. Experiences of a secondary betrayal thus operated not only through governmental silences but also through the internalization of perceived legal barriers that prevented test veterans from integrating radiation in their health histories.[1]

COLLECTIVIZING ILLNESS AND MEMORY

Patients' needs can exceed the care biomedicine offers. When patients fail in their quest for the sick role, what then? As Petryna notes, the sick role conventionally contained a biomedical locus, a social contract between doctor and patient to work towards wellness.[2] Yet, increasingly the sick role has shifted to 'paramedical spaces of authority' (2012: 377). These spaces blur law, politics, and new social configurations. Militarism provides veterans with one such space, and with values and social infrastructures to recognize illness. In veterans' communities, self-care and mutual responsibility meet (cf. Robbins-Rubszkowski 2017).

[1] As Fiona Bowler deftly points out (2022: 159–161), the degree of secrecy required by law remains unclear. Media reports during and directly after the nuclear tests publicly disclosed details of the tests, and some test veterans were open in discussing what occurred operationally with their families, communities, and the media.

[2] Talcott Parsons (2013[1951]) theorized social norms for illness. The 'sick role', he argued, enabled a person to be relieved of certain social expectations (such as work) but necessitated other obligations, such as working towards wellness, seeking diagnosis, and engaging with medical authority.

Test veteran collectives in New Zealand and the UK are grounded in the unique features of military social life. There are multiple reasons why military personnel often maintain lifelong bonds. Military training and service seek to build intense forms of solidarity through practices that isolate personnel from civilian life, that strip back an individualized selfhood, that immerse them in shared rituals, and which promote narratives of loyalty and selflessness (Gutmann and Lutz 2010). And it is achieved through infrastructures of military sociality that endure post service. In New Zealand, veteran reunions are an often-annual occurrence, and a national network of Returned and Services Association [RSA] venues offer veterans a shared space in most New Zealand towns to talk, drink, remember, and reconnect.

In these gatherings and collective spaces, test veterans began crafting three concurrent narratives. These were the memories of risky service, the experience of slowly emergent injury, and the neglectful silence of the state in the face of their suffering. Roy recalled,

> in the early 80s I became aware, well convinced in my own mind that Operation Grapple had affected us. And ... that opinion was boosted by a number of others who felt the same thing – we weren't many, but they were sort of congregat[ing], they were sort of noticing that, to their reckoning, that guys were dying fairly early, from cancers and stuff. And a lot were suffering illnesses, particularly ... joint and muscle problems.

In 1995, Roy formed the New Zealand Nuclear Test Veterans Association, with the explicit aim to investigate any links between radiation exposure and ill health.

At their first meeting they heard stories not only of servicemen's ill health but also of miscarriages and babies born with congenital conditions. Not content with the lack of action from the government, Ruth, a test veteran widow, started a spreadsheet database of veterans' and their children's ill health. As there were no surviving ships logs or crew lists, two test veterans, Gerry and Authur, painstakingly spent two years manually searching through Naval Posting Cards in order to identify the 551 New Zealand servicemen who had served at Operation Grapple.

A Scottish test veteran, Ken, suffered from infertility and other ailments. He wrote a letter to the Glaswegian paper, the *Daily Record*, in November 1982. He asked if 'any readers had suffered medical problems after they returned from Christmas Island'. This generated reader interest, and the paper wrote an article on the tests. The following week Ken was interviewed on BBC Radio Scotland, and a few weeks later his story featured on the BBC Nationwide programme. Test veterans from around the UK got in touch. Within a year, he had formed the British Nuclear Test Veterans Association. By 1984, it had hundreds of members and representatives across the UK and sent out a regular newsletter.

Kim became aware of these groups in the 1990s and became increasingly involved. She decided to take a more active role after hearing and seeing too many test veteran families struggling with ill health. Kim's work, like many who took on leadership roles in the test veteran communities, involved supporting test veterans to meet others who had similar health concerns. She began by giving them a hug and telling them they weren't alone. She often referred to them as a family. Emotional labour and hard work build valued ties from a shared sense of nuclear exposure. They became nuclear kin (Brown 2013, Kalshoven 2021) and nuclear community (Kari 2020, Kalshoven 2022), where health risks are made more manageable through post-nuclear relationality. As Reverby and Moran Thomas argue (2024), recognizing the facts of injury alone are insufficient for redress, but rather, facts are activated for justice by the repeated building of relations and shared practices over time, galvanizing collective emotions and memory into public and community consciousness.

Collective life involved remembering together. Scholars use the term *collective memory* to signify shared accounts of the past that utilize powerful sociopolitical narrative templates (Wertsch 2008). These constitute history into a lively ongoing social force, mapping past events onto present concerns and debates, as well as imagined futures (Armstrong 2000). In practice, however, the rituals of collectivizing memory do not always operate by standardizing memory (Robbins 2019). In coming together, test veterans shared diverse personal memories from service and its aftermath. Depending on their service role, each had their own vantage of the bombs, bodily reaction, sense of danger, and tactile engagement with the environment. And each had a particular constellation of diverse ailments to report. Telling personal stories together involved crafting unique and highly personal points of view that refused standardization. Indeed, it was this level of specificity that reinforced the legitimacy of having 'been there'.

Such personal stories were, however, socially constituted within shared evaluative frames and practices of ethical witness. Together, test veterans re-evaluated memories in light of illness and together found 'the right way to be concerned' (Kimura 2016: 6). In doing so, they offered each other care by refusing to replicate the sceptical treatment they received from others. They built spaces in which veterans and their families could disclose their stories and, no matter how tentatively told, they treated such stories as believable and trustworthy on their own terms. These practices were an ethical counterclaim to official denial, just as speaking and hearing illness became a 'collective counter-emplotment of facts' (Dumit 2006: 285).

FORGOTTEN

Overcoming isolation and uncertainty can, as Açiksöz (2012: 4) shows, harden veteran injury into a political force. As test veterans articulated their claims publicly, they were often met with disbelief and sometimes ridicule. Roy recounted how 'in those early days, [we] were laughed off by everybody, including the RSA [Returned and Services Association], who published a front page article [that said] … Operation Grapple concerns was a nonsense, something like that, and that didn't help our cause at all, they were laughing it all off.' Overall, Roy recalled how, in those early years, 'I was subjected to a lot of ridicule [from] politicians and even from some navy people, senior navy people.'

A friend of Roy's, Barry, a New Zealand veteran in his late seventies, recounted that in the 1980s and early 1990s few politicians had any knowledge of New Zealand's involvement in the British nuclear testing programme.

> I was a member of the Labour Party, and I made an appointment to see [my MP]. I told him my story … and he told me to stop listening to old sailors' stories, and there was no recollection down in Wellington of any

> New Zealand Navy ships ever being there [at Christmas Island] . . . He said, "Just get on with your life." . . . I'll never forgive that [MP] for that.[3]

Another New Zealand veteran, Steven, said, 'originally, they denied we were there, didn't they. [They said] "No, you weren't there". Well, I mean we had documentation, but the government's saying, "no, no, no, you weren't there"'. Because of political ignorance, participants explained, fuelled by military secrecy and a dearth of knowledge in the education system and media, most members of the public lacked any knowledge of the test veterans' experiences.

Beyond government officials and military bureaucrats, this ignorance and denial cut deepest when it came from fellow service personnel. Sam, a New Zealand test veteran in his late seventies, thus reflected:

> Even the crew of the new Pukaki and Rotoiti [ships], when it came here I [went on board and I] mentioned the fact that Rotoiti was at most of the tests in the Pacific. The crew didn't know . . . and I just can't understand why. We're part of their history. You'll have to scrape quite a long time before you find any mention [of us] in any publications of the Navy, and . . . it's very short. . . . We were sent there by this government. . . . No one knew about nuclear test veterans, we had to fight to get recognized.

Test veterans articulated fierce criticism of state organizations with an expressed purpose to memorialize, preserve records, and raise awareness of veterans' experiences. Some participants discussed a national naval museum, which in the 1980s and 1990s had nothing to commemorate servicemen who participated in the bomb test programme. John recounted: 'I am quite upset about that. I love the Navy, I am loyal to the Navy, and there is nothing on record there to tell others.'

Roy recalled how veterans of the nuclear tests could also participate in acts that dismissed and silenced other test veterans' growing public concerns.

> I got a lot of letters from our own people who abused me . . . they were of course, as we *all* are, even to this day in the main . . . very loyal to the Navy

[3] Barry's quote, the quote that follows by Sam, and the quote following by John, were previously published in my book chapter *Memorialising the Veteran Body: New Zealand Nuclear Test Veterans and the Search for Military Citizenship* (2013: 248–249).

> still . . . although the [Navy has] treated us abominably really. And the [test veterans] were protesting that there was nothing to be concerned about and I was a traitor . . . [The] duty manager at the RSA [Returned and Services Association] here one night banned me from the RSA and I never went back for about 10 or 15 years.[4]

Alan, a New Zealand veteran, recalled attending the first test veteran reunion.

> I told [a test veteran friend I'd pick him up and take him. He said, 'No, no, no, I'm not going . . . the way I look at it . . . I was on that ship when it [went to Kiritimati Island] and that was just luck of the draw. I was doing my duty.' And I said, 'Yeah, but, you know . . . what about your grandkids, that's what you've got to think of.' 'No, no, no, I took the luck of the draw', he said.
>
> When I came back, he said, 'Good conference?' and I said, 'Yep'. And he never asked me another question, he didn't want to know what happened. . . . Bloody suffered in the long run, in the end. He could of got something out of it [a war pension]. . . . One of his grandkids suffered too!

The trust many test veterans came to place in collective memory work and embodied modes of knowledge worked against a social tide of erasure and denial. That not all test veterans partook in these acts of embodiment and memory reveals the diverse ways that history can occupy or vacate the work of selfhood over time. These counternarratives index the multiple possibilities for trying to make sense of past experience in the aftermath of nuclear tests (Stawkowski 2016, Zonabend 1993 [1989]). For some test veterans, the past was meaningfully held together through repeated acts of remembering. For others, managing the past required wilful forgetting.

[4] The enemies that test veterans have vested with blame – callous politicians, risky scientists, even invisible radioisotopes – are characters that do not fit easily within mainstream narratives of militarism. Theirs is a story of being harmed by one's own side, motifs that threaten war's nationalistic and unifying force, as well as its dependence on binary oppositions.

AT THE LIMITS OF MEDICINE

Merleau-Ponty (2012[1945]) argued that the process of knowing, popularly cast as a rational, cognitive matter, in fact begins with bodily and sensorial acts of perception. This is knowledge understood as emerging out of 'being-in-the-world', one that foregrounds the sensory bond between body and world.[5] Embodiment is thus never an individual process, but, as Thomas Csordas (1993, 2002) argues, one that entails cultural worlds of meaning.[6] The ability to know through the body, indeed, the *need* to know through the body, is often mediated by the role of medical expertise, its technologies of visualizing, probing and measuring the body, and its successes and failures in drawing the body into view in ways that allow intervention (Mol 2003). For test veterans, bodily attunement became an ethical and existential anchor point because, in the face of medical uncertainty, it offered a shared language for explaining pain, debility, and disease.

Throughout the 1960s to the 1990s veterans found few doctors prepared to take seriously their claims that radiation had contributed to their health concerns. As one New Zealand test veteran, Simon, explained, 'My GP wouldn't listen to me ... he wasn't interested. I told him, you know, what I had done, and I said ... I attribute a lot of it to radiation. "Oh no," he said, "It can't be that, I know nothing about that".' Many test veterans reported that doctors refused to equivocally link their illnesses and those of their children to radiation exposure and nuclear testing. Craig explained, 'You go to these specialists and doctors, [and they say] "Oh maybe, could be", but no one will come out and say yes, and that seemed to be one of our major problems.'

Brian's medical consultants offered positive but equivocal support for his case. His GP felt unable to substantively confirm the link to radiation, and instead presented it as her client's opinion, stating, 'Mr Davis has approached me today for support in pursuing a claim for compensation

5 The process of embodied objectification allows objects to emerge into view as they meet the body and self. Objects in the world are thus not already finished things but come into fullness in particular ways as we interact with them, as our attention, intention, and desires engage them into being.

6 As Csordas argues (1993: 138): 'Somatic modes of attention are culturally elaborated ways of attending to and with one's body in surroundings that include the embodied presence of others.' This thus entails both attending 'with' and attending 'to' the body.

for his pancreatic carcinoma explaining that he has been exposed to the fallout of nuclear testing. . . . He explains that in these circumstances US test veterans automatically receive compensation on a presumed link.' Brian's oncologist wrote with slightly more assertion, but remained equivocal: 'I write to confirm that he has an adenocarcinoma of his pancreas which I understand is one of 21 conditions which are now recognized to have radiation as a possible aetiological factor.'

Roy's frustrations with the medical sphere began with being either undiagnosed or misdiagnosed. He visited many medical experts, but 'nobody could tell [me], could diagnose what I had'. Finally a local rheumatologist 'treated me for a long time, and his diagnosis was that I had a thing called ankylosing spondylitis, which is a disease . . . where the spine fuses and drags you forward so that you're [bent over]'. However, the diagnosis did not seem to fit, Roy recalled, noting that he is not bent over. 'I never ever believed that I had it.' Another doctor whom Roy saw also remained sceptical. This doctor was also the first to take seriously his growing belief that Kiritimati Island was a possible cause. 'He always supported me, the fact that he says, "I think it's something to do with a nuclear service that you've been involved in". But of course we couldn't prove it.' Even when doctors were sympathetic or open to the test veterans' building narrative of radiation harm, their roles and expertise were circumscribed.

Years later, doctors confirmed that the diagnosis of ankylosing spondylitis was indeed wrong. Roy never received an accurate diagnosis of the bodily discomfort that he experienced mid-life. Later, in retirement, Roy was diagnosed with polymyalgia rheumatica, which caused severe stiffness in his joints, particularly in his arms, shoulders, and neck. 'If you take away the prednisone [steroid], I'm totally useless again, pain.' These missing or shifting diagnoses reduced Roy's faith in the medical system to uncover and tell an accurate story of his body and affirmed that his own hunches were worth following. This experience helped to prioritize his own embodied knowledge of his ill health as valid, constant, and consistent in contrast to the partial and contradictory knowledge offered by biomedical and diagnostic systems.

For Kim, recounting the period leading up to Adam's suicide involved telling a story in which they desperately sought answers to his psychic pain. Medicine did not deny his suffering, but admitted the limits of its explanatory power. 'He used to hold his head and say, "Oh My God, what is happening in my head." . . . and I felt so helpless'. She reassured him, 'Darling the doctor can help with the pain', to which he responded, 'You don't understand it is agony, but it isn't pain and I can't explain it except that it is like a dark cloud . . . it is as if it is coming from under the floorboards, it is encasing just me.'

> So we went to a psychiatrist, an excellent one . . . and for the last session . . . Adam and I sat there and [the psychiatrist] said "Squadron Leader, I have to tell you that I have never felt so helpless in all my life". And my stomach lining went straight down to my boots, because he was our last hope. And he said . . . "You see in medical terms you are not a manic depressive, you are not a psycho whatever it was, you are not a split personality . . . there is no medical term for what is happening to you, and I have no idea what is the matter with you, but I do know you are not mad and you are not insane and I know you are suffering agony and I can't help you." . . . and the poor boy [Adam] came out of there and he went downhill very rapidly . . . there was no help anywhere. [7]

Such stories decentred medicine's role in offering the truth of their suffering. In the wake of medical equivocation, test veterans and their families looked elsewhere for answers, inward to their own embodied knowledge, and outward to their collective narratives. This tactic was not a rejection of medicine, but a claim to agency when medicine failed them. In facing the limits of medical care, they still regarded medical explanation, as Kim's memories make plain, as a force powerful enough to hold pain and death at bay, and as a route to vital and desired treatment.

LOST LOYALTY

Soon after returning home to the UK following service on Kiritimati Island, Alex began to experience stomach problems. After many years, and many sceptical doctors' assessments claiming there was nothing wrong with him, he was finally diagnosed with diverticular disease. In 1960, he also noticed 'lumps on my groin the size of bantams' eggs'. In

[7] Kim's quote was previously published in my article, *Biopolitical Endpoints: Diagnosing a Deserving British Nuclear Test Veteran* (Trundle 2011: 885).

hospital for observations and tests, doctors removed a lymph node from his arm and sent it for tests, the results of which were never shared with Alex nor entered into his medical record.

After leaving the Army, Alex worked for six years as a mechanic. But he realized that he 'liked the Forces, and I thought, well I would like to go back in. So I went into the Air Force which was more relaxed ... it was a better service I suppose, no doubt about it. The Army was good for companionship, but the Air Force was good for job prospects.'

After twelve years in the Air Force, he left the forces for good. After working a range of civilian jobs, Alex retired at sixty years of age and expected to get a pension for his service in the Army and Air Force. However, 'the Army turned around and told me, "Oh no, you are not getting a pension". I said, "Why not ... I'm a holder of the long service medal ... for 18 years' service I'm given a 12-year pension". "No," they said, "you had a break of over 5 continuous years between the Army and the Air Force"'.

Feeling betrayed by the Forces, to which he has shown commitment all his adult life, Alex's sense of loyalty began to waiver, and he began to look upon his service at Kiritimati Island in a new light. Until then he hadn't thought 'any more about it'. After his pension was turned down, 'I thought, I am going to start checking up on the radioactivity.'

For Alex, loyalty to the Forces involved a certain orientation in time. The past could be left undisturbed, as long as the future bore the promise of ongoing state care. This was the reciprocal bargain of military sacrifice. Set adrift from this bargain and its entitlements, Alex felt free to excavate his service memories, and the history of his ailments, for all that remained unsettled.

In injury, does causality lead to responsibility or responsibility to causality? In his discussion of American tort law, Malone (1956) argues that in both legal and everyday forms of reasoning, causation does not logically lead to a process of deducing responsibility. Rather, responsibility and expectations of how people ought to behave lead to theories of causation. Thus, what we think one *should* do to prevent or protect self or others from injury – the responsibilities and duties one expects in such situations – leads to understanding of the cause of the injury. As Engel explains: 'When ordinary people experience injuries, their interpretive process may begin with ideas about risk and responsibility in society and move from there to a search for causal explanations that are consonant with those ideas' (2009: 253–254). Thus, it is from people's perceptions of in/judicious precaution and care or im/permissible risk that causal explanations emerge.

POLITICAL AND LEGAL OPENINGS

In order to hold the state responsible for a past wrong, to level a legally recognizable grievance at the offices of state, law must be geared to define the state as an agent of its actions, that is, a liable actor. The *Crown Proceedings Act* 1947 (UK) made it possible for parties to sue the British Crown in civil actions for the first time. It contained, however, several limitations, including for the armed forces. Section 10 stated:

> Nothing done or omitted to be done by a member of the armed forces of the Crown while on duty as such shall subject either him or the Crown to liability in tort for causing the death of another person, or for causing personal injury to another person, in so far as the death or personal injury is due to anything suffered by that other person while he is a member of the armed forces of the Crown.

Test veterans lobbied hard to repeal section 10 of the Act, succeeding in 1987 and paving the way for service personnel and ex-service personnel (or by proxy their families) to sue the armed forces or members of the military for injury or death due to negligence.[8]

This legal change represented shifting societal attitudes towards service personnel, their place in society, and the moral obligations of society and the state towards the wounded soldier. The legal principle of Crown immunity, first introduced in the thirteenth century, that 'the King can do no wrong' reflects the principle of absolute sovereign power (Street 1948). The state justified the continuation of the principle of Crown immunity for the armed forces after 1947 in two ways. First, they argued

[8] While the repeal of section 10 was not retrospective, an action for damages and later appeal, *Pearce v Secretary of State for Defence* ([1988] 2 All ER 348), brought by nuclear test veteran Melvyn Pearce, established that the MoD could not rely upon Crown immunity. Pearce later abandoned his claim when his lawyers determined he could not sufficiently prove illness causation due to radiation exposure.

that effective military activity – in war and during preparations and training for war – required personnel to face exceptional hazards and degrees of risk. Society had to accept and expect this state of exception, and the possibility of civil action might curtail the effectiveness of the military to carry out its risky work. Second, and relatedly, they argued that the threat of civil action would negatively affect the social bonds of trust and loyalty upon which effective military action depended (Barnes 1948).

By the 1980s, after four decades of sustained peacetime, public attitudes regarding the necessary risks and sacrifices expected of the armed forces had shifted. Entry into the European Community, as well as the influence of the *European Convention on Human Rights*, elevated the idea of inalienable human rights in UK legal and political spheres (Slynn 2004). Service personnel began to challenge their exception status as one that deprived them of fundamental rights granted to ordinary citizens, recasting it as a form of social marginalization. This critique was framed through the language of the social contract, in which the security that military protection granted civilians required the state, in turn, to protect and care for service personnel. In the House of Commons debate on the Crown Proceedings (Armed Forces) Bill, the MP for Twickenham Toby Jessel argued:

> This is a moral issue. It is a matter of justice that service men should not be placed at a disadvantage when compared with their civilian counterparts. It must be a matter of principle that Parliament and the Government should accept that families of service men who are prepared to risk their lives in the service of our country so that the rest of us may live our lives in freedom and peace should not suffer from any injustice in comparison to others (Hansard 1987).

Test veterans' claims in the 1980s thus became intelligible at a precise moment when the law recognized veterans as vested with a new rights-bearing status.

For test veterans, debates about the legal right of service members to become claimants were foreshadowed by another important moment of political theatre. Public resistance to the threat of atomic war and nuclear annihilation was growing more organized and vocal (Burkett 2012). In 1985, New Zealand's Prime Minister David Lange travelled to Britain to compete in the Oxford Union debate against American evangelist Jerry Falwell.[9] He argued in favour of the motion that 'nuclear weapons are morally indefensible'. Dressed in a formal black suit, black bowtie, and his signature large glasses, Lange argue against the 'manic', 'relentless', and 'inhuman' logic of the nuclear arms race with its 'macho lurch into mutual madness'. He challenged the political argument that nuclear weapons and their mutually assured destructive potential were the new guarantors of peace.[10] 'Nuclear weapons make us insecure, and to compensate for our insecurity we build and deploy more nuclear weapons.'

Lange's argument was ultimately a moral one.

> I hold that the character of nuclear weapons is such that their very existence corrupts the best of intentions; that the means in fact perverts the end. And I hold that their character is such that they have brought us to the greatest of all perversions: the belief that this evil is necessary – as it has been stated tonight – when in fact it is not. . . . A system of nuclear defence guarantees only insecurity. The means of defence terrorize as much as the threat of attack.

For Lange, who characterized nuclear weapons as holding the world to ransom, as keeping us all hostage: 'Rejecting nuclear weapons is to . . . restore to humanity the power of the decision' (Lange 1985). Lange portrayed the bomb as inherently evil, by which he meant it contained an agentive consequentiality that far outstripped human control and moral fortitude. Lange was articulating what many critics of the arms race knew, that nuclear

9 In a bold diplomatic move in February 1985, New Zealand Prime Minister David Lange refused to let the US naval vessel, the USS Buchanan, dock in New Zealand ports. Lange's government's stance banned all nuclear-powered warships and submarines from entering New Zealand waters and ports, causing a minor diplomatic stand-off with the US (Priestley 2013). A few months later, two French spies bombed the Greenpeace Rainbow Warrior ship docked in Auckland and preparing to protest a French nuclear test in French Polynesia. One crew member, a thirty-five-year-old Portuguese photographer, drowned. This terrorist act, ordered by the French Foreign Intelligence Service, galvanized public condemnation of nuclear testing and helped to stall the French bomb programme for a decade (Priestley 2013).

10 In a cheerful and self-assured southern US accent, Falwell accused New Zealand of freeloading protection off the nuclear might of its allies and of 'living in the peaceful shadow of the bomb'. The risk of nuclear destruction, according to such a logic, is in fact a stalemate of safety, which all nationals now bear responsibility to uphold.

weapons created a moral paradox: in the new nuclear age, where 'there are no peripheries to humanity' (Turner 1997: 95), global safety and destruction became absurdist mirrors of each other (Gusterson 1998).

Lange won the debate. His victory spoke to a receptive audience.[11] The 1980s – a time of increasing tensions between the USSR and Western Europe – was marked by disarmament peace protests throughout Britain and New Zealand. In 1983, 300,000 people marched on Hyde Park to protest nuclear weapons. It was the largest anti-nuclear march in British history (Burkett 2012).[12] While the peace movement's anti-war, anti-militarism, and anti-nuclear beliefs sat uneasily with many test veterans' identities as proud supporters of the armed forces, it did raise the public profile of nuclear injury and risk.

Test veteran collectives were also part of an emerging and increasingly critical and vocal international veteran polis who, from the 1980s, were forming groups to contest governmental modes of care and responsibility and rigid military hierarchies (Kilshaw 2009). During the 1980s and 1990s, test veterans contacted and formed alliances with a range of veterans exposed to dangerous toxins, such as veterans exposed to mustard gas at the UK military research facility Porton Down, and nuclear test veterans in the US. These communities in turn reflected the broader emergence of health and environmental social movements on a global scale, movements that were increasingly utilizing democratic, human rights frames to challenge biomedical authority, the links between chemical industries and environmental safety regulations, and health entitlements in the wake of toxic harms (Brown et al. 2000, 2011). Public concerns were growing over

[11] Beyond atomic war fears, Lange's debate played into an increasingly post-colonial narrative in New Zealand. In 1962, Britain's Prime Minister Harold Macmillan described New Zealand as an 'English farm in the Pacific' (in Singleton and Robertson 1997: 327), a description that signified both the extractive ties between colony and Motherland, and the status of dependent economic satellite that New Zealand occupied since colonial occupation. By 1973, when Britain joined the European Economic Community, New Zealand had lost preferential trade access to Britain, and a shift towards political, economic, and cultural autonomy had emerged. In the 1980s, New Zealand was focused on developing geopolitical influence in the Pacific and realigning itself with emerging Asian economies.

[12] In sites of Pacific nuclear testing, rising localized and regional nuclear free movements emerged. For example, see Johnson (2013), de Jong (2023), Maillochon (2024), and Siwatibau and Williams (1982).

toxic exposures and the failure of regulation in the wake of high-profile toxic disasters such as Chernobyl, Bhopal, Love Canal, and Three Mile Island, as well as revelations about the health effects of industrially produced substances once declared safe by government and industry, such as formaldehyde, tobacco smoke, asbestos, and lead (Trundle et al. 2014).

AFTER BETRAYAL

The poet Stanley Plumly writes: 'Real time is when a thing happens but you're only aware that it really happened later' (2020: 72). Time is made experientially real when meaning and narrative are folded back into it. Making sense of the second betrayal required dwelling at the limits of bureaucratic care and etiological certainty, in the moments when institutional knowledge failed to offer coherent meaning, and bodies brought their own truths to the fore. For test veterans, a sense of fidelity towards embodied and community accounts emerged. This required many test veterans and their families to first instantiate care beyond the public eye, in intimate and community realms.

Equally emergent was a growing duty to help shore up each other's unique accounts of injury. Memory becomes a collective resource for understanding and storying the body, just as bodily experience and illness have the capacity to enliven and activate memory over time. Throughout these years, test veterans took crucial steps, mostly in private spaces, in arguing back against the authority of military records, doctors' assessments, and state practices of history making. This chapter has thus revealed how quotidian everyday encounters with illness and medicine can, as Herremans and Destroooer argue, 'open up the justice imagination, what is imaginable in terms of justice' (2023: 523), and can 'function as rehearsal space . . . prepar[ing] victims and their families to share their stories publicly' (2023: 527).

Test veterans' accounts of this stage in their lives were shared with me between fifty and sixty years after the bomb tests. The ways in which test veterans marked the long passage of time in their accounts were crucial to how they reckoned with injurious law. For test veterans, the physical harms of radiation were only the first instantiation of state negligence. Equally harmful for many were the long silences, the reluctant responses, the officious denials that went on for decades. The rising need for an account of causation, for state responsibility, the increasing awareness of its absence, became in their narratives grievously entangled with the injuries of radiation. Indeed, it became difficult to narratively separate such injuries as the years progressed.

In attempting to understand the second betrayal I found myself often returning to the idea of static, as mentioned at the start of this chapter by Robert in his rose garden. Understood through the weave of narratives explored above, static offers a metaphorical possibility beyond stasis and confusion. Static electricity describes a charge, one that doesn't budge and move, but instead builds up, often through friction. It is released once touched by a conductive material. Static acts as a state of preparation, of accumulating power, of the growing potential for movement. This chapter has thus shown how experiences of silence and denial in the face of illnesses can prefigure the ethical and political stakes of claim-making. Test veterans urge us to consider the challenges patient groups experience engaging with medicine, law, and politics that become the bedrock for 'injury narratives' (Engel 2005) and new claimant selves.

These questions of silenced injuries and injurious silences did not take test veterans away from medicine, but further into it. The accounts of their illnesses offered by medicine and the military were flawed, they believed, because they rendered certain types of radiation invisible and untethered them from the social processes of recording harm. The work of medical science, in enumerating illnesses with enough certainty to support claim-making, was as much an ethical process as it was a technical one. To this topic, the next chapter turns.

CHAPTER 3

Bad Numbers and Good Science

I STOOD WITH PETER IN HIS HOME OFFICE AS HE RIFFLED through neat folders containing medical studies and records from his medical history. Peter pulled out a thick, well-worn document, stapled several times to stop the front cover from falling off. He muttered about '*that* NRPB study', adding quietly, 'Waste of time'. He beckoned me down the stairs to the dining table where his wife was laying out a meal. We'd talk about it after lunch, he suggested, as if the topic might put us off our food.

In this chapter, I explore the evaluative practices that test veterans like Peter brought to bear on health studies about them. Test veterans and their families laboured within what Scott (1988: 156) calls 'the politics of facts and certification', where 'the time lag between exposure and consequence strains the methodologies of science, medicine, and law to the point where it is difficult to establish evidence'. From the 1980s, government agencies in both the UK and New Zealand began to sponsor health studies in order to adjudicate claims. Such studies have proven instrumental in enabling or foreclosing new entitlements to disablement pensions, compensation, and healthcare.

Test veterans came to understand that nuclear harm became visible within claim-making only under a narrow set of epistemic conditions. In test veterans' practices of evaluating medical studies, 'good' and 'bad' numbers emerged. As this chapter shows, Good numbers were for test veterans temporally responsive, contained the right entanglement of detachment and relationality with study subjects, and were distanced from the state's control, co-option, and influence. Moreover, they contained epistemic openness and humility, were future- rather than past-focused, attending to the living and not the dead, and allowed for exposure data to be strategically contextualized within the social processes of their production. As test veterans show, scientific practices enumerating illness could themselves be experienced as harmful. In evaluating such studies, test veterans revealed a desire for what Paul Ricoeur (1992: 172) terms 'little ethics'. These are claimants' attempts towards 'a good life lived with and for others in just institutions', made possible by scientific knowledge.

During fieldwork participants regularly invited me to read and discuss epidemiological studies about their health, to engage in this evaluative practice. Test veterans worked hard to understand and engage with such research. They waded through technical prose, discussed study designs and limitations together and, with the aid of medical experts, dissected methods and findings. It was strange, a British test veteran named Evan told me, to see yourself recorded like that, 'as a number'. When discussing some studies with participants, I encountered eyerolls, disgruntled grunts, or stony shakes of the head. I became curious about what lay beyond these reactions. Like many communities engaging with science and scientists, 'debates *within* science are simultaneously debates *about* science and how it should be done – or who should be doing it' (Epstein 1996: 3).

Health sociologists and medical anthropologists have shown that epidemiological practices reflect wider social and cultural values about what and who should be counted, what aspects of human illness experiences can and should be rendered numeric, and the relational conditions through which enumerative practices should occur.[1] They note that inequitable economic and political systems shape the possibilities for and nature of exposure data.[2] In a similar vein, test veterans evaluated epidemiological studies about their own illnesses and health through a range of ethical lenses. These included considering the politics of delay and dissemination, the institutional construction and control of exposure data, the attitudes and approaches of scientists to

[1] See for example, DiGiacomo (1999), Fenton and Charsley (2000), Krieger (2000), Reubi (2020), Mason (2021), and Wemrell et al. (2016).

[2] See for example Brown (2007), Jobin and Tseng (2014), Phillips (2015), and Vanderlinden (2011).

study subjects, the ethics of enumerating life and death, and the engagement of epidemiological scientists with the political afterlives of their studies.

'*THAT* STUDY'

In the 1980s, as nuclear test veterans grew increasingly vocal about their health concerns, the UK government sponsored the National Radiological Protection Board (NRPB) to conduct an epidemiological study of test veterans' health. They did so despite test veteran scepticism that the NRPB, a public authority and government-funded nuclear body, would be impartial enough or epidemiologically skilled enough to do so. For many test veterans, the thirty-year lag between exposure and research indexed a troubling politics of delay and undercut their trust in the study from its inception. This in turn exemplifies an enduring ethical critique from toxic exposure communities. As Vanderlinden (2011: 33–34) observes of the scientifically underexplored nature of toxic exposure, the 'active discovery of environmental health effects is a central agenda neither of governmental health and environmental agencies, nor independent research centers'.

Some of Britain's most senior epidemiologists worked on the NRPB study, which involved a labour-intensive compilation of military records in order to create a list of around 22,000 British armed forces personnel and civilian scientists who had attended the nuclear tests, and a similar number of military men to act as controls. By the established epidemiological and statistical standards of the day, its sample was comprehensive and its design robust.

The NRPB study focused upon underlying and contributing causes of death. It relied upon data from death certificates and a national cancer register, data that did not require patient consent. The study authors explained why they chose death as their primary health measure. 'Firstly, death is unequivocal, its recording is compulsory and unbiased, and information that it has occurred can be obtained effectively and rapidly from national records. Secondly, mortality rates are believed to be the best available general indicators of the health of a community, even though they provide no information about the incidence of non-fatal diseases' (Darby et al. 1988: 2). Stabilizing death into data and rendering it an uncontroversial and reliable scientific object relied upon what Zwart (2007) calls a 'pragmatic reductionist approach'. Such epidemiological reasoning aimed to make persuasive claims based on the strength of mono-causal relationships, connecting exposure to illness. Exposure–disease relationships are necessarily treated, as Wing notes, as 'self-contained, homogeneous, and independent phenomena ... appropriately studied in isolation, one at a time' (2000: 33).

In 1988, the first NRPB study concluded:

> On balance ... that there may well have been small hazards of leukaemia and multiple myeloma associated with participation in the programme, but their existence is certainly not proven, and further research is desirable. The only carcinogenic agent that has been shown to cause an increase incidence of both these diseases is ionizing radiation, but there is no specific evidence that the test participants who developed these diseases were exposed to unusual amounts (Darby et al. 1988: 85).

Some test veterans emphasized the lack of proactive dissemination of the study results to study subjects. This represented another moment of injurious engagement with the MoD and, by extension, with science. 'I didn't know about that study for a decade', said Carl, a British test veteran.[3] A fellow British test veteran, Michael, said laconically, 'you'd think they would have let us know they'd done a study on us', while Carl mused, 'it makes you think, what were they hiding?' Some test veterans understood the inaccessibility of epidemiological knowledge through their experiences of military culture and its weaponization of secrecy to their disadvantage and disempowerment. They drew links between the 'secret' NRPB epidemiological study and the legislated secrecy that they believed prohibited participants from talking about their participation in the tests with others in the subsequent decades.

[3] By Contrast, the MoD insists that 'The nuclear test veterans' organisations were involved in discussions with the researchers as the study was developed and the progress and the results of the work have been openly published and widely publicised' (UK Government 2022), suggesting that the routes the government took to consult on and disseminate the study did not reach and engage with all nuclear test veterans.

THE INSTITUTIONAL CONSTRUCTION OF EXPOSURE

Test veterans emphasized how proof of exposure and the lack thereof were built out of a set of social dependencies established between state-funded scientists and military institutions. The test veterans argued that just as there was no evidence to show they were exposed to low-level radiation, there was also no clear evidence to show they *were not* exposed to low-level radiation; the monitoring had not been sufficient to support either conclusion. At the British nuclear testing sites only 21 per cent of test participants were given dosimeter badges to record radiation dose, and very few participants wore them consistently across their participation in multiple bomb tests (Darby et al. 1988). Such records thus offered a limited picture of individual dose and exposure rates. Importantly, they focused on high-dose gamma radiation, and did not measure low-level radionuclides (ionizing alpha and beta particles, or fallout) that can be inhaled or ingested and can lodge within the body for decades.

While acknowledging that the film badge exposure records did not record internal contamination from radionuclides, the NRPB still relied upon the MoD's assurances, who they stated had 'advised' that the estimated doses from internal emitters 'were negligible' (Darby et al. 1993: 10). For test veterans, this signified a problematic degree of proximity between the commissioning government department, the MoD, who was simultaneously the party accused of harm, and the study authors who relied upon the MoD for funding, basic data, and 'advice'. The NRPB appeared to have built such advice into the study's core assumptions.

Test veterans and their advocates argued that the radiation monitoring records were unreliable and inaccurate. Participants' gamma radiation doses from film badges and dosimeter readings were recorded in 'Blue Books'. These were a set of records with blue covers held by the Atomic Weapons Establishment. They were explicitly marked as 'provisional' and contained information transcribed from a number of original sources. They often contained incomplete, sketchy information, such as only the surnames of participants, making it impossible to link them to particular test participants (*AB* v *Ministry of Defence* [2009] EWHC 1225 (QB), [378]). Indeed, the authors of the NRPB study pointed out that the Blue Book 'list is not claimed to be free from errors, incorrect assertions, or omissions and … the information available was sparse, of varied quality, and often ambiguous or indeterminate' (*AB* v *Ministry of Defence* [2009] EWHC 1225 (QB), [378]).

Despite at first detecting an increased risk of blood cancers, the study scientists soon queried this and, through further statistical interpretation and follow-up studies in the proceeding decade, the study team declared this 'a chance finding' (Darby et al. 1993, Muirhead et al. 2003). Test veterans could not understand how the positive results, slight as they were, could disappear in the follow-up study. Word spread amongst test veterans that some of the sample's participants were excluded from the four-year follow-up study. 'They did it to change the results', a British veteran in his seventies, Toby, explained to me. The rationale given by the study authors for the subsequent removal of 1,503 participants, and the addition of 514 previously unidentified participants was, however, seemingly straightforward. Most of these men who were excluded had left the testing site before any bomb tests occurred, or had worked on military sites away from the bomb testing sites (such as Edinburgh Field and RAAF Pearce). They were deemed to have not been 'involved in cloud sampling or handling contaminated aircraft' (Darby et al. 1988: 4), activities that could have exposed them to radiation. Peter pointed out that the military files of the 1950s were patchy and, most of the time, simply inaccurate, meaning posting locations might not always be accurate or complete.

Many test veterans also argued that exposures to radiation were not simply the result of high-dose gamma radiation, nor were they limited to being near the bombs or highly irradiated aircraft and equipment. Their experiences speak to the enduring challenge of making low-level radiation and fallout medically visible, and of mapping human movement and exposure within nuclear spaces. As Zonabend (1993[1989]) has shown, despite spatial segregation, role differentiation, and safety plans, in practice nuclear workers often move between zones deemed risky and non-risky in unmonitored, or unmonitorable ways.

'HE NEVER CAME TO TALK TO US'

A mistrust of the records was compounded by a mistrust of those who handled and interpreted them. Such complaints point to an ethical critique of the attitudes of scientists who collected individual exposure rates while failing to reckon with the inequitable contexts of their production. British test veteran Kevin explained to me one reason he regarded the NRPB study as 'junk'.

'Those scientists, Doll and his men, just believed whatever the government told them. They told them there was nothing to worry about. They took government money to do that study, they were susceptible, to government lies.'

Such statements are easily dismissed due to their conspiratorial veneer. But my conversations and debates with test veterans about the scientists revealed a more subtle evaluative stance. Sir Richard Doll, who was actively involved in the NRPB studies, received particularly bitter and sharp critique from test veterans. They pointed out how Doll, a lauded British epidemiologist, spent much of his career refuting worker claims and scientific studies that linked low-level occupational exposures, such as asbestos, dioxins, and radiation, to cancer rates (Clapp et al. 2008, Greene 1999, Tweedale 2007). After Doll's death in 2005, many participants added, it was publicly discovered he received significant undisclosed funding from chemical industries, including from Monsanto and Dow Chemicals (Tweedale 2007).

The occupational health and safety specialist Richard M. Park argued that, when researching environmental workplace exposures, Doll tended to rely heavily upon company records and company narratives of exposure. 'Doll's dealings with occupational issues were almost always with individuals from the management side, the data he analyzed was usually collected, described and documented by the management class. His deliberations in interpreting findings were within that same social context' (in Greene 2011: 517–518). Such a critique echoes test veterans' frustrations at the trust Doll and his team placed in the evidentiary documents produced by the MoD. As scholars of environmental exposure demonstrate, industries producing and controlling the potential evidentiary record of workplace exposure represents a clear conflict of interest and source of epidemiological advantage (Brown 2007, Phillips 2010).

Test veteran Kevin complained that Doll 'never came to talk to us … he was too busy living his life of luxury'. Such a complaint highlights how social class and the distances it generates come to matter when illness communities ethically evaluate the scientific production of evidence. Doll's upper-class life as a knighted professor in Oxford, stories of his elegant suits, classic convertible car, and large country house (Greene 2011) contrasted sharply with test veterans' more modest incomes and class backgrounds, and their experiences as rank-and-file servicemen.

When I pointed out that Doll had also proven a link between tobacco and cancer, and that disclosure of industry funding was not commonplace in the 1970s and 1980s, participants were unmoved in their judgements. The grudge, they explained, was personal. 'He didn't have time for us, people like us', Kevin concluded. In evaluating epidemiology, illness communities pay attention to the ethical attitudes of scientists towards them (Brown 2007). As test veterans had discovered in their own online research, and as the scholar Greene (2011) confirms, Doll's attitudes towards the workers, communities, and activists fighting for recognition of environmental exposures grew more publicly dismissive across the 1980s and 1990s. During this time, he railed against 'environmentalists' who

> 'whip up irrational prejudice, unfound in science' (Daily Telegraph, Feb. 7, 1983). He cautioned, in a letter to the Daily Mail, that environmentalists represented 'an irrational ideology opposed to science, to industry and to progress' (June 3, 1992). He urged the public 'to trust industry and industrialists, science and scientists' – these are 'the people with the key to the future' – and ignore warnings by the powerful 'anti-science Mafia'. (Greene 2011: 513)

In foregrounding the attitudes of a scientist as ethically important in evaluating their science, test veterans did not consider themselves 'anti-science'. In accusing the NRPB study of 'bias', they tried to challenge the purification of science, wanting science to see its failings on its own epistemic terms. This was the presence of political and economic influence from which the NRPB authors strived so hard to maintain a distance (Harvey 2020: 16). Test veterans sought to show, to borrow the words of epidemiologist Steve Wing (1998: 245), 'how assumptions and values shape the practice of epidemiology and determine the character of explanations'.

Peter expressed a further concern with the underlying logic of epidemiological population studies. The NRPB study, he said, 'wasn't based on evidence like health checks or individual veterans, on blood and tissue'. These arguments raise the question of how and why test veterans were framing the enumeration of flesh and blood as more truth bearing than the enumeration of death. The very factors that the NRPB study scientists regarded as the source of scientific rigor (statistical mortality studies based on death certificates) became the very features that test veterans most disliked and distrusted.

Some test veterans I spoke with objected to a study design that required deaths to occur in numbers deemed 'significant' before evidence reached thresholds of truth and political action. The moral logic invested in such epidemiological reasoning meant, perversely, waiting for the death of their peers in order to make legitimate claims. 'We'll all be dead by the time they finally decide something's wrong', Cyril, a British veteran, complained. The head of the medical department at the NRPB agreed. In an interview for the *New Scientist* magazine about the nuclear test veteran health database, Chris Sharp argues that 'the epidemiological investigation cannot be completed until the cause of death of all the test veterans is known. Until, that is, they have all died' (Edwards 1996).

Environmental epidemiology, as sociologist Sara Shostak points out (2013: 19), traditionally relies upon tracing 'the relationship between exposures, disease and death at the population level', and does not require examining live bodies. Some veterans found such 'population imaginaries' (Whittaker 2022) objectionable, questioning why such studies were so utterly detached from the living test veterans' own ill bodies. Such studies appeared unconcerned with present suffering, and its prevention in the future. Such studies offered no way through which their ongoing illnesses might become scientifically visible.

PREFIGURING INJURY

The only thought British test veteran Eric wanted to offer me about the NRPB study was this: 'They saw what they wanted to see, [they] got what they wanted.' Eric's critique invites us to consider the impact of established 'facts' that prefigure epidemiological interpretation. Such facts act as a lens to think through the possibilities of harm. Environmental epidemiological studies are required to tell two parts of a story: both the 'what' and the 'why' of illness. The 'towering obstacle' within epidemiology is exposure: 'When exposure can be measured reliably, a subtle association may be credible' (Taube and Mann 1995: 164). If exposure cannot be measured, then scientists must at least offer a reasonable theory of how exposure has occurred, estimated rates of exposure based on available evidence, and proof from other studies that show such rates of exposure can be harmful for human health (Jobin and Tseng 2014).

Drawing from earlier research on radiation exposure, especially from Hiroshima and Nagasaki, the NRPB argued that blood cancers are the only illnesses that can be definitively associated with high-dose radiation. As Goldstein and Stawkowski (2015) show, the American-affiliated Hiroshima and Nagasaki studies, and the narrow range of carcinogenic effects they account for, have dominated both scientific understandings and political responses to nuclear dose, exposure, and disease. This paradigm continues to marginalize other epidemiological communities, including Soviet studies and low-dose nuclear worker studies (see also Wing et al. 1999). Science develops, as Galison (1997: 840) notes, as a 'set of subcultures bound together through a complex of hard-won locally shared meanings'. Building upon the dominant post-war scientific paradigm shaped what the NRPB study could postulate as a plausible account of disease. The authors thus assumed a 'chance finding' and dismissed the results from a follow-up NRPB study (2003) finding that test veteran rates of bladder, liver, and prostate cancers were significantly higher than rates amongst controls.

Test veterans resented the ways in which the studies required them to become neatly comparable to other groups, which Nelson (2015) called the power of mathematical 'equivalence' underpinning such numbers. In building upon Japanese studies, the NRPB invoked a universal biological body. This reflects epidemiology's quest to find replicable exposure–disease associations with wide applicability. This is what Cram refers to as 'the nuclear body', one that constitutes 'a universal human template . . . designed to be applicable in every radioactive environment' and which is thus 'profoundly a-spatial' (2015: 802).

The epidemiological toolkit can, however, be used in subtle enough ways to account for 'interaction' or 'effect modification', the ways in which specific bodies and specific environments shape responses to exposure and disease outcomes. Effect modification can be particularly salient when studying low-level exposures. As Wing argues, 'variations in exposure-disease associations under different conditions may make the difference between no relationship and an important one'. For low-level exposure, he points out, 'it is recognized that associations may be modified according to age of exposure, sex, and perhaps factors including diet, presence of other chemicals, and genetic characteristics' (2000: 33).

Test veterans often pointed out to me that the wider synergistic effect of radiation in concert with other exposures at the testing sites was likely to have been significant in contributing to their risk of ill health (see Engelmann 2022). They recalled the ubiquitous and heavy presence of cigarette smoke in confined spaces, the poor diet, a range of chemicals and dangerous elements released by the exploded bomb components, the weekly spraying of DDT, and the common presence of asbestos. In other words, while the NRPB study utilized pragmatic reductionism to isolate a singular exposure disease relationship universal to study subjects, test veterans wanted their specific, complex experiences of exposure to count. As Yates-Doerr argues (2012), the reductionism of science and its translation into policy often fails to resonate with the complexity of people's understanding of their own bodies, environments, and health.

The NRPB studies did linguistically reflect the limits of epidemiological certainty. Tentative language peppered the findings to reveal interpretive challenges. As test veterans reflected, the problem of epidemiological interpretation often lay outside science, in the political realm. The UK government used the study to assert that a definitive proof now existed, showing that, aside from a few known exceptions, the men had not been harmed in any way. An absence of certain types of evidence became evidence of an absence. In other words, politicians turned the study's negative logic – the ongoing illnesses and non-cancer deaths that it could say nothing about – into a positive result. For test veterans, the retooling of uncertainty into certainty turned the government's efforts at robust scientific inquiry into a morally callous denial of harm.

Test veterans were not prepared to defend or acknowledge the subtleties of the studies in the wake of political co-option. 'After [the NRPB] did their study they washed their hands of it. They didn't care', a nuclear test veteran's widow, Carla, reflected. The scientists did not, as far as test veterans knew, attempt to publicly counter or correct simplified political claims about the results. Test veterans thus asserted the need for an epidemiological ethics in which scientists claimed responsibility across longer time frames, to engage with the political flattening of epidemiological evidence into black and white truths about health.

AN ETHICS OF PERMISSION

In the late 1980s, a team of epidemiologists conducted a study that found New Zealand test veterans had an increased rate of death from haematological cancers (Pearce et al. 1990). The authors did not dismiss the results as a chance finding. In contrast to the NRPB study, New Zealand veterans talked with ease about this study, rarely expressing strong emotions. 'That was the beginning, that study', New Zealand test veteran Roy explained to me. 'The government couldn't ignore us after that.'

The Pearce study entered conversation as an accepted form of proof, a part of the veterans' claim-making toolkit. Given that this study was also based on death rates, given that it had been commissioned by the New Zealand Department of Defence, and given that it had been conducted 'at a distance' and beyond the control of veterans, I wondered why it did not generate the same acrimony as the NRPB study.

An easy answer to this would be a utilitarian one: its findings were of more use to the veterans, and its political afterlife conferred resources. As a result of this study, test veterans could more easily claim military disablement pensions for a range of cancers. This contrasted with the way the UK government had used the NRPB study to deny liability. But the answer to this question also lies in an ethics of counting which veterans desired and expected from epidemiological science. And it reflects the ways that test veterans sought to legitimize studies that supported their illness claims through the language of ethicality.

'Good science', as Douglas-Jones notes (2015: 56), is increasingly understood to be 'based on both reliable and ethical data' that reveals reliable and ethical conduct. The test veterans explained to me that the Pearce study authors did not as a rule take money from industry to conduct research. One of the study authors recalled to me first hearing about the contract to conduct the first epidemiological study of New Zealand test veterans. 'I was a bit sceptical, because it was from the Department of Defence [funding it], but it seemed to have no strings attached ... providing the contract says we have absolute right to publication, and they can't interfere and so on.'

Despite asserting an unequivocal right to design and conduct the study beyond the oversight of all interested parties – both claimants and accused – the scientists of this study recognized the importance of an ethics of permission. Such an ethic understands that, regardless of legal status, data about the test veterans' deaths were not the inert property of the state or science. Test veterans had a moral claim over them. The research team did not want to conduct the study without the expressed approval from the New Zealand Nuclear Test Veterans' Association, which they duly received.

The authors of the study expressed both confidence and humility in their studies. They were careful to avoid extrapolating their findings too far. As one author told me, acknowledging the open-ended, financially curtailed and refinable nature of scientific facts:

> It is quite possible that other cancers have increased since then, we don't know, we haven't done a follow up, but certainly up to the time we looked at there was nothing much else happening. It's quite possible there are other health problems. ... We never looked at birth defects and stuff because we never had the money to do it.

While many similarities existed between the epidemiological logics of the NRPB and New Zealand studies, subtle interpretive differences existed. Unlike the NRPB study, the New Zealand scientists ceded less certainty to government-produced evidence of exposure. A scientist who worked on the study recalled how 'the British Ministry of Defence was adamant that no one got exposed'. For those who accepted the MoD's assurances on exposure, this negated the validity of the Pearce study's findings. Thus, as one of the study authors recounted, a prominent radiation scientist in New Zealand had

> issued a press statement before [our] study was done saying we wouldn't find anything because no exposure had occurred, and after the study came

> out, he issued a statement saying what we found out couldn't be real because no exposure had occurred. Basically, all we did was say, "well, this is what we found, this being speculation that exposure occurred through this route [fallout], we don't really know, but it's possible".

The Pearce study was prepared to consider the risks of fallout, in part due to the comments on some test veteran questionnaires about 'rainout' – irradiated rain that fell on their ships – occurring after some tests. The test veterans' recollections were not dismissed out of hand in favour of official MoD records or assurances. 'The accuracy of the recording of the official data has been disputed by some men who participated in the tests' the scientists wrote dispassionately (Pearce et al. 1990: 7). A lack of records detailing exposure to low-level fallout radiation did not prove a lack of such radiation exposure, they reasoned. 'No data are available on internal radiation exposure' (Pearce et al. 1990: 8), they wrote in their report, highlighting the gap.

Other studies, furthermore, offered the theory of exposure that is needed when evidence is lacking: 'the possibility of significant exposure through inhalation or ingestion has previously been raised for United States Army participants in the Smoky nuclear test' (Pearce et al. 1990: 8). The interpretive grounds of the Pearce study reflect what Jasanoff describes as scientific 'technologies of humility', systems of expertise and knowledge that, in contrast to a science grounded in certainty, 'take better account of uncertainties and unknowns ... that are more attentive to history, to past failures of understanding, and to persistent inequality and injustice' (2012: 14, see also Phillips 2010).

THE ETHICAL LIMITS OF THE POLITICAL

I interviewed Tom, an environmental epidemiologist who had been involved in veteran health studies. We met in his sparsely decorated urban office in New Zealand. Our conversation ranged over environmental health and the ethical work of producing epidemiological knowledge. He explained that autonomy from all parties – both claimants and defendants – ensured scientific objectivity. Yet such objectivity involved more than removing himself from the influences of each side's claims.

He was also aware that, in the real world, unequal power relations determine who defines and generates exposure data. Only through a detached evaluative stance and mode of scientific reasoning could one counter the power imbalance and allow multiple sources of potentially useful information to count. For epidemiologists like Tom, practices of scientific objectivity come into focus through an ethics of justice, which in turn requires a conscious detachment (Candea et al. 2015).

The detachment that Tom described involved dividing science from politics. This entailed making distinctions between the question of 'what happened' and the question of 'what should happen next', between description and prescription, or between fact and value (Douglas-Jones et al. 2022).

'I never get involved in conversation', Tom said.

> I've always turned down every request to go to court or to get involved with [compensation] or anything like that. And . . . because if I get involved with things like that, and I go along and say what I've found, then I have to go along and say what I've found irrespective of which side I'm sympathetic to, and I'd rather not get involved in that sort of argument, so it's good to have some people like me just collecting the evidence and saying what we found.

Despite disavowing the political realm, Tom's avoidance of environmental health claims contained its own ethical commitments. Tom wished to remain detached and neutral in his engagements with claim-making because of the uneven and unequal political risks epidemiological knowledge produced. Like test veterans, Tom understood how the political appropriation of science led to injustice. Becoming involved was unwise, he argued, because it just as likely would entrench such inequalities as challenge them. He demonstrated this point to me by discussing the recognition and support that different victims of dioxin poisoning received from the state.

He pulled up a graph onto his computer screen. 'This is the background levels of dioxin in the general population. This is 2.' He pointed to the shortest bar of the graph. 'Now, U.S. [Vietnam] veterans would be about 4. So actually, if you've got Agent Orange exposure in Vietnam . . . unless you're actually mixing this stuff, the general exposure to the veterans was quite low.' He traced his finger upwards and along the graph. 'This was what was found in the [contaminated] Paritutu community [around the timber mills using dioxins], in the survey that the Ministry of Health [did]. . . . That's about 11'. He moved right along the graph, to an even high bar. 'But then . . . this is what we see in timber workers [in these mills], which is about 50.'

He then pointed to the tallest bar on the graph. 'And this is what they've found in US production [factory] workers, which is about 200. . . . All the exposure is in the people producing [the chemicals]. What they do is that they try and filter out most of [the toxicity], . . . and the exposure happens to the people who are doing the filtering [in the chemical production factories].'

Tom then explained what each of these affected communities had received from the state.

> But in New Zealand, what you get is with . . . a level four [Vietnam veterans] get a parliamentary level of enquiry and an official apology from the government. If you're living in Paritutu [near the timber mills], you um, after 20 years or worrying, eventually you get your blood tested, if you're in the community . . . *and* you get some health services.

He pointed to his screen, resting the tip of his pen on the second highest bar in the graph of dioxin exposure. 'If you're a timber worker, after 20 years of lobbying and us doing the study . . . they're still not paying to test people but they are providing some health services'. He moved his pen to the highest bar on the graph. 'And if you're a worker in the factory [producing the dioxin] you get nothing. Absolutely nothing at all. . . . And it shows that the decisions are political.'

Tom's reflections on the inverse relationship between toxic exposure levels and compensation starkly reveal a double burden for the most vulnerable: increased exposure to environmental risk tends to parallel decreased access to social power, political clout, and institutional recognition (Brown 2007). It speaks of the relatively venerated moral position of military veterans in social and political life that leads to health entitlements deemed 'above and beyond' civilian entitlements, like disablement pensions, as discussed in Chapter 5. While test veterans wanted scientists to be reflexive about how they and their knowledge were imbricated within systems of power, scientists could invert the gaze. A scientific vantage point revealed that veterans occupy positions of both privilege and vulnerability, a positionality that ensured not only exposure to military risk but also a social status that warrants evidence about their ill health being produced in the first place.

NEW NUMBERS, SAME OLD PROBLEMS

Increasingly molecular approaches to epidemiology reconfigure the ethical engagements of scientists. Yet a range of tensions continued regarding the temporality of research and its political legitimacy and efficacy to address claimants' urgent health needs. In 2008, a genetic epidemiological study of New Zealand test veterans was published measuring chromosomal translocations (abnormalities) (Wahab et al. 2008). The average number of translocations for a normal healthy male is 10 per 1,000 cells. The strength of the result surprised the scientists conducting their study. As one explained to me, 'For the veterans it was 29 translocations per 1000 cells, three times the average [of the controls]. ... This sends a red alert signal in terms of health, it normally means a higher chance of cancer.'

Genetic research changes the ethics of epidemiological engagement and detachment in fundamental ways. For example, blood must be taken from living participants. The objects of science become the subjects of science and cannot be treated at a distance, as death certificates allow. Generating the best sample size depended upon individual consent, ongoing community support, intimate engagements with bodies, and relations of collaboration. The study authors and their research assistants worked with leaders in the New Zealand Test Veteran community. Relationality and detachment depended upon each other. The test veterans and scientists were clear in how, after establishing trust, the study's labour was divided. As a test veteran explained to me, 'They were the experts. We trusted them to do the science part.'

The visibility and trustworthiness of scientists who 'fronted up' and shared initial ownership of the study were not the only reason test veterans put their faith in the emerging realm of genetic science. They hoped it might provide more temporally expansive evidence. 'We're sick, we're suffering', said test veteran Ben. 'The Rowland Report shows that.'

This speaks to genetics' capacity to constitute a category of generalized illness based on latency and risk, in part through the links between chromosomal mutations and immune system effects that can manifest in multiple ways and over long time frames.

Some of the strongest criticisms of the Rowland Report came from other scientists who could not accept the results because they refused to believe that exposure to radiation had occurred. A review conducted by the Australian Radiological Protection and Nuclear Safety Agency argued that 'There is documented evidence that the NZ sailors present at the Grapple tests were not subject to significant radiation exposure' (Johnston et al. 2010).[4] These familiar critiques reveal the roadblocks genetic epidemiology face in toxic exposure claims. Without direct evidence of environmental exposure, the 'causal chain becomes unmoored' (Shostak 2013: 127). In other words, when chromosomal changes cannot be conclusively linked to measurable, bureaucratically recognized levels of dangerous exposure, it 'dramatically diminish[es] their epistemic and political power' (Shostak 2013: 127).

Test veterans were invited by a government expert advisory panel on veteran health to discuss the research. Before the two meetings, I sat with a small group of test veterans in a cold kiosk café beside the New Zealand Defence House. Wrapped in our coats we sipped water and avoided coffee, knowing that a morning tea meet-and-greet was part of the agenda. Conversation conveyed a mixture of hope and dismay. They were pleased the government was paying proper attention to the study, but they were dismayed with the lengthy review. The Rowland study had been conducted by respected scientists. It had appeared in a respected peer-reviewed journal. Why did the panel deem it necessary to arrange further reviews, some from scientists who weren't genetic specialists?

[4] During peer-review for an academic journal, one referee queried the findings, noting that in Europe the normal rate of translocation in controls was 13 per 1,000, higher than the New Zealand veteran control group. But the geneticists counted that it was obvious that the less healthy worker effect in Europe related to New Zealand being less polluted with radiation. The healthy worker effect refers to the phenomenon of active workers having lower rates of morbidity and mortality than the wider population. This is particularly the case in the military where recruits are medically screened before acceptance into service (Chowdhury et al. 2017).

The panel's assessment of the cytogenetic study revealed how genetic epidemiology gets 'stretched to its limits' (Taubes and Mann 1995: 164). The panel accepted that the study proved the men had chromosomal damage. However, their report to the Minister of Veterans Affairs concluded that, while the translocation rate suggested some radiation exposure in the past, 'The clinical consequences of this, if any, are not known' (Campbell 2010). For genetic damage to transform into medical entitlements, it still needed to be hinged to the proof of manifest illness or recorded death.

A scientist on the panel suggested the veterans needed another epidemiological study measuring recent illness and death rates, and he offered to conduct one. The veterans' reaction was adamant and furious. Test veteran Roy wrote in a response letter:

> When research is in progress, many issues are unnecessarily put aside under the pretext of 'waiting until the research is completed'. Further delays on important matters to the veterans are created. . . . Given the time frame of two years, plus the unexpected delays to complete the research, then [the time it takes to] initiate the use of the results, there will be few veterans alive ... the research could take up to 4–5 years to complete. Hardly of use to very aged and sick vets.

In other words, if veterans ceased to be alive for the counting, what was the point of counting? Pointing out this injurious logic – that counting the dead this way would only let more men die – once again critiqued the temporal unresponsiveness of science, the slow violence of its rigour. It was, to borrow the words of Jane Guyer, to reveal enumeration as riven with metaphorical irony (2004: 64).

Test veterans tried to place limits on the quest for a more perfect proof, on the unending role of numbers to tally their lives and deaths. Here test veterans used refusal to negotiate a tension between 'the obligation to end the dispute and deliver some kind of justice for the victims and the radical uncertainty inherent to toxic' claims (Jobin 2021b: 1). Test veterans' concerns with 'endless studies' is mirrored in concerns within epidemiology about 'the ethics of delay'. In response, some public health scholars advocate for a 'precautionary principle', a bioethics idea of 'doing good by preventing harm to public health from delay: when in doubt about the presence of a hazard, there should be no doubt about its prevention or removal. It shifts the burden of proof from showing presence of risk to showing absence of risk' (Richter et al. 2005: 17).

In 2021, a new British study of test veterans revealed 'exposure worry', high rates of anxiety, anger, a sense of responsibility for ongoing family illnesses, and guilt. For many participants, the study findings were validating. In discussing what test veterans needed to alleviate their suffering, the study concluded that recognition was vital. 'For some, recognition meant acknowledgement for their service, while for others it meant admitting negligence and, in some cases, deception' (Collett et al. 2021: 8).

Psychological studies are commonly double-edged swords for toxic exposure claimants. In the absence of biological proof, psychological proof of harm reveals the problem as 'all in their heads'. Like in tortious claims for multiple chemical sensitivity or repetitive strain injury, defendants attempt to reframe claimants' pain, illness, and injury as sociosomatic condition, as 'psychologically generated symptoms from social paranoia' (Phillips 2015:27) which has the effect of delegitimizing and masking the structural conditions within workplaces that generate injury (Reid and Reynolds 1990). Rather than encourage political recognition and restitution, psychological proof can engender the opposite. For test veterans, harm can be seen to originate from within test veterans' own psyches. Both UK and New Zealand government veteran agencies turned to education and lay appropriate information sharing. They sought to allay veterans' clinically elevated anxieties by assuring them that they had never been placed in harm's way. Attempting to address psychological injury by denying physical injury compounded many participants' sense of injustice. It reaffirmed their belief that political institutions misuse science. Once again, the state used the enumeration of health to deny physical harms, harms psychological studies neither explored nor drew conclusions about.

ENUMERATING INJURY

Through experiences of epidemiological reason, test veterans honed ethical ideas about 'good' and 'bad' science, critiques that ultimately cautioned against 'the license [that quantification] provides to leave out much of what is difficult or obscure' (Porter 1992: 645). An ethical science, test veterans argued, depended upon scientists practicing appropriately calibrated detachment and relationality with study subjects. At the same time, an ethical epidemiology was, for test veterans, one that kept the state or other institutions responsible for toxic exposure at arm's length. This was a science that sidestepped rather than embraced institutional control of unreliable evidentiary exposure records, either through not weighing them heavily in a study's explanatory frames or in producing new forms of biological evidence beyond institutional control.

Unethical epidemiology, by contrast, hid the political relationships and political failures that turned exposure into numbers. It ignored the suffering of the living in favour of the dead, and refused relational accountability to the subjects of science over time. Utilizing an uncontroversial means of critique within science, test veterans saw 'biases' in a priori assurances that low-level radiation exposure had never occurred, or that low-level radiation could not act as a convincing exposure pathway for disease. Unethical epidemiology, test veterans believed, too readily discarded plausible, but hard to quantify pathways for exposure, creating thresholds of proof that were insurmountable. The linear story epidemiology needed to tell – tracing exposure to dose to plausible disease mechanism to elevated disease rates – became unreachable.

In trying to make their injuries visible for claim-making, test veterans offered an epistemic critique of biomedical knowledge production. 'Good' science required illness communities and scientists to acknowledge and work upon the specific social and political contexts that shape epidemiological evidence of injury. This critique in turn challenged those engaging in claims – politicians, scientists, lawyers, and advocates – to more carefully contend with the potentially injurious temporalities, certainties, invisibilities, and social impacts that epidemiological reason produced for claimants.

CHAPTER 4

Into the Documentary Hinterland

I STOOD IN ARNOLD'S HOME OFFICE, SURROUNDED BY TALL STACKS of archival documents. Several teetered on the verge of collapse. 'Maybe this is how the MoD will finally get me', Arnold joked. 'My wife will find me one morning, squished flat under these.' Arnold's elusion to documentary overload was echoed in legal courts. In a High Court ruling in favour by a group of test veteran claimants (discussed in Chapter 6), Justice Foskett pointed out a challenging feature of the case. 'The bundles of documents in this case exceed 100 lever arch files, many containing up to 400 pages of documentation. ... I make no complaints about this ... but it is important that anyone reading this judgement should understand the extent and depth of the documentary hinterland' (*AB* v *Ministry of Defence* [2009] EWHC 1421 (QB), [549]).

An experienced archival researcher worked for test veterans in the 1980s and 1990s searching the British National Archives for nuclear test files. In evidence before the High Court he observed that anyone without 'specialist knowledge of the Public Records Office would find it virtually impossible to fully research as extensive a subject such as British Nuclear Weapons Testing' (in *AB* v *Ministry of Defence* [2009] EWHC 1225 (QB), [547]). Justice Foskett also argued that 'the collation by an individual, or even a group of individuals, of all potentially relevant documentation concerning the tests from public sources would be an impossible task' ([549]).

In this chapter, I turn attention to the 'impossible' documentary hinterlands of law and nuclear testing, the maze of documentary trails that claimants attempted to traverse and the 'states of searching' (Coutin and Yngvesson 2023: 80) in which they perpetually found themselves. Documents are a 'paradigmatic artifact' of governance (Lowenkron and Ferreira 2014: 78) and the materialization of the state and its power (Borrelli and Andreetta 2019, see also Hull 2012a, 2012b). The production and use of documents is a cornerstone of the knowledge practices within law.[1] Documents provide the material aesthetics and allowable meanings through which nuclear injuries become apparent or are denied. And they contain 'the promise of wholeness' (Coutin and Yngvesson 2023: 77): the ability to settle claims and complete the search for evidence once and for all.

In daily life, test veterans attempted to engage with a plethora of documents, many of them buried deep and stored at a distance in inaccessible state files. Test veterans and their advocates experienced these hinterlands as paradoxical. They regularly faced documentary overload, encountering a voluminous number of documents in building and making claims. Yet amidst the piles of documents that they navigated, the ones they most needed were too often missing, restricted, or withheld. Scarcity and overabundance are twin cornerstones of documentary claim-making (Coutin 2020).

The quest for documentary evidence butted up against the 'discursive containment' (Kinsella 2001) that commonly surrounds nuclear risk and its communication, as state actors and agencies constrain the meanings assignable to evidentiary documents within legal and political arenas. Horton shows how documents become (2020: 4) 'the tangible evidence of bureaucratic inscription'– the process by which actors are written into documents and made visible to the state. Yet documents can also function inversely, to expunge legal responsibilities. Rather than render state responsibilities to injured claimants visible, test veterans experienced documents through acts of bureaucratic and legal refusal. Their illnesses and experiences became unrecognizable within the form and content of documents.

Despite these risks, the work of claim-making through documents was central to test veterans' quests for justice. Yet seeking, receiving, reading, and responding to documents revealed anew the very thing that test

[1] See King et al. (2024), Mathur (2016), Shore (2008), and Strathern (2000).

veterans attempted to use documents to fight against: a sense of governmental neglect. Contestations over documents in legal arenas exemplify efforts by injury claimants to turn the spotlight of claim-making onto itself, to articulate the injurious stresses of ongoing claims (Kumaki 2022).

This chapter reveals how British test veterans' legal claims came to centre on the right to information. In exploring three case-studies spanning the 1980s, 1990s, and the early 2000s, this chapter shifts between the European Court of Human Rights, the UK Pensions Appeal Tribunal, and a First-Tier Tribunal dispute arising from a decision of the UK Information Commissioner. In each case, a claim about negligent exposure to radiation became a claim about the delay and denial of information, which in turn they used to reveal the government's neglect and moral indifference.

THE FIRST CASE: KEN AND THE EUROPEAN COURT OF HUMAN RIGHTS

Ken was born in the small Scottish town of Johnstone in late 1930s, sharing a modest council house with his parents and seven siblings.[2] At seventeen, while in Glasgow one day for work, he visited the Royal Engineers recruitment centre. The sergeant recruiter told Ken that he would receive better treatment and privileges as a regular than the other boys who would be called up for compulsory national service at the age of

[2] I have used Ken's real name here as all the details of his story conveyed here are already well detailed in his autobiography and he was a publicly known figure in the test veteran community. Ken was the only participant I did not interview in person, but by phone. My interview recording failed, and given my full reliance on his public autobiographical account, and public legal documents about him, anonymity became both impossible and unnecessary. To my dismay after the interview, a strange loud buzzing overlaid his words and made the recording unintelligible. The digital voice recorder worked perfectly before and after this interview. It was something about the interference from the phone. I couldn't help feel a rising suspicion that something or someone had interfered in the phone call. I'd barely worked through the thought when I found myself laughing at the absurdity of it. I'd been conducting research for three years and I realized that decades of solidifying suspicions amongst my participants was wearing off on me.

eighteen. There and then, Ken signed up to the army for twenty-two years, with the option of leaving after three years. At the age of twenty, Ken's regiment sailed to Kiritimati Island via the Panama Canal. On Kiritimati Island Ken worked as a sapper and spent much of his time driving a bulldozer. Ken recalled that three or four days after witnessing the first nuclear test, he woke to find the upper parts of his body covered in watery blisters. He also described suffering from nausea, diarrhoea, and watery, weeping eyes. After a medical exam he was treated with rash cream and given a pair of sunglasses. To his relief, within two or three weeks the rash had cleared, and he didn't think much more about it. Over the course of his posting, Ken witnessed five bomb tests in total, three of which were in the megaton range. Soon after his return to the UK, he was admitted to a military hospital with a severe duodenal ulcer and was discharged from the Army, deemed unfit for further duty in 1959. He received a 20 per cent military disablement pension for his ulcer.

Upon discharge, Ken filled in a statement about his health history. The nature of the form's questions, however, meant that only certain illnesses and incidences that had a clear start point and ongoing progression were deemed worthy of official record. They could not capture the moments when ill health struck then disappeared. The form asked him: 'If you are suffering from any diseases, wound, or injuries, state what they are, and also when and where they first started', and 'Give details . . . or any incidences during your service which you think caused or made worse your disability' (*McGinley* v *the United Kingdom,* [1998] ECHR 51, [19]). Ken recorded a torn cartilage, a broken ankle, and in relation to factors that could have exacerbated his ulcer, he noted the compound ration meals he had recently received.

From the time of his discharge, Ken's civilian health records began to list a range of disorders, including a sebaceous cyst, infertility, acne, and renal colic. In the early 1980s, through a series of newspaper and TV documentaries, Ken became aware of radiation-related illnesses and began to attribute his ill health to Kiritimati Island. Thus marked the beginning of his advocacy for test veterans through the British Nuclear Test Veterans Association, and multiple appeals to the Scottish Pensions Appeal Tribunal to increase his pension. In one application, in which he attempted to get a war disablement pension for depression, sterility, and arthritis, he wrote:

> I consider my problems to be directly linked to radiation exposure. Since leaving the service I have experienced bouts of moodiness and at time[s] unexplained attacks of very quick tempered actions. Then later regret them. I have been examined ... and diagnosed as sub-fertile ... I have also suffered from mysterious paralysis of the legs and arms and have been for the past four years ... in extreme pain sometimes 24 hours per day.

Throughout this process, the MoD continued to assert that Ken's radiation dose at Kiritimati Island was zero and, without evidence of exposure, his appeals were unsuccessful. The doctors who assessed him often asserted that they lacked the expertise to conclusively link his illnesses to radiation exposure. Moreover, general practitioners or medical specialists in non-radiation related fields, essential for the progress of war pension claims, asserted that the available evidence did not meet the levels of proof and certitude that they were comfortable or familiar with when assessing the aetiology of disease and illness.

In 1985, Ken appealed his pension claim again, arguing that his military medical records had been doctored, and crucial evidence had been removed. They contained no records of the examination or treatment he received directly after the first blast for blisters, vomiting, and nausea. Ken believed that this demonstrated at best negligence, and at worst, wilful corruption. The records also contained evidence, he argued, that the doctor commissioned by the War Pensions Board to assess him was biased, politically motivated, and dismissive towards test veterans. Written in a hand-drawn box on the side of a war pensions clinical report, the doctor had written 'politically sensitive case' and just below he has labelled Ken a 'paranoid appellant', noting his role in the British Nuclear Test Veterans Association.

Within pension appeals at this time, medical documents did not circulate easily to those whom they assessed. At first Ken only received an edited version of the pension Statement of Case. The unsympathetic doctor's assessment was missing. As noted in a similar veteran claim ruling, *Roche* v *United Kingdom* ([2005] ECHR 956, [103]),

> Prior to 1991 all medical records (civilian and service) were only disclosed in a 'medical in confidence' basis. It was a matter for the doctor to decide if it was in the patient's best interests to see his or her records ... the Act [*Access to Health Records Act,* 1990] ... sets down the rights of persons to access, inter alia, their service and civilian medical records. It applies only to records compiled after the date of its entry into force and to records compiled in connection with the care of the applicant.

The Pensions Appeal Tribunal rules allowed them to omit information if it was 'undesirable in the interests of the applicant to disclose to him'.[3] That Ken did not get to determine what he saw as 'in his own interests' infuriated him. However, the PAT did send an unedited version to Ken's tribunal representative, the Royal British Legion, through which he gained access and was dismayed by the unsympathetic doctors' side-comments. Without evidence of exposure or mainstream medical support for causation, Ken lost the war pensions appeal case. Ken's story is one in which the body and its medical encounters are steadily politicized. The work of politics becomes increasingly visible to all involved, and weaponized by each party against the other. In such encounters, mistrust becomes an ethical register for claimants to seek truth.

THE RIGHT TO INFORMATION

In 1993, Ken and another British test veteran Edward initiated complaints with the European Commission for Human Rights.[4] They complained of several breaches to their human rights, including that they had not been warned of harmful exposure to radiation at the tests, that they were systematically denied access to any state records about such radiation exposure in making military pension claims, as well as denied access to their military medical records, and that such omissions had 'exacerbated their suffering and denied them access to, and a fair hearing before the Pensions Appeal Tribunal' (*McGinley* v *United Kingdom* [1998] ECHR 51, [64]). Given that the nuclear testing events took place before 1966, when the UK first accepted the right of individual petition

3 Rule 22 of the Pensions Appeal Tribunal (Scotland) Rules 1981.
4 Application numbers 21825/93 and 23414/94.

to the Commission, the Commission asserted that the question of historic radiation exposure was outside their jurisdiction. Yet they deemed the joint case admissible under articles 6, 8, and 13 of the *European Convention on Human Rights*, and in 1995, they produced a report expressing the unanimous opinion that the non-disclosure of records resulted in the men denied access to a full and fair trial (article 6 § 1), and the near unanimous opinion[5] that the UK government violated the applicants' right to respect for their private and family lives (article 8). They considered rights violations under article 13, the rights to an effective remedy, more adequately covered in articles 6 and 8.

In 1997, Ken and Edward brought their case against the MoD to the European Court of Human Rights in Strasburg, France (*McGinley* v *United Kingdom* [1998] ECHR 51).[6] While continuing their claim of the unjust withholding of documents under articles 6, 8, and 13, they once again attempted to broaden their claim. They argued that failing to monitor their radiation exposure at Kiritimati Island violated their rights under articles 2, the right to life, and article 3, which prohibits inhuman or degrading treatment. Moreover, with respect to article 3 they complain that 'as a result of the unfair pension procedure, each of them had suffered severe mental stress'.

Falling in line with the Commission, the Court ruled that only a consideration of violations relating to the non-disclosure of documents, under articles 6, 8, and 13, fell within its jurisdiction. And they ruled that the suffering caused by the applicants' lack of access to documents could be folded into the non-disclosure argument. Article 6 § 1 states that 'everyone is entitled to a fair and public hearing within a reasonable time by an independent and impartial tribunal established by law'. Article 8 asserts that 'everyone has the right to respect for his private and family life, his home and his correspondence'. According to the Court, article 8 applied to the two claimants because having access to

[5] This ruling was decided 23 votes to 3 votes.

[6] As Greenberg (2020) outlines, the ECtHR was formed in 1959 to adjudicate contraventions of the *European Convention on Human Rights*. Its mandate was not fact-finding, nor to assess original evidence, but rather to assess if member states' national laws were upholding human rights obligations.

information necessary in assessing one's health risks and the dangers to which they might have been exposed is a right tied to the full enactment of private and family lives. Thus 'where a Government engages in hazardous activities ... which might have hidden adverse consequences on the health of those involved in such activities, respect for private and family life under Article 8 requires that an effective and accessible procedure be established which enables such persons to seek all relevant and appropriate information' ([101]). Regarding the applicants' right to access information about their health, the Court found that a positive obligation existed beyond a lack of interference in accessing information.

Indeed, the Court argued that the issue of providing access to information was crucial in that it could 'either have allayed the applicants' fears in this respect, or enabled them to assess the danger to which they had been exposed' ([97]). The Court acknowledged that 'given the fact that exposure to high levels of radiation is known to have hidden, but serious and long-lasting, effects on health, it is not unnatural that the applicants' uncertainty as to whether or not they had been put at risk in this way caused them substantial anxiety and distress' ([99]).

In their legal defence, the MoD asked the Court to find the application inadmissible. The Court was restricted to consider cases in which applicants had exhausted all domestic legal routes for remedy. The UK government argued that they had fulfilled their duty to enable access to information through the *Pensions Appeal Tribunal Act* 1943 (UK). Under Rule 6 of the Act, in the event of a pension appeal and after the Department of Social Services issued a Statement of Case containing all of the applicant's service medical records, the applicant had six weeks to request disclosure of relevant documents that they believed a government department held. The UK government argued that neither applicant had utilized this legal recourse.

In reality, however, Rule 6 was not a guaranteed avenue for access. The tribunal president had to assess the request as relevant to the appeal before forwarding it on. The Secretary of State could then place an indefinite stay on the documents in question, asserting that their release was not in the public interest or a threat to security. In the case of documents deemed a security risk, an appeal could be adjourned 'until such time as the necessity for non-disclosure on the ground of security no longer exists' (*McGinley* v *United Kingdom* [1998] ECHR 51, [59]).

In an interview Ken explained to me that he never knew about Rule 6 at the time, and the Pensions Appeal Tribunal had never informed him of his right to receive information through it. Speaking at a test veteran conference, widow and member of the BNTVA Shelia Grey said:

> We have . . . been informed that we should apply for pensions using Rule 6 of the War Pensions Agency. That would be alright – IF ANYONE KNEW WHAT IT WAS! We have even asked some of our Members of Parliament and they do not know of it. We are also told, should we want to know about it, we should give full details, including in which office [documents are] held! How do we do that when even the officials don't know! (Grey 2002).

In their response to the applicants' claim, the MoD portrayed Rule 6 as a robust and accessible avenue for information gathering, claiming that, in test veterans' pension appeals, no impediments would have prevented disclosure of all relevant state documents. They argued that had the applicants availed themselves of Rule 6, 'there would have been no security reason for withholding such records' (*McGinley* v *United Kingdom* [1998] ECHR 51, [89]). While the judges asserted in their ruling that there existed no reason for them to doubt that all relevant records have been released, and no security proviso would have prevented their release under Rule 6, test veterans were highly sceptical. Records of environmental radiation records on Kiritimati Island were not 'released into the public domain for reasons of national security' ([83]) until requested for the ECtHR case in 1997. These included historical documents regarding the safety plans for the bomb tests, and environmental radiation records from the air, ground, water, and fish on and around Kiritimati Island, all of which showed safe levels of radiation. Reflecting on the case over a decade later, Ken said: 'It's obvious. They cherry-picked a few documents to release, showing no danger. . . . If we'd asked for anything under Rule 6, they would have just said, national security. Denied.' The evidence for this, he argued, was right there in the case. The documents used by the MoD to proclaim their innocence and demonstrate a culture of transparency had, after all, been 'forced out' and 'pressed into legal service' through transnational litigation (Elander and Hughes 2024: 840).

Ken and Edward lost their case. The Court held, by six votes to three, that no violation to article 6 § 1 had occurred, and by an even closer five votes to four, that no violation to article 8 had occurred. The decision deemed that Rule 6 had provided sufficient guarantee of a fair trial and access to information, arguing that 'where a procedure was provided for the disclosure of documents which the applicants failed to utilize, it cannot be said that the State prevented the applicants from gaining access to, or falsely denied the existence of, any relevant evidence, or that the applicants were thereby denied effective access to or a fair hearing before the PAT' (*McGinley* v *United Kingdom* [1998] ECHR 51, [90]).

The dissenting judges offered robust disagreement with the ruling. They disputed what, in this case, a positive obligation to provide information entailed. In a joint opinion, three judges argued that, given knowledge existed at the time of the tests of the harmful nature of radiation exposure, the state bore responsibility for monitoring health at the testing site. 'They should have established the state of health of both of the participants before and after the tests and monitored developments, at least for as long as the soldiers remained in service.' By contrast, the Opinion noted, 'their medical records, as produced by the government contained hardly any information as to their physical condition before and after the tests, or as to the possible consequences of their presence near the places where the tests took place'. They noted that Ken's military medical records contained nothing at all from his arrival on Kiritimati Island in late 1957 to September the following year, after all but the final test was detonated.

> The government implied that that information did not exist. That would mean that the authorities had been grossly negligent in not gathering it. It is also possible that such information exists or did not exist and that it has been deemed necessary to keep it or destroy it. That would be even more serious. Whatever the case, the information should have existed and ought to have been communicated to the men concerned. . . . The applicants had the right to be informed of all the consequences that their presence in the test area could have for them, including those it could have on their pensions. They had the right to know what might happen to them, without having to ask ([annex]).

Unlike the Majority View, the joint Dissenting Opinion expressed a mistrust similar to test veterans' regarding the UK government's claims of transparent and honest production and treatment of documents. The Dissenting Opinion quoted documents that test veterans had found in archives and presented to court, noting in a footnote that,

> A tendency to deny or to minimize the effects of the explosions is to be found in particular in a telex of 31 July 1956 where there is a request [from Penney] for the words 'shows an increase' [in radiation levels] in a particular document to be replaced by the words 'has not shown an increase' ... and in a letter of 22 December 1955 which contains a recommendation not to give the Australian Government certain samples for a number of days, 'so that some of the short-lived key isotopes have decayed a good deal' ([annex]).

A second dissenting opinion by Judge Pekkanen argued that, given the men had a general and ongoing interest in information about their health, Rule 6 did not provide a general enough avenue for accessing information. Judge Pekkanen thus argued:

> I do not consider that [Rule 6] was sufficient to fulfil the State's positive obligation under article 8, since the Rule 6 procedure was contingent on the applicants' claims for pensions whereas, as the majority have found, in addition to and independent of their interest in establishing pension entitlement, the applicants had a general and continuing interest in obtaining access to information relating to the extent, if any, to which they had been exposed to harmful levels of radiation ([annex]).

While not a legal win for test veterans, the case generated new grounds for enunciating claims. As Greenberg's study of the ECtHR revealed, such 'legal institutions offer people venues and language that they can use to produce shared vocabularies of change' (2020: 419). By framing the absence of historically collected health information through the lens of human rights, the case increased test veterans' awareness of the vast documentary records that remained, and the different measures possible to reconstruct radiation and explain its biological effects. It made visible the documentary records' flaws, gaps, silences, and absences. The case formed the basis of a new demand: documents became a locus for contrasting the state's reactive approach to care with a new anticipatory ethic of care.

Anticipatory care, as McKearney (2018) shows, means claimants of care need not articulate or even know in advance their needs or the practices that will bring about their flourishing. Instead, for those who care, being responsible for another involves building durable practices to envisage and imagine future need. And as Greenberg argues, 'legal frameworks, styles of argumentation, case law, and documents give specific shape to people's experience with violence or harm' (2020: 420). Through engagement with law, injuries are reframed as human rights and their breach. While unelaborated within the judgement, the Court accepted the suffering generated from having documents withheld in claim-making as a legitimate grievance and form of harm, admissible within a human rights frame.

While Ken and Edward's case was not purposively pursued as strategic litigation, its effects were thus. Strategic litigation and legal mobilization focus on longer-term social, political, and legal goals over single case victories, enabling a 'wedge' approach. They aim for incremental shifts in legal legitimacy, irrespective of winning or losing cases. Incremental wins can include proving admissibility and legal jurisdiction, and generating more favourable interpretations of law, legal precedence, and duties of care. Strategic litigation can generate public visibility and collective mobilization, highlight injustice and suffering, and spotlight moral transgressions, 'those "lawful, but awful" acts and omissions' (Natali 2015: 64). They can, moreover, produce dissenting opinions, and clarify rights already existing in law and the conditions and procedures needed for their compliance (Guerrero 2020, Smart 2024). Understood this way, Ken and Edwards case was a pivotal moment in articulating the injurious impacts of document-based claim-making.

THE SECOND CASE: TESSA, BRIAN, AND THE PENSIONS APPEAL TRIBUNAL

I sat on the carpet, amongst the stacks of documents. Pile after neat pile of letters surrounded us. Tessa had lined them up in the lounge before I arrived. Here was what materially remained of her late husband's battle with the British Secretary of State for Defence. Hunched over these weighty, officious paper towers, we glanced through the top leaves in silence. It didn't take long for me to feel awash in their mild-mannered refusals.

Making war disablement pension claims and appeals, test veterans and their widows discovered, was a temporally arduous process.[7] It was largely conducted on paper, by mail and through medical intermediary assessors who wrote and sent off reports and did not have the power to make decisions themselves. Most of the time, the process was occurring elsewhere, mysteriously, in locations they did not know. Documents were always moving, albeit glacially. Responsibility was distributed across such a wide and opaque network of actors it seemed to disappear entirely.

In describing her late husband Brian's application for a pension, Tessa described it as 'a torturous experience, because it was letters backwards and forwards, it took a long period of time, there were a lot of obstructions through time wasting'. It was normally months before the Agency would even acknowledge the receipt of documentation and applications with brief, 'standard letters'.

> The way it works is that you could then get a case officer for this particular claim, it was a lady who was the case officer, and Brian would write to her and say, 'What's the position of my claim?' and then it would take weeks and weeks and weeks before she responded. ... It all felt very stalling from a time perspective. And then, the suspiciousness would come out, we'd get a letter that said, 'we wrote to your consultant and we haven't heard from him, hence the time delay', and Brian would then phone up

[7] Once personnel of the British Royal Armed Forces have completed their military service, they could apply under the War Pension Scheme for a war disablement pension if they believed that they suffered from a physical or mental disablement (an injury, illness, or disease) caused or made worse by their military service. Depending on a service personnel's rank and the duration of their service, as well as the severity of their illness, eligible veterans received a lump sum payment and, for those deemed over 20 per cent disabled, weekly tax-free payments. While there was no time limit for submitting a claim, after seven years from the date of military discharge the onus of proof reversed from being the state's responsibility to prove that an illness is *not* attributed to service to the claimant's responsibility to prove that it is, and to raise 'reasonable doubt' based on 'reasonable evidence' that service was the principal cause of an illness.

the consultant's secretary and they'd say, "We sent the form off three months ago."

In re-listening to the interview later I realized that the painstaking, methodical telling of Brian's experience was crucial to the pace of the story and its injurious lesson. Through it she sought to offer proof of the slow grind of unrelenting small barriers, one after another, through which she and Brian laboured and were worn down.[8] She wanted to convey the deep weariness central to such rituals of claim-making, the unspectacular yet cumulative harms, the non-events of claim-making (Gupta 2012, Nixon 2011). Povinelli (2011) calls these harms 'cruddy' in that they fall below the moral visibility of 'eventness', those spectacles of suffering that demand political action or answerability. Tessa's experience reflects the embodiment of bureaucratic and legal time, what she described as the slow wear and tear of administrative indifference.

Tessa and Brian's frustrations emerged at the same time as a society-wide critique, what du Gay describes as 'anti-bureaucratic thought' (2005: 2). This provides an 'image of malfunction' within which to situate experiences that are 'part of a larger universe that we might call . . . the ideology and practice of accountability' (Herzfeld 1992: 3–4) emergent in the late twentieth century. These accountabilities blend 'the economic imperatives of neoliberalism with the technologies of New Public Management' (Shore 2008: 278) and aim to interpolate audit cultures into the fabric of workplace policy, language, and subjectivities (Strathern 2000).

[8] This reveals how Brian's combative, determined stance was a virtuous character trait in the face of such barriers. As Zoë Wool demonstrates, while victimhood affords veterans some resources, 'it also has an ambivalent and tense relationship with forms of masculinity that are so central to the military personhood to which diagnosed soldiers seek to remain attached. This is the puzzle of what we might call "military victimhood"' (Wool 2013a:140). As a non-combat conscript, it is hard to know how much Brian identified with such a military masculinity, although his ongoing regular engagements with other test veterans, many of whom were career service personnel, are likely to have shaped his self-identity. In a similar vein, Gutmann and Lutz (2010) note that soldiers who experience traumatic stress and who 'break ranks' and come to oppose war can refigure the valued soldiering virtues of service, loyalty, and duty to the nation, compelling them to oppose war.

In the British context, when Brian was making his claim, addressing bureaucratic malfunction became both a political technique and a cultural performance through which the ruling Labour government attempted to garner and assert democratic legitimacy. They rolled out a series of reforms aimed at instilling new norms of 'responsiveness' within the public sector in the early 2000s. These new policies demanded of government agencies regular inspections, target-setting, a focus on outcomes, new systems of audit, competitive tendering, and the increased recognition and role of 'users' or 'customers' in bureaucratic action. Prime Minister Tony Blair (1997–2007) also sought to legislatively encourage more direct citizen participation in service provisions (Taylor and Kelly 2006). Tessa and Brian's complaints reflect an emerging language of public sector accountability that simultaneously crafted newly active citizen selves.

The War Pensions Agency (renamed the Veterans Agency in 2003) was not entirely indifferent to such critiques, as reflected in a departmental review in 2001–02 (House of Commons 2004), during which time Brian was making his claim.[9] The Agency was becoming increasingly reflective of its temporal failings to 'clients' like Brian. Monitoring over the 2001–02 time frame revealed that it took the Agency four months to clear a first claim for a war disablement pension and on average 135 working days for the first stage of an appeal. The report suggests that Agency staff did not dictate the temporal trajectory of claims. Documents travelled slowly into their orbit.

The Agency relied on an entirely paper-based records system. They spent much time waiting for others to provide them with information. Despite a target of ten working days, it took around 24 working days for hospital case notes and 38 working days for reports from general practitioners to arrive. Moreover, the Agency had to wait on the MoD to deliver claimants service records. Despite an agreement that such records would arrive within twenty days, the report observed that 'over a quarter were not provided within 25 working days' (House of Commons 2004).[10]

[9] For more other veteran examples of such critiques against the British Veterans' Agency, see Martin (2007).

[10] The Agency relied on an entirely paper-based records system, with two aging computer systems that did not communicate with each other. This compounded inefficiencies and delays, the report noted. Furthermore, the Agency explained that they

Despite the often-significant bodily suffering test veterans faced while making their claims, the documentary process curtailed the urgency and visibility of their needs by making it vie with acute, emergency care. The war pension review concluded that some of the delays were due to 'a lack of resources in [the] hospital records department who faced continual demands for records for immediate clinical purposes against which the Agency had to compete' (House of Commons 2004). By emphasizing the corrosive, harmful effects of waiting at a distance, Tessa's story resonated within a wider politics of statecraft. Brian was making his claim for a pension at a moment when bureaucratic temporarily itself became political, a data point to quantify responsive and responsible government.

Brian was eventually awarded a one-off war disablement pension payment of £4,300. As the pension scheme is a no-fault system, the MoD asserted no moral liability, contrition, or blame. Tessa read to me a letter from the Veterans Agency stating: 'We've accepted the following diagnosed conditions as being caused by your service. We call this attributable to service: Keratosis of the skin.' The attribution of keratosis came as a surprise to Brian and Tessa. Brian's GP and dermatologist had never made such a diagnosis. 'At no point in this particular claim, do they link that to anything to do with the nuclear fallout. And in fact, there is a letter somewhere, that says the claim, "attributable to service", was due to "over exposure to sunlight".' Tessa placed the letter back down on the top of the pile. 'He was recompensed financially for that, but not morally.'[11]

No-fault schemes express an intrinsically modernist logic regarding the necessary costs and trade-offs of progress, as Feldman and Bayer

struggled to meet the demand for their call centre. 'The Agency operates a freephone helpline which handled 418,284 calls in 2001 ... of which 11.4% were lost calls. ... Since its call centre is small the Agency said it was difficult to match the number of people working to the volume of calls received' (House of Commons 2004). This reflects what Mathur (2014: 148) describes as struggles to reconcile different forms of time within bureaucracy. Waiting and failure result from 'impasse arising out of attempts to bring incommensurable forms and representations of time into congruence'.

11 Tessa's quotes in this paragraph were previously published in *Tinkering Care, State Responsibility, and Abandonment: Nuclear Test Veterans and the Mismatched Temporalities of Justice in Claims for Health Care* (Trundle 2020b: 208).

(1999: 12) demonstrate in their study of haemophiliac claimants seeking justice for HIV-tainted blood transfusions in the 1980s. Underpinning this logic is the assumption that necessary 'technological achievements inevitably bring with them the possibility of unintended harms'. Yet no-fault schemes 'fail to "make whole" when they do not recognize the psychological needs of individuals or the social needs of communities to hold to account those deemed responsible for actions that caused injury'. And as Pillayre (2021) demonstrates, claimants within no-fault compensation still regularly use them to assert normative frames and assign blame.

After Brian received his lump sum payment, they received devastating news. Brian was diagnosed with pancreatic cancer. Certain that Kiritimati Island was to blame, he put in another pension claim. It was rejected. Before a Pensions Appeal Tribunal date could be set, the MoD requested more information and to see all the evidence that Brian would submit to the tribunal. 'He had to keep sending things in', Tessa explained. Brian was responsible for getting his doctors and medical consultants to write to the MoD, 'they [the MoD] wouldn't search for it anymore'. This documentary responsibility revealed the double bind of informational excess and scarcity. Proliferation led to overload, which in turn led to gaps in the record. Brian's pension appeal offers a tragic example.

When a date for the appeal was eventually set, Brian and Tessa received a copy of the case notes from the MoD that contained both parties' supporting documentation and evidence, and the correspondence between them. Tessa showed me the two large folders, each around three inches thick, filled with medical reports, research articles, and photocopied letters. As the appeal drew near, Tessa and Brian received crushing news.

> Brian's cancer had returned. And he knew it was terminal. And he had refused further chemotherapy. So we knew we were talking time. So, when we had the tribunal hearing, Brian at that point – it was three and a half weeks before he died, so he was an ill man, he was an ill man. And you know, Catherine, when they talk about people who wait for children to come before they die, they wait to see somebody, they hang on? He hung on for this tribunal. And it was quite emotionally distressing to see that

> something, which for me was not important, but for him, was crucially important, life holding important. ... So, at this point, he was struggling with walking, he was a very, very ill man.[12]

Arriving at the Tribunal, 'armed with our documents' Tessa explained, Brian 'struggles to get there'. Tribunal officials then informed them that the hearing had been cancelled. 'At which point Brian broke down. So they told us to sit down, and then we went into the tribunal room.' Tessa recalled that the tribunal judge explained:

> we're terribly sorry, but we are going to have to cancel this. ... Because we're very surprised at the lateness of the hearing. It was at 3 o'clock, these offices close at 4 o'clock. In the light of the case notes ... it is our view we will need at least a whole day to hear your tribunal, so we can't possibly do it in an hour.

Tessa and Brian were furious that the Tribunal and MoD had scheduled the case so late in the day.

Tessa recounted how Brian said to the judge, '"I'm a very sick man, I haven't got the time". And then ... the Tribunal judge said something about the amount of paperwork, and Brian said then, "Oh yes, I'm just going to focus in on the work of Professor Sawada".'[13] Tessa described how the Tribunal judge responded, asking, '"And who is he?" So, Brian said, "I sent his report to my case officer in September. ... And I sent it 'recorded delivery', and I have proof it was signed for ...". But it wasn't in the [case notes]. So they said, "Well, that's a second reason now, we can't have the tribunal. Because we haven't seen that document".'

On reflection, Tessa realized they had been too trusting of the documentary system underpinning the pension claim system. 'The mistake I think we made was that we didn't thoroughly go through those [case notes]. It was clear when we arrived that it was a mistake.' Tessa and Brian had assumed that the MoD would include all of the information that they had sent them. 'And I know you shouldn't assume, but we assumed.' For Brian this represented a final loss of hope. 'He said, "Well, it's not going

12 Tessa's quote was previously published in my article, Biopolitical Endpoints: Diagnosing a Deserving British Nuclear Test Veteran (Trundle 2011: 886).

13 See Sawada (2007).

to happen in the next however many weeks or months, because we know what they're like". So he gave up.'

Despite a failure of hope, Brian was incited to one final fight when, the following week, they received a letter from the War Pensions Agency stating why the Appeal had not gone ahead. One reason given was that 'Mr. Rielly has produced further medical evidence.'

At this point, Brian's quest for justice gave way to a desire for truth, to influence how the story of his loss would be inscribed in the official record. Brian was determined to, as Zussman labels it, challenge 'a moral universe of limited liability' (1992: 33) appearing in the records of his case. Tessa and Brian drafted a letter to the Tribunal Services. 'It's his words, but it's my typing', Tessa explained. It read: 'I am writing to inform you that I strongly refute one of the reasons as listed, [that I] produced further medical evidence.' ... I did not produce any further evidence at the adjourned tribunal. ... It is, in my opinion, seriously erroneous and a distortion of the truth'. Using both deferential and forceful language, Brian attempted to rewrite the official bureaucratic record. 'May I humbly suggest that Point 2 should read – the Tribunal members had not been supplied with all the relevant information by the Ministry of Defence. ... I do not accept the decision on appeal and I wish it to be reviewed in light of my comments.... Please do not insult me further by delaying with your response.'

In response to their letter, Tessa and Brian received a letter stating, 'Unable to change a tribunal decision', as well as a statement from the Tribunal judge, which explained that Brian had produced the medical report and deemed it crucial to his case. It went on,

> This was looked at by the medical member whose view was that it might have relevance, but that it was too complicated to consider that day. In any event the Tribunal was running very late and was not in a position to proceed. I cannot understand why Mr. Rielly should appear to be saying that this Report was not produced.'

Tessa was deeply disturbed by the cold formal response, its lack of attention to detail, and its failure to comprehend Brian's assertion and the facts at hand. 'When you're talking about, you know, so, a man who is dying is receiving this level of.... And it is a lie. It is a lie.'

Despite this, the Tribunal did explain that they would attempt to try to reschedule the case in the coming weeks and hold the Tribunal in Tessa and Brian's house if possible. However, Tessa realized that this was unrealistic. 'In the last week of his life, Brian was in, I don't know, a coma, conscious, but he wasn't really speaking, and so we knew ... it wasn't going to happen.' When Tessa heard back again from the Tribunal, she was instructed that it would be held in a nearby city, in just under a month's time. Five days later, Brian passed away. 'And so ... there was no compassion shown to Brian or to us at all.'

Javier Auyero (2012: 156) reveals in the waiting rooms of bureaucratic offices how 'people learn through endless delays and random changes that they have to comply with the requirements of an unpredictable state' (see also Carswell and De Neve 2020). But as test veterans show, 'chronic waiting' (Jeffrey 2008) does not always lead to an ethic of compliance. Waiting can instil an ethic of refusal on both sides of a claim (Petoukhov 2023). Just as government actors refuse or scupper claims, so too clients can refuse and vocally criticize the temporal consequences of documentary practices in law. And like Brian, test veterans used their bodies, their diseases, even the end stages of their lives to instantiate their refusals. In the mismatch of governmental refusal and claimant need, documentary practices get detached from what Sarah Franklin (2014) calls 'biologized time'. The body moves towards death faster than the paper-driven systems of legal redress can account for. Legal processes outlive bodies. Tessa's story is perhaps the starkest yet of how injury law injures, and how over time such legal processes become the centre of the injury claim, the core moral driver to continue pursuing justice.

THE THIRD CASE: ALEX AND THE INFORMATION TRIBUNAL

On Kiritimati Island Alex was assigned to clean up debris at Ground Zero and make sure the bunker located beneath the bomb site and the various instruments inside it were undamaged after detonations. He spent five hours at Ground Zero and was given two types of dosimeters to wear but little protective clothing. Even in retirement, he could recall the overall dosimeter readings: 25 rads in total, or 12.5 rads of beta radiation by the end of each of two clean ups.

Decades later, Alex applied for a war pension for a raft of ongoing health concerns. His application was denied. 'And the first thing I did was ask for the results of my radiation film badges. So I got an answer back telling me they went missing, there was no result.' Alex did not give up. 'Well, my MP at the time was the Minister of Veterans Affairs, and when he made the questions, they sent them the printouts of all ... well out names were blanked out, but the names of all the radiation badges [for our group] that were issued [were there].'

> Prior to the bomb going off we did do a dummy run and we were all issued with a badge which we wore around the area, handed in for decontamination exactly the same as what we did after the bombs. Now every single badge that was handed in on the dummy run was recorded and it was put down against that name as 0.2 millisieverts. It was just the background radiation. So that went down, all into records. Now after [the first bomb] as I say 12 [badges] went missing, 2 were returned. After [the second bomb] 8 [badges] went missing and 7 returned, all 7 recording nil dose.

In seeking to provide Alex with his radiation dose, the MoD extrapolated from the limited readings that they had. 'Because both of my badges went missing they averaged it out, but [from] the one that I had for the dummy run. So my dose rate was put down as 0.6 millisieverts for all the bomb blasts. So you can see it was one big fiddle.' By contrast, Alex was certain that he had received 250 millisieverts from his dosimeter readings, and further dose due to his time spent living in 'Camp B' located only three miles from Ground Zero.

When Alex requested his dosimeter records, he reported that the MoD replied: '"No we didn't keep them for servicemen, we have them for civilians [scientists], but not for servicemen". They didn't keep the results.' Alex was indignant and wrote a letter to the then Prime Minster of the United Kingdom Gordon Brown. In it, he noted: 'They didn't even bother to have an incident book at the decontamination centre to register any person found to show signs of radiation on their clothes or body. It would appear no consideration was given to the welfare or health of the ordinary British Serviceman.'

Alex was determined to get a more accurate reading of his radiation dose and believed that the MoD had more information available from which to reconstruct his dose. 'I realized I was in one position, Ground Zero.' From safeguarding the bunker, 'I knew there were instruments in there that were recording all the levels of radiation. So I decided if I got the radiation levels from the bunker that would show the levels that I had picked up because I was within an inch of that bunker when I was working, I thought, that would have been my levels.' Alex put in a freedom of information (FOI) request[14] in 2008 to the MoD and was eventually sent a graph which recorded the radiation decay levels for the 150 hours after both bombs at Ground Zero. Alex showed me a copy of the graph and pointed out a crucial detail was missing from the y-axis of the graph, making it impossible to read accurately. 'It was just one square, one cubed, one to the power of four. So I put in an information request asking . . . what measurement they actually were.' Thus began Alex's five-year battle with the MoD to gain the information he sought that would eventually culminate in a hearing at the Information Rights section of the First-Tier Tribunal.

The MoD responded to Alex that he could get this information from the Public Records Office (PRO) at Kew (now The National Archives). When Alex requested this information from the PRO, they informed him that as the request would take longer than twenty minutes to action, he needed to come down to London himself and access the records.

> There were only 195 pages in the entire section that I was after, so I said 'I'll buy [a copy of] the whole section, rather than coming all the way from

[14] The *Freedom of Information Act 2000* (UK), championed by Tony Blair's 'New Labour' government, aimed to make the British state services accountable to every citizen, creating clear procedures through which the right to access state documentation could be enshrined and enacted, and create a proactive duty on over 100,000 public authorities to release information. Beyond this legislation, earlier laws, namely the Public Records Acts of 1957 and 1968, require that once official records are thirty years old, they must be held by the Public Records Office as 'historical records' with exception to some documents, such as cabinet documents. In 2010, this time frame was reduced from thirty to twenty years. The *FOI Act* sought to increase transparency, accountability, robust government decision-making, government record keeping, public understandings of government decisions, and public trust in government (Birkinshaw 2010). Birkinshaw argues the Act has improved accountability and transparency, but not met its other objectives. In terms of trust in government, Birkinshaw illustrates the paradox thus: 'How can it increase trust when it constantly reveals shortcomings in government?' (2010: 318).

> home having to pay for accommodation and everything down here, I thought it would be a lot cheaper doing it this way. . . . And they came back and said it's restricted. . . . Now I could have come all the way down here, spent this money and not been allowed to see them.

Alex refused to give up and continued to put in FOI requests. Eventually, the MoD sent him a scale that their officials had deduced, which put the reading of radiation at the time of the Burgee[15] bomb detonation at one rad.

'I was getting five rads from the dosimeter, so there was no way that was accurate. So I told them that was false. . . . I think it was ridiculous, and I'm not that sort of an idiot.' Alex insisted that such a reading could not be accurate, and reflected dryly in a letter to MPs that 'if this was the case: the test could have been held in complete safety on Salisbury Plain or Dartmoor and saved countless millions. But we all know this is ridiculous'.

The MoD insisted that neither they nor any other government departments held further information on the graph, but Alex persisted in his search for information. He put in FOI requests after request, hoping to uncover radiation records by trying a range of angles, and potential documentary paths. Since the release of environmental monitoring records at Ken and Edwards' case before the European Court of Human Rights, Alex had some knowledge of what might be available. He began to seek all the possible records that might provide answers to his questions. His requests included such questions as the following:

- What was the average radiation level at Camp C?
- If there was monitoring, was it perpetual or several times a day?
- What was considered the maximum permissible radiation dose allowed for servicemen?
- What was considered the maximum permitted [dose] for Civilians?
- What were the radiation levels [recorded in aircraft sampling] for each of the five tests [that I witnessed]?

[15] While each test was code-named Operation Grapple X, Y, or Z, the devices themselves had other names, such as Burgee, Pennent, Flagpole, and Dickens.

Over the next two years he sometimes sent three or four requests in a month. Then, he would send a prompt and often curt reminder if he did not receive a reply within that statutory period of twenty days. At times Alex engaged in what Aimee Meredith Cox calls 'shapeshifting' (2015), he was shifting the normative terms while engaging with them, utilizing the 'performative capacities embedded in law by bending them toward new and unexpected arcs' (Cohen and Morgan 2023, 1063, see also Ewick and Silbey 1998). He expanded the ambit of the *Freedom of Information Act* 2000 (UK) as his information requests became the means to publicly and officially express grievance. His questions became morally and rhetorically pointed. For example,

> Due to sepsis, many Servicemen lost all their teeth within five years of returning from nuclear test zones and many also suffered several years of boils. Why was no action taken to medically examine these men? Did the MOD know about these problems and deliberately refuse to inform the Servicemen? If so, for what reason were the Servicemen denied an honest explanation?
>
> On the 17th of March 2011 the Foreign Office advice to UK citizens in Japan was to remain indoors, keep windows and doors closed and not use ventilation between 20km to 30km from a damaged nuclear facility. Why was such advice not given to participants of the British Nuclear Tests following detonations in the 1950s? Why were servicemen lodged in open tents within 5kms of Ground Zero after detonations when it was recognised dangers existed from breathing in contaminated dust blowing around?

In many instances, the MoD replied that they did not hold the information he sought. At other times they informed him that the information would be available at The National Archives and therefore they were not obliged to look. Documents perform the deferral, dilution, and redistribution of responsibility as it rhetorically circulates within the state (Trnka 2017). On occasion the MoD gave some information about which files to request at The National Archives. These rarely proved helpful. When Alex requested information about the movements of one of the squadrons on Kiritimati Island, a MoD researcher informed him that a file existed in The National Archives covering the periods of 1956–58. Alex duly requested the entire file at a cost of £59, but found that 'there was a section missing from

March 1957 till March 1958,' prompting him to write asking 'were the pages removed for censorship purposes?' Having already fulfilled their obligations under the *FOI Act* (2000), the MoD did not reply.

Alex's FOI requests were, however, not entirely futile. They revealed to him the sheer lack of records that had been collected, preserved, or released on the topic. In one FOI request, Alex summarized in a long list the health and safety records the MoD had not collected during the testing, that his FOI requests had revealed. To this he simply asked: 'my question under the Freedom of Information Act is: what information was recorded?'

Eventually, the MoD used the force of the Act to ignore Alex's claims. 'The appropriate limit is specified in regulation and for central government is set at £600.' They explained in a letter. 'This represents the estimated cost of one person spending 3.5 working days determining whether the department holds information within the scope of the request, and then locating, retrieving and extracting the information.' Alex's requests were, they argued, too costly to fulfil.

Quantifying the democratic right to information gave Alex numerical ammunition to assail governmental spending. In his interview, Alex compared the cost of his requests with the millions of pounds the MoD had spent on the High Court case fighting the veterans' group action, as well as the fact that the MoD staff 'picked up £39.7 million in the last six months of last year as bonuses'. For Alex, these letters and their legally specified refusal to answer his questions represented the 'embodiment of contempt' (Struthers Montford 2023) he had come to expect from the government in documentary form.

VEXATIOUS CLAIMS

The MoD responses grew firmer. Alex explained: 'I tried again and I was told that if I carried on putting in any more questions regarding radiation levels it would be treated as vexatious . . . . And so I wrote back and said, "The only person being vexatious is you", I said, "I have asked a legitimate question".' According to the British Information Commissioner's responses to Alex, a request is considered vexatious when it is obsessive, when it harasses or distresses staff, 'causes a significant burden in terms of expense and distraction', 'is designed to cause disruption or annoyance', or lacks 'any serious purpose'.[16] In categorizing a request thus, government departments are not required to apply any public interest test and can assert a significant degree of discretion.

Alex disputed the label of vexatious. Through such a system, he argued, the MoD could dismiss the persistence of a legitimate claim and cover up their own failure to respond. 'The reason I am asking again', he explained, 'is because they didn't answer the first time'. Alex took his complaint to the First-Tier Tribunal.[17]

Before the tribunal judge, Alex quoted the Lesvos Declaration (2009), produced by the European Committee on Radiation Risk,[18] which 'consider it to be a human right for individuals to know the level of radiation to which they are exposed, and also to be correctly informed as to the potential consequences of that exposure'. He argued: 'my Human Rights are being violated due to the deliberate concealment of all records which would prove I have received large dose of ionising radiation during my tour at Christmas Island', and he complained, 'the onus is on the individual to prove evidence that the Ministry of Defence is culpable, the Ministry of Defence are not required to prove their innocence'.

In invoking the language of human rights, Alex hopes to flip the burden of responsibility in ways that foregrounded precaution and classified radiation exposure as intrinsically dangerous. Presumption benefits those who have the least power to prove a case of exposure and causation. The party with an archive and significant budget at their disposal must prove otherwise. Human rights for many test veterans

[16] See *Freedom of Information Act* 2000 (UK) 14 §1.

[17] The Information Commissioner and Information Tribunal act, according to Birkinshaw, as 'a champion of the legislation; an adviser on good practice; a publisher of advice, guidance, and decisions; and an enforcer'. Many of the Tribunal's decisions have demanded more robust practices of disclosure than those practiced by British Public Authorities, suggesting it performs a check and balance to government (Birkinshaw 2010: 317). The Information Tribunal was later subsumed into the Information Rights division of the First-Tier Tribunal.

[18] The European Committee on Radiation Risk regards most mainstream international standards for radiation risk as inadequate, and takes a more precautionary approach to low-level radiation exposure, in contrast to, for example, the International Commission on Radiological Protection (whose International System of Radiological Protection is used worldwide as the common basis for radiological protection standards). The UK Health Protection Agency has criticized it as unscientific in its approach.

ideally signified a set of safeguards that proactively mitigated the power imbalances inherent within documentary systems.

Alex claimed that the MoD had violated article 8 of the *European Convention on Human Rights*, the right to respect private and family life, by making his search for information so difficult. Alex believed the ECtHR ruling on Ken and Edward's case had created a precedent at odds with the MoD's FOI process, which was reactive, defensive, slow, and unyielding. The fact that so many of Alex's medical and radiation records were missing was not a burden that Alex felt he should have to bear. Instead, it evidenced the state's failure to enact his rights.

Near the conclusion of the tribunal, the judge asked the MoD to provide more information regarding its search processes for the graph before he could form a judgment on the case. Several weeks later, Alex received a letter from the MoD. It explained that as there had been 'a lack of definitive record' of the searches they conducted for the graph and further information about it, they had conducted a new search.

They reported: 'I am pleased to be able to advise you that this search has identified a hand written log book, a copy of which I am sending you . . . which contains information relating to the graph.' The log was 90 pages long. They explained,

> 'During the recent search we found another electronic version of the graph in the AWE archive. Unlike the version available for public viewing in TNA since 1998, it contains the descriptor DOSE-RATE mr/h.' By way of excuse for the delay they stated that,
>
> Both the MOD and AWE have, in dealing with this case, relied solely on the electronic and publicly available version of the document in the National Archives. Public authorities are not required to search for information in scope of the FOI request where it is in the public domain and reasonably accessible to the requestor. Consequently, we did not search with MOD or AWE for the graph . . . it would appear a single reprographical error has unfortunately given rise to a significant volume of work for everyone involved.[19]

[19] The MoD's expert witness's statement at Alex's hearing revealed the complex nature of how military information circulates and is stored. The Atomic Weapons

The detail and specificity of this response reveal how bureaucratic systems express their authority through mastery and failure of the technical. It is, as Weichselbraun describes (2020: 131), the ability to stabilize 'the spectacular political entailments of nuclear weapons . . . by capturing nuclear things in their most banal, technical form'.

Alex shook his head as he showed me this letter. The fact there were two different versions of the same document revealed to him how untrustworthy the state's documentary processes were. Yet the letter's admissions were deeply satisfying for Alex to receive, especially the recognition that the MoD's approach had caused him hardship. Here the technical gives way to the ethical. The letter concludes: 'I sincerely regret that the department's long-sustained position in response to your request meant that it was necessary for you to Appeal to the Tribunal. This will undoubtedly have caused you considerable inconvenience and I apologise unreservedly on behalf of the department.'

The tribunal case was dropped and the MoD agreed to pay Alex's costs. For the MoD, the case was now closed. They concluded their letter to Alex by stating that 'While it has taken a very long time to reach a conclusion, I am pleased that finally we have been able to satisfy your request for information on this occasion.' For Alex however, the documents finally produced had brought to light more uncertainty and doubt, and raised more questions. As Françoise Zonabend (1993[1989]: 55) demonstrated, the long-standing secrecy within nuclear informational realms often leads to stubborn perceptions of widespread governmental manipulation.

The completed version of the graph that the MoD supplied to Alex confirmed their earlier explanation of its measurement scale, and the low reading of the radiation levels for Pennant and Burgee tests. Alex

Establishment held most of the MoD's documentary archives from the nuclear weapons programme. As a 'Government-Owned Contractor-Operated' organization, the AWE's land, facilities, and archives are owned by the MoD, but are managed and operated by AWE 'on their behalf'. Consequently, the AWE was not a public authority and was not subject to FOI requests. However, the AWE had devised a convoluted process by which they could seek such information. In response to Alex's request to AWE for more information about the graph with missing details, an Information Request Delivery Manager replied: 'information held by AWE on behalf of the MoD can be requested via [the MOD's website] . . . or with your permission we can pass on your details to the MoD who can process it'.

remained convinced that his own missing radiation readings were much higher. He told me that, after careful thought, another explanation looked increasingly likely to him.

'All these measures are taken from the instruments in the bunker ... the bunker was half submerged underground.... So I will put in a freedom of information request, asking what the materials were surrounding the instruments.' He needed further answers. 'So I'll ask [the MoD] how thick the iron [walls and roof] was. I think half an inch of iron reduced the radiation level by half. It was more than half an inch thick, and the bunker was also covered in sand and the instruments were below ground level.' Based on this, he calculated that 'there was a 3 or 4 value, half value thickness, surrounding the instruments. So if it was one rad inside, it would actually be eight outside.'

Documents that enter legal claims are both evidentiary and fictitious. They are seen to record and reflect facts, at the same time that they craft 'the very facts that they allegedly authenticate, and hide truths that exceed that which can be documented' (Coutin and Yngvesson 2023: 80). Alex's account reveals how little faith test veterans placed in state documents extracted through legal routes to reveal what they professed to measure. Yet test veterans remained doggedly determined to uncover such documents. They understood that the state respected their own documents as legal proof above all else. Test veterans hoped that even untrustworthy documents, if understood within the wider contexts that they hid, might prove supportive of test veterans' claims.

OUT OF THE DOCUMENTARY HINTERLAND

Historic injury claims hinge upon documentary records and the proof of harm that can be gleaned from them. Yet documents were not simply evidentiary but could become the very focus of claims. Documentary practices could themselves injure. Ken, Tessa and Brian, and Alex often failed to gain the elusive, definitive information that they sought, and rarely managed to shift a skewed balance of power in the control of documents. But their efforts revealed a woeful lack of record keeping, a woeful lack of transparency, or a woeful lack of attention to the needs of claimants to receive and control information about themselves. In these moments, claimants helped to re-word the record, generating dissent and critique that came to reside durably within state files and legal rulings.[20]

These stories of injurious documentary practices are not simple narratives about the compounding harms of law. Many test veterans persevered with gritty resolve in the face of minimal success. Seeking information became a moral good, a 'David and Goliath' fight, as Alex and many other veterans referred to it, a motif that cast their struggles with the power of the state as unequal, unlikely, but ultimately heroic. Persisting on despite ongoing setbacks infused test veterans' lives with a sense of justice and larger purpose.

Tessa recalled that in making his pension appeals, Brian became deeply engaged in the quest for recognition, compensation, and redress. Tessa was firm in describing his motivations as selfless and collective, rather than personal and monetary. He acted, she stressed, out of 'a sense of friendship, of shared acts' with other veterans who also sought recognition. In a similar vein, a fellow widow, Betty, reflected upon her duty to keep going. Many veterans, she noted, couldn't and wouldn't put up a fight, because they were 'old and they're not well. So it's up to us who are fit. To just keep battling on, you know.' Through documents, obligations were made to continue the work of claim-making. As Heimer (2006) argues, state documents do not simply reproduce legal rationality, but enable diverse modes of action beyond and against such rationality. Indeed, as the next chapter shows, the shades of reason that legally constitute veteran injury entitlements are diverse, exceptional, and often morally fecund.

[20] By generating ethical critiques, but rarely managing to punitively punish the government for negligent record keeping, test veterans give us pause in theorizations of an increasingly decentralized era of information. Centralized archives remain resiliently influential in claim-making. Such power can be even more bitterly experienced by social movements that have come to believe in the promise of a democratic, 'accountable' information age.

CHAPTER 5

Shifting Thresholds of Proof

HOWARD, A NEW ZEALAND VETERAN IN HIS SEVENTIES, witnessed three nuclear bomb tests at Kiritimati Island. In his interview, he recounted recently drinking beer with a fellow nuclear test veteran at a Veterans' Association.[1] 'It was a kick in the guts', he said, recalling finding out his friend and fellow test veteran Sam had won a veteran disablement pension on appeal. 'I think it depends on which day your [appeal] case goes up. Sam, won [a pension for] diabetes ... and he doesn't take any medication for it whatsoever, but he's paid out on it, about 80 percent.' Howard's voice grew agitated. 'And I put in, I'm on insulin three times a day, can't do this, can't do that.... Unless I can prove to Veterans' Affairs that it was caused by nuclear radiation, they won't give me that.'[2]

I later interviewed Sam. 'They granted me a pension for diabetes, type two', he confirmed. His voice was flat, as if he didn't want to seem too pleased with this result. Gaining this benefit, however, was not a straightforward or easy process. Sam put his success down to having a dedicated doctor who was prepared to take the time to read through a range of Japanese studies that Sam had spent time researching and gathering. These studies concluded that the incidence of diabetes was higher than

1 The Royal New Zealand Returned and Services' Association (commonly known as the RSA) is a nationwide veterans association that advocates for and provides social opportunities for veterans and their families. Local RSA posts often centre around a bar and restaurant for members.

2 Howard's quotes in this paragraph were previously published in *Memorialising the Veteran Body: New Zealand Nuclear Test Veterans and the Search for Military Citizenship* (2013: 244).

normal for those exposed to radiation. 'The chairman [of the Appeal Board] said: "We must congratulate you, you've opened the door for quite a few of your shipmates by the look of things".' Sam's account did not linger on his own success, but the failure of the system to live up to the chairman's promise. 'Well, it didn't, because they opened the door for me and slammed it shut behind me.'

Placing Howard's and Sam's experiences side by side reveals the seemingly inexplicable, uneven results of two similar environmental exposures and illness accounts. This chapter explores New Zealand military disablement pension appeal processes as a lens into contested environmental illness and the social construction of plausibility and proof that undergird veteran healthcare, showing how the appeal process relied heavily on the narratives of service, illness, exposure, and debility that claimants and assessors succeeded or failed to construct together.

Despite legislation ensuring presumptions of illness, benevolent reasoning, and lower burdens of proof for test veteran claimants, medical and legal reasoning still grappled with the uncertain work of building associations between exposure and disease (Beyea and von Hippel 2019: 627). Test veterans' accounts of pension claim-making reveal the complex ways in which bodily debility grafted or failed to graft onto venerable disability status (Açıksöz 2020), a process that, when it worked, marked veterans as both 'damaged and deserving' (MacLeish 2020).

Experiences of proof-making processes can become incommensurate for the varied actors involved. While legal and medical assessors in the appeal process saw flexibility as the hallmark of benevolent reasoning and exceptional veteran entitlement, test veterans often experienced such flexibility as untransparent, confusing, inconsistent, and ultimately unfair. This chapter explores why, even when the burdens of evidence are flexibly construed, claimants of radiation injury still experience proof-making as deeply unjust.

CONTESTED ENVIRONMENTAL ILLNESSES IN MILITARY LEGAL SETTINGS

Test veterans' pension claims reflect many of the core features of contested environmental illnesses. Such illnesses challenge established medical and legal models of evidence and require patients to fight for recognition (Dumit 2006, Dumes 2020, Phillips and Trundle 2023). Contested illnesses reveal the limits of medicine to understand and establish biomarkers and clear diagnostic categories for the chronic, shifting, and debilitating illnesses that result from toxic exposures (Brown et al. 2000, Vanderlinden 2011). As Chapter 3 revealed, legal denials of harm by industry and government are often entangled with a lack of exposure data or inequitable power relations that lead to institutional control over and even manipulation of exposure records, stymieing patient access to information about their health (Cable et al. 2008, Shriver and Bodenhamer 2018).

The ability of industries to pollute and harm communities is in turn set by environmental policies that normalize such harms and make them politically and socially permissible and even mundane. The environmental regulatory framework in New Zealand has, as Pearce and Kingham (2008) describe, 'desocialised environmental concerns', meaning questions of social equity and environmental justice have failed to drive environmental debates and inform public consciousness, despite clear evidence that socially underserved neighbourhoods, households, and workers are disproportionately exposed to harmful levels of environmental toxins and pollutants.[3]

In this chapter, I explore how contestable proof of exposure gets shuttled through different types of legal rationality, becoming more or less persuasive in different moments of adjudication and investigation in injury claims, and how the work of meeting evidentiary burdens dynamically shifts between claimants and those who judge their claims. Such a close-range account reveals how different claim-making arenas contain

[3] In New Zealand, scholars have shown a positive correlation between socio-economic disadvantage and proximity to toxic substance sites (Salmond 1999), as well as to polluted air, water, soil, and workplaces. While environmental justice approaches have been formally incorporated within British environmental regulatory frameworks (Chalmers and Holvin 2005), scholars note that New Zealand planning legislation governing pollution, toxic exposure, and environment focuses overwhelming on enabling free market development while ensuring the protection of biophysical environmental 'bottom lines', an approach that has failed to address the uneven social distribution of toxic harms, social equity impacts, and environmental justice concerns (Pearce and Kingham 2008).

their own unique logics of illness legitimacy, evidence, and patient deservedness.

This chapter thus engages with the unique social, medical, and legal contexts that shape military personnel's and veterans' experiences of injury claims. Militarism generates a distinctive mix of risks and responsibilities for toxic environmental harm. The inherently risky nature of warfare and the experimental drive to develop and deploy new weapons of war have exposed veterans to a wide range of toxic substances (Trundle 2013). Beyond radiation, these have included dioxin from Agent Orange in Vietnam, organophosphates and bromine exposure amongst Gulf war veterans, and toxic compounds from burn pits amongst veterans of Iraq.[4]

Beyond the unique environmental exposures that soldiers face, records of exposure are severely constrained in military settings. Exposure records are hampered by the unmonitored nature of war activities and war zones, military cultures of bodily risk, and the acceptance and expectations of war injuries (Trundle 2012). This is compounded by legally sanctioned secrecy practices and the resulting controls militaries exert over records and information about veterans' health, as already explored in Chapters 2 and 4 (see also Shriver 2001).[5]

Military healthcare can also represent sites of unique and sometimes exceptional entitlements, lowered burdens of proof, and flexible medico-legal reasoning. Understanding these requires placing the structural burdens that veterans experience seeking entitlements for toxic exposures in conversation with the complex tactics through which veterans and state actors wrangle over proof and deservedness. What emerge are a set of paradoxical practices that blend ideas of benevolence reasoning, improvised proof-making, acts of attentive listening, and

[4] See for example, Trundle (2017, 2020a), Brown (2007), Floyd and Kroll-Smith (1997), Kilshaw (2009), Morgan and Fortun (2020), Scott (1988, 1992), Shriver and Waskul (2006), and Wool (2023).

[5] As Jung (2024) argues, military settings are not the only workplaces that rely upon a culture of secrecy. In examining workers in high-tech industries exposed to chemical compounds, such as workers semiconductor fabrication, many contemporary industries refuse to disclose the chemical composition on their products in efforts to protect trade secrets.

experiences of an unjust, unaccountable state. Practices of proof-making thus localize biomedical and legal norms in unique ways.[6] Test veterans reveal how thresholds of proof and exposure become negotiable and unstable objects of law and medicine that shift dynamically throughout the proof-making process. As this chapter shows, flexible proof-making systems that aim to overcome unfair evidentiary burdens of exposure can ultimately reinscribe a sense of injustice amongst claimants.

DEFINING THE DESERVING VETERAN

Veteran disablement pensions are legally distinguished from other workplace compensation scheme or disability benefits in New Zealand as a 'special' entitlement in two ways.[7] First, in both the applications and appeal processes, a lower burden of proof should exist than in common law when veterans attempt to prove that their injuries or disabilities are service related (attributable or worsened by service). Second, a veteran's disablement pension must be more generous than any similar civilian entitlements in terms of weekly monetary amount, duration, and extra benefits (Law Commission 2008: 12).

Unique articulations of veteran deservedness emerge through localized histories of nationalism and war. Compared to Commonwealth countries like New Zealand, in the post-war period, British veteran

[6] Cultural norms of justice, inequity, and fairness as they play out in law are culturally shaped and vary. For example, as Takao Tanase (2009) shows, in the US, injury litigation is underpinned by an ethos of individual justice aimed to maximize legal redress, while in Japan, the notion of 'equal justice' points to the moral framing of injury in more collective terms. Correspondingly, in New Zealand, a cultural ideal that all citizens, regardless of class and social status, should receive a 'fair go' (Bromell 2014) echoed within test veterans claims as they compared their unequal treatment. This also spoke to a military ideal of solidarity, comradeship, and equality between service members.

[7] In New Zealand, there exists a state-run, no-fault, and universal compensation insurance scheme for personal and work-related injuries and accidents (the Accident Compensation Corporation scheme, or ACC), funded through workplace levies. However, this scheme does not apply to debilitating illnesses (such as cancer), or congenital disabilities, and has been critiqued for creating a two-tiered system of disability entitlement. People with permanent disabilities or ongoing illnesses can alternatively receive a disability allowance, through the state's welfare system.

advocacy groups struggled to garner political influence or ensure generous entitlements. Class and political divisions within the services and veteran organizations weakened advocacy for veteran pensions and social supports, and veteran organizations struggled to marshal large membership numbers. In New Zealand, by contrast, service in the world wars functioned ideologically as defining moments – the 'birth of the nation' – constituting a national identity distinct from Britain (Crotty et al. 2020). The still-popular annual rites of war commemoration, sanctified since the 1930s in a national public holiday, dawn services, and military marches, continue to ensure that the political theatre of war sacrifice justifies veteran deservedness as 'a class apart' from other injured, aged, or vulnerable bodies (Walker 2013).

Being the recipient of a veteran's disablement pension meant receiving a fortnightly pension payment, and cost-free medical treatment and prescriptions for accepted disabilities, including reimbursements for travel costs associated with medical checks and treatments. While New Zealand's healthcare system is a public model, and heavily subsidized, it still often requires co-payments at the point of service, particularly for treatment by general practitioner doctors. A disablement pension also included financial support for some tasks that disability and ageing made difficult, such as gardening, window cleaning, and other home maintenance services. Veteran disablement pensions were, for many test veterans, a significant form of support that tangibly and immediately improved their lives. Now on a disablement pension, Cliff said, 'I don't just struggle along [and] survive. . . . I don't have to worry if I can afford this or that, pills . . . [or to get to] the doctors.' Highly prized, test veterans were prepared to spend months, even years, going through an often-arduous application process, and even longer contesting decisions that went against them.

Veteran deservedness sits within wider social norms regarding the social contract of care. Disablement pensions are discursively embedded within the wider politics of welfare reform in both New Zealand and Britain. From the 1980s, universalist models of state social security and support in both countries shifted towards welfare conditionality, personal responsibility, and workfare. Veteran entitlements came to be classified increasingly through the lens of contribution, in which deserved compensation flows naturally from an idealized citizen sacrifice. This in turn acts to 're-enforce the broader principle that provision of public goods is contingent on personal endeavour' rather than a fundamental right (Martin et al. 2024: 1).[8]

The veteran pension appeal process also reflects the global growth in decentralized, lower-level courts and tribunals that focus on 'problem-solving' for specific groups, such as the homeless, drug users, or veterans (Metzner 2017, Rusch and Banner 2024). Judges in such courts 'largely repudiate ... the classical virtues of restraint, disinterest, and modesty' (Boldt and Singer 2006: 83) and instead enact a more flexible, engaged, collaborative, and therapeutically geared mode of justice (Rusch and Banner 2024: 279). The ethos of interaction within the Pensions Appeal Tribunal thus worked against the grain of other judicial settings in which the legal legitimacy of judges relies upon the performance of detached impartiality (Bornstein et al. 2016), and epitomizes 'the rational face of the law' (Barry et al. 2023). Instead, emotional work and therapeutic talk were a key part of the redress the Board offered and the benevolence they hoped to embody. Constructing reasonable proof required an investigative and proactive judicial approach, and appeals were frequently intimate and collaborative, containing within them an elaborate understanding of benevolent rationality by both

[8] Since the 1980s, both Britain and New Zealand shifted from universalist welfare systems to welfare conditionality. In New Zealand, in the wake of the Great Depression, the rights of citizens to a state-guaranteed minimum standard of living, 'from the cradle to the grave', was instituted through the *Social Security Act 1938* (NZ), which extended a broad range of welfare provisions (Kingfisher and Goldsmith 2001). In the wake of World War II, Britain's Labour Party sought to build a welfare state offering a 'fair shares for all' (Whiteside 1996: 83), founded upon free healthcare and education, comprehensive social assistance and social security programmes, and full employment. However, in the 1980s, New Zealand and British governments shifted towards a new social contract commonly defined as 'welfare conditionality'. Entitlements now required fulfilling specified conditions of deservedness and individual responsibility, such as job seeking and ongoing training. In New Zealand, universal family benefits were abolished and means tested, with obligations and sanctions instituted to reduce 'dependency' and ensure the compliance of beneficiaries. The provisioning of services to vulnerable populations were deregulated and increasingly outsourced to non-governmental providers. Under Margaret Thatcher, the UK limited entitlements to benefits, adopted workfare, and promoted the privatization of housing and market-based solutions to social need (Gray et al. 2022, Lunt 2008).

claimants and assessors. At the same time, and as Welsh (2023) shows, such informalities can obscure decision-making and undermine claimants' abilities to engage.

MAKING 'WAR' INJURIES COUNT

Before all claimants access war pensions, multiple thresholds of military and medical designation must be traversed. For test veterans this began with the official classification of their military service. Since 1866, the beginning of legislation governing veteran disability support schemes in New Zealand, pension law implicitly assumed veteran disability deservedness as stemming from injuries inflicted by a recognized enemy in hostile and violent warfare (Uttley 1994a: 7). To be eligible, test veterans had to have served in a 'war' or an 'emergency', categories that lacked any clarity in the *War Pensions Act 1954* (NZ), the legislation under which the vast majority of test veterans claimed for pension.[9] War indexed a government-declared conflict and a violent threat by an identified enemy. Emergency was a foggier, scaled-back category, implying a situation of imminent bodily risk and threat.[10] New Zealand test

[9] While this law has been subsequently superseded by the *Veterans' Support Act 2014* (NZ), all of my interlocutors conducted the vast majority of their pension claim-making across the 1990s and early 2010s, and most referred to historic experiences making claims as governed by the previous Act. See the Law Commission (2010) on the new Act.

[10] For New Zealand veterans seeking disablement pensions, all qualifying military service involves overseas theatres of operation, revealing that the designation of emergency does not apply to national civil emergency situations, but rather to international conflict. The formal designation of the term emergency applied only to the Malayan Emergency (1948–60), in which the British colonial forces in Malaya crushed a communist liberation movement, deploying British, Australian, and New Zealand troops. Using the label emergency rather than war ensured colonial plantation owners could be compensated by insurance companies for damages to their plantations. It allowed the British rulers to declare a state of emergency, bypassing the Geneva Conventions on the rules of armed conflicts, and suspending the rule of law regarding the arrest, home raids, and detention of dissidents and guerrillas, and the use of chemical warfare and internment camps (Hack 2009). In the UK, the *Emergency Powers Act 1920* and its revision through the *Emergency Powers Act 1964* operate by royal prerogative. The Monarch is the head of the armed forces and thus retains the right to declare war or military emergencies. While convention dictates Parliament should be engaged and informed, Parliament does not have a legal role in decisions to authorize

veterans fit awkwardly into such categories. Officially they took part in peace-time activities. The Cold War threat that drove the British nuclear testing programme was neither temporally immediate nor geographically near. An identifiable enemy was even harder to pinpoint.[11] As Zoë Wool makes clear, the notions of 'combat', signifying 'kinetic enemy contact ... where killing and being killed are pervasive and realistic possibilities' (2013b: 427) remains central to many schemes of veteran entitlement and the ideals of solider sacrifice that underpin them.[12]

Decisions designating service as a war or emergency were not questions of legal categorization, but political decree. The Minister of Veterans' Affairs made decisions to declare deployments as emergency or war. In reality, the Department of Veterans' Affairs and the New Zealand Defence Force made a recommendation to Cabinet, and which the Minster signed off. However, as the New Zealand Law Commission commented, 'the legislation provides no guidelines or criteria to inform this decision. Nor does it establish a process for when and how the decision is to be made' (Law Commission 2008: 132). Scant documentary traces remain that account for how and why such decisions

military operations. This is unlike the US where Congress has delegated the right to decree most emergencies to the president(Anderson 2020).

11 The New Zealand Defence Force acknowledges that designations of conflict and war have broadened beyond organized, state sanction violence governed by international law. The 'operational environment has become increasingly indistinct and increasingly urban. Civilians are more directly or indirectly involved or affected. The distinctions between military and non-military forces, civilians, combatants, and non-combatants have become increasingly blurred' (NZDF 2017: 32).

12 The edges of these categories of war and emergency have come into clearer view when legally disputed. One such case, *Hikaka* v *Social Security Appeal Authority* (2007) (CIV-2007–485-330), tested the limits of the definitions of an 'emergency'. The appellant served in the Navy as part of deployment to the Malayan emergency, and was refused a war pension due to his non-combat role and service, which the Pension Board argued did not placing him 'at risk' of harm or death. Finding for the Appellant, the High Court judgment asserted that a requirement for the serviceman to be put in situations where there was an actual 'air of urgency' or a 'heightened level of physical, psychological or environmental risk' was not required. Simply serving in a declared emergency was sufficient to meet the threshold (Law Commission 2008: 126). This ruling still asserted that a pressing emergency situation still needed to exist somewhere in the deployment, and the notion of a threatening enemy was still essential to the category.

have been made.[13] The legislation granted the government considerable arbitrary power in determining to which theatres of operation, and by extension, to which veterans, a social debt was owed.[14]

Understanding the importance of a ministerial classification of service, nuclear test veterans lobbied doggedly for decades until, as Sam phrased it, they 'got lucky'. In 1998, the MP Winston Peters, a long-time public supporter of test veterans, became the deputy prime minister. Using ministerial prerogative, he reclassified Operation Grapple from 'routine service' to emergency service. In a press statement he justified his decision using the charged language of military sacrifice, shedding no light on what exactly had changed in the government's assessment of deployment and deservedness. 'Those sailors, some as young as 17', he declared, 'were exposed to considerable risk from nuclear fallout while observing detonations, and it is only fitting that we recognize the sacrifice these veterans made while serving their country'.[15] Test veterans and their widows could now claim full war disablement pensions or surviving spouses' pensions.

[13] The only public traces of such decisions could be found in brief comments by MPs during parliamentary debate. Such speeches relied heavily on the tropes of risky combat, of deservedness being tied to having 'fought' bravely for one's country. For example, MP Katherine Rich argued, when debating veterans' entitlements, and the special status of veterans, that 'people who have put their bodies on the line are quite different' from other needy social groups (Hansard 2003). The deserving veteran was one accustomed to extraordinary degrees of bodily risk vis-à-vis an enemy. Despite this apparent reverence, this scripted political language could disadvantage veterans. For those seeking to challenge the rules of inclusion around veteran entitlement, such 'debt' talk obscured exactly how decision-makers arrived at the idea of veteran deservedness upon which the law rested.

[14] Rather than war and emergency, current legislation, the *Veterans' Support Act 2014* (NZ), makes a distinction between 'routine' and 'operational' service. Similar to the *War Pensions Act 1954* (NZ), the Minister of Defence designates service operation based on an assessment of 'threat' level, defined as a 'significant risk of harm to deployed personnel'. Section 9(6) of the Act lists 'risk associated with chemical, biological, radiological, and nuclear exposure' as included in operational threats. Only operational service qualifies veterans for a disablement pension, while injuries associated with routine service have, since 1974 been recompensed through ACC, a national no fault workplace accident compensation scheme (*Accident Compensation Amendment Act 1974* (NZ). Thus, while the categories of war and emergency have been sidelined from current veteran pension legislation, a similar underlying logic prevails regarding the necessity of threat and risk to exceptional military deservedness.

[15] See Peters press release in full (New Zealand Government 1998).

BENEVOLENT REASON

Test veterans described travelling to New Zealand's capital city and government hub, Wellington, in order to attend War Pension Appeal Board meetings. Wearing their best suits, and sometimes accompanied by their wives or veteran advocate, they sat in pale, non-descript meeting rooms within the offices of Veterans' Affairs New Zealand in the heart of the busy central business district. Across laminated tables and under the light hum of air conditioning, four Appeal Board members listened to test veterans' stories of service and asked them questions about their health.

The Appeal Board members I interviewed had served as members of the War Pension Appeal Board[16] across the time frame when my participants were making claims, from the 1990s through the 2010s. Kelly and Beth had legal backgrounds, while Hugo and Jason were doctors. With military experience and years of experience working on the Board, they offered an array of reflections. All described a military approach to proof that was designed to be less onerous on claimants than civil and criminal codes. Injury law within English-speaking jurisdictions normally dictate that the burden of proof – who is responsible for proving harm and fault – falls on the injured claimant. To meet the civil law balance of probabilities test (that a claim is *more likely than not* to be true), the plaintiff in an injury case must prove a specific causation – that the injury happened to them – rather than a general causation: that exposure to a particular risk statistically leads to increased injuries at a population level (Phillips 2015: 89).

The evidentiary levels were lower than a civil court, Appeal Board members confirmed, but it varied at different stages of the process. As Kelly explained, 'You didn't have to corroborate, there is no onus, it is not like a criminal standard, where you bear the onus' of proof. But

[16] Claims and appeals were assessed by panels of up to four members with medical and legal expertise. In the first claim panel, one member was appointed by the veterans' advocacy group, the Royal New Zealand Returned and Services' Association (RSA). At the appeal board level, however, all were appointed and approved by the Minister of Veterans Affairs; however, the RSA was able to recommend a medical practitioner who represented the Forces as one of its members. Veterans' influence over the make-up of these panels thus remained limited.

a balance of probabilities test still applied to proving that one had the illness or disability. After this, however, a beneficial evidential provision applied. Kelly explained:

> [it was] to do with causation [of the disease or injury], and that was reasonably benign, but … you still had to have reasonable evidence, but that wasn't on the balance of probability, it was just reasonable evidence, and you could be as flexible with that as you liked on the evidence, and then you kickstarted the presumption. And then [the state] had to prove otherwise.

The Appeal Board members stressed that despite this shifting responsibility for proof, valid proof never fell below the threshold of 'reasonableness'. Reasonable evidence meant plausible evidence. In other words, the question was not whether an injury was attributed to service, but *could* it have been? Such plausibility was most easily achieved through medical endorsement. An initial application required a medical specialist's assessment. As one test veteran advocate explained: 'The specialist will say, "I believe it's possible that this could be from nuclear …" – and normally that's enough to get it through.' Without this, the task of assessing plausibility fell to the Appeal Board.

In seeking plausibility, Appeal Board members used their own knowledge of the past, of human anatomy, psychology and injury, and of military service, as well as military records, to assess the feasibility and believability of claimants' accounts. Claimants needed to craft accounts that were internally coherent and uncontradicted by official records. Such accounts needed to conform with accepted standards of cause and effect, with assumptions of social normalcy, and with expectations of correct behaviour and morally sound action. As Gluckman argued, 'legal truth involves the assessment of what happened in terms of both legal and moral norms' (1973 [1955]: 82). Test veterans were actively engaged in the process of producing this social and 'scientific credibility', which Epstein (1996: 3) defines as 'the believability of claims and claims-makers' and 'the capacity of claims-makers to enrol supporters behind their arguments, legitimate those arguments as authoritative knowledge, and present themselves as the sort of people who can voice the truth'.

Personal narratives of military experience, illness, decline, and suffering were often the central evidence of test veterans' claims. As Jason explained, this was in part pragmatic. 'There were significant issues with obtaining [military] medical information, records, from years before. We would rely upon family stories.' This placed a particularly heavy weight on test veterans to offer persuasive narrative accounts of injury.

Test veterans, by contrast, did not always like the weight of evidentiary credibility resting on their own accounts. Many expected that their military medical records would be useful in proving their claim. Military medical records could be used to prove attribution, that the early stages of their conditions emerged during service. But such records were too often inaccessible. Test veteran Caleb recounted that when he requested his medical file from the archival services of Veterans' Affairs, they replied, '"No, we haven't got them". They have been taken away. [They said] "We've got your records in the Navy . . . but your medical file is not here".'

Even if their military medical records were available, test veterans recounted that the culture of service censured their content and rendered them inaccurate. Test veterans recounted suffering from a range of ailments during service. But they mostly avoided seeing a doctor during deployment. According to test veteran Trevor, 'medical records, to a great extent, are not much good. Because there's nothing on them'. Servicemen's stoic expectation that some degree of sickness was a routine part service abroad limited engagement with doctors during deployment. Stigma and masculinity, solidarity and fear, and the rigors of military labour all coalesced in the underreporting of illness.

Test veteran Trevor explained: 'There's an old saying about some people who are, like hypochondriac type people. In the services they used to call them the "sick bay ranger" because they'd go down to the sick bay and never get out of the bloody place.' Over time, he explained, 'that stigma sticks with you. So you didn't go. Didn't want to be called it, a sick bay ranger. Because if you're gonna go [off] sick, someone else has got to fill your boots and do your job, it's because you're so limited in the amount of people that you've got.' Another test veteran, Andrew, concurred. He explained that sick bay rangers were liable to get 'beat up' by their fellow servicemen for shirking their duties.

THE PLAUSIBILITY OF INJURY

Appeal Board members admitted that certain claimants did better than others. Some persuasively engaged in the dialogical process of appeal, performing the right medical and legal narratives of cause and effect, while others failed. Hugo explained: 'People who came with a well-prepared structured outline of where they were coming from and where they were going to, did better. But by the time they had that produced, they probably had a better idea themselves.'

Kelly noted very few naval officers came before the Appeal Board, and she speculated they did better than rank-and-file seaman in their first applications. Hugo added: 'So if you can afford a big law firm [to help prepare and present the appeal], generally they were better. They look at the law and make the evidence fit it.' Education and income mattered to legal reasoning. Kelly reflected, 'well educated veterans ... could articulate their claim, and they understood the correlation between presenting evidence and what they were presenting it for'. As Conley and O'Barr (1990) have noted, for claimants in low-level courts and tribunals that have a narrow legal scope to offer remedies or redress, presenting a limited, rule-based narrative is often essential to claimants' success, as it aligns with and shows deference for the procedural logic of legalist thinking.

The Appeal Board faced a problem. Test veterans' own evidence often worked against their claims. As Johannesson argues, legal processes often assumed that orality enables voice when often 'orality can place claimants at a disadvantage and amplify' their vulnerability (2023: 399). The Appeal Board's discretion allowed them to override claimants' narratives and take matters into their own hands. They often acted diagnostically, supplemented medical facts with direct observation. External medical assessments could be brief, dismissive, or uninformed.

Hugo gave an example. 'And if you just get them to walk through what had happened to them, what their life has been like, and you get a picture of someone who has been performing really well and then sometimes they turned up with daughters or sons who would say, "I remember that Dad was fine, [then] Dad would never go out on ANZAC [war memorial] Day, he would always sit in the shed at the back [of the house] and would never interact with us, loud noises startled him, and he never saw a doctor because they didn't do that sort of stuff". So no one had actually diagnosed the fact that this guy had been traumatized by what had happened.'

Beth characterized the process as 'investigational, not adversarial'. This enabled them to be, as she described it, 'very proactive and interactive'. At the same time, 'we still want to hear the evidence from the claimant. We don't just want it presented by someone else. So you actually engage with the people. ... It was an advantage to be there because we could ask them things, you could actually almost do an examination. "Can you turn your head this far?"'

Veterans could thus be prompted to offer physical evidence and be guided by experts to offer persuasive accounts. They could be guided to adhere to the right 'temporal and content boundaries' (Bergman and Minissale 2022: 247) necessary for law stories, to offer up the right 'isolated fragments' of their wider life experiences (Bergman and Minissale 2022: 248). Hugo recounted a veteran who described receiving ordered to clean up the bodily remains of fellow naval men blasted by torpedoes. When asked how he experienced this, he stoically replied that he'd just 'done his job'. Against his own assertions, the Appeal Panel categorized this grisly experience as a plausible cause of undiagnosed PTSD. In another case, a veteran had lost his vision. A medical member of the panel knew of a bacterial infection that existed across the region where he served that could cause eye problems, even though the claimant, his advocate, and his original medical assessment did not suggest or argue for this. In such cases, benevolent reason overruled claimant evidence and afforded hypothetical plausibility. At times advantageous to claimants, hypothetical plausibility relied upon the Appeal Board's breadth of knowledge and their collective understanding of the body, disease, and history on any given day.

At other times, appellants accounts needed above all to demonstrate credibility and coherence (Daiute and Di Donato 2023), to logically align and accurately recount the material and natural surroundings of service, technologies of war, and historical moment of service. Hugo had a keen sense of what an implausible claim sounded like. 'So if someone says they jumped off a helicopter from 20 feet for instance, and in their description they describe stepping out onto the front of the helicopter, where the helicopters of the day had no struts. So a lot of conversations about that. The reasonableness was, could he show us there was something he did, and it was fine and it worked, was linked to the illness. It was plausible.'

Hypothetical plausibility could also draw upon statistical reasoning, biological determinism, and ethnic generalizations. Jason explained this obliquely. 'So if you were of a certain ethnic persuasion, and your body mass index was of a certain dimension, then your chances of getting type two diabetes was near 100%. But if you were the exact opposite, and you had type two diabetes, and there is no family history, no predisposing risk factors . . . then you would view that person quite differently to another one. If, for instance, a certain type of service gave you diabetes, then why haven't all the other [servicemen] got it? Because that is what you would expect, more [among the veteran cohort].'

Appeal Board members worked varied paths to draw plausible evidence forth. And so did veterans, in their own ways. Test veterans' accounts of the pension appeals process focused less on thresholds of hypothetical plausibility and more on the believability of intimate knowledge.[17] One test veteran, Bill, who helped other veterans make pension applications, gave me several examples. While test veterans submitted claims for radiation-related illnesses, they also included other service-related illnesses, such as hearing loss from machinery noise and explosions, and lung conditions due to the ubiquity of cigarette smoke in service. He explained: 'I put in an application for this widow, for a surviving spouse's benefit, and they said to me, they said to the lady – they turned her down, because she didn't meet her husband until two years after [service]. So therefore, it's been assumed that she doesn't know whether he smoked or not during service.' To the pension Appeal Board, he argued, 'for God's sake, wives and husbands *talk*, they talk about things! And this is the thing, they've got this mantra there, that if you were married to your husband after service, then your evidence is no good.'

[17] In legal terms, their accounts often amounted to hearsay. Hearsay refers to out of court statements, made by people who are not legal witnesses, which witnesses recount in a formal legal arena. In civic and criminal cases, hearsay is usually discounted as unreliable and inadmissible. While the *War Pensions Act 1954* (NZ) technically allows for such evidence to be included in veteran claims, test veterans recounted how pension assessors still found ways to discount it.

Bill explained how 'One [panel] said, wrote to this lady, turned her down – on the smoking thing'. In response, 'they said to her, "Your husband, prior to joining the service, worked in a hairdressers and tobacconists. Therefore, we presume that he smoked prior to his service".' Understandings of social norms could trump personal memory and intimate knowledge.

For test veterans, the stubborn problem of causation persisted, despite benevolence. Radiation exposure and disease causality resisted hypothetical plausibility. As Appeal Board member Jason explained: 'The relationship in the science literature, between the conditions and radiation, at the time was pretty dubious. . . . So in terms of them proving that they had been exposed to a sufficient dose, on the knowledge of the day, that was the dilemma for them. The people we saw were unwell, no two ways about it.'

Test veterans' illnesses were often unremarkable, blending too convincingly with the ailments of ageing. Jason explained:

> The counter [claim] was always as they got older, we were starting to see more and more of what you would expect in the older population, and in terms of them, as a subgroup of that population, the studies just weren't there. So they would come in and say, 'I have got this [disease or disability] . . . and you would think, but then so did six out of ten men of your same age.

The Appeal Board assessed pension claims not only for internal coherency but also for collective consistency. Benevolent reason was built through corroboration. Individual test veterans, Hugo said, 'had such varying stories' about Operation Grapple. So varied they undermined each other. Recognizable similarities across claimants' accounts reinforced their claims, and marked collective memory as reliable.

The Appeal Board's approach to benevolent reason was highly effective. So said Appeal Board members. They accepted and reversed half the rejected case decisions they reviewed. 'Because we saw them', Beth said. While the initial pension application was done entirely on paper, without any face-to-face engagement with government agencies, the Appeal Board met in person and could take time to hear the veteran's story and flesh it out through questioning and dialogue. 'It was that whole face-to-face thing, you got a different story with the guy in the room', Kelly said, which 'allowed them [the veterans] to eyeball us, so we are not these mysterious lawyers and doctors closeted away, who are going to say yay or nay.' Kelly further explained: 'It was their opportunity to say what they wanted to say . . . it could be free-ranging, very free-ranging . . . they could go everywhere. They got to be heard, and I felt that what we offered was a forum where they could say what they wanted to say.' This, Kelly argued, benefited veterans.

> For many they were quite grateful, they lost a lot of their anger, it was almost as if they had been heard. I think it was a catharsis. And I think that's why, if you handled it well, that why it was interactive, it was a chit chat, we didn't have any procedures. We sat around a table, and they would hand their pictures around, and show us their leg that was sore. It was very informal. Some of them were very angry, and we got the wrath.

Appeal Board members acknowledged, as legal scholars have observed, that 'courts affect people's well-being not only through their decisions but also, no less important, through the behaviours of those involved in court proceedings' (Dancig-Rosenberg and Gal 2024: 44). Dixon and colleagues (2024: 26) note how the types of relationships that institutions of justice foster with claimants may become 'of equal relevance to what these institutions ultimately deliver'. Indeed, the relationality offered in tribunal sessions can become a cornerstone of redress and a signifier of responsibility assumed or denied. As Welsh (2023) notes, however, this emphasis on intimate collaboration can obscure decision-making and stifle claimants' ability to disagree with developing decisions.

Like assessors, test veterans' narratives also centred the pension system's effects of veterans' emotional well-being. But rather than focus on any cathartic process or end point, they described an ongoing sense of disempowerment and hopelessness. 'They are just worried', Terrance said, describing his fellow test veterans' sense of precarity in a system that many felt couldn't be trusted to deliver deserved resources. 'Disbelief is the other thing. They no longer have faith in the system and that is a big thing to try and handle.' Anthony spoke directly from his own experience. 'It makes you feel ratshit ... it's bloody criminal.' Drawing on military metaphors, Martin said: 'We are having a war of our own, just existing.' Nathan described it all as a 'big fight'. The seeming uneven, arbitrary nature of pension entitlement felt particularly cruel for the ways it pitted test veterans against each other. 'You are on the scrap heap, created real bitterness amongst the guys, because some of them got it and some of them didn't' Doug explained.

PRESUMPTION

In 2007, the New Zealand government reduced the burdens of proof-making for some nuclear test veterans by introducing a 'presumptive list'. This contained a list of cancers automatically accepted when claiming a disablement pension. Test veterans no longer had to provide a medical opinion recognizing the illness' attribution to service. Instead, attributability was assumed to exist. In this way presumption seeks to set down a correct 'correspondence' (Pottage 2004: 13) between the legal ascription of a norm and the object it governs. This presumptive list included leukaemia, multiple myeloma, heart, lung, and bone cancers.[18] At first glance, this list appeared generous, with twenty-five different types of cancer now attributed to radiation exposure during service. Still test veterans' complaints of unfairness and a lack of generosity remained.

The list was meant to make claims easier, faster, and smoother. But the list did not cut the considerable time it took to receive a disablement pension. Test veterans still needed proof that they had the illnesses on the list. After months on a waitlist to see the specialist required to assess their medical condition, test veterans then had to wait for the Claim Panel or Appeal Board to rule, and to decide the percentage of disability that they were to be awarded. As a test veteran named Tim explained: 'So if you're in an area where this orthopaedic surgeon has a nine-month waiting list, you're going to wait nine months. . . . And what's happening in that time is your quality of life

[18] The illnesses that are presumed to be attributable to Operation Grapple service are all forms of leukaemia (except for chronic lymphocytic leukaemia); cancer of the thyroid, breast, pharynx, oesophagus, stomach, small intestine, pancreas, bile ducts, gall bladder, salivary gland, urinary tract (renal, pelvis, ureter, urinary bladder, and urethra), brain, bone, lung, colon, and ovary; bronchiolo-alveolar carcinoma; multiple myeloma, lymphomas (other than Hodgkin's disease), and primary liver cancer (except if cirrhosis or hepatitis B is indicated).

is deteriorating. … But in those months [you] still had to pay for medical, if you needed it.'

As a test veterans' pension advocate, Pete, explained: 'If anything is on the presumptive list, of course it's supposed to be almost instantaneous that you get the thing.' This was, however, 'Not so. I had to wait a year from the time of the application to the time it was approved … you get the back pay … but it's still annoying because it's stress upon stress, and you keep on worrying about it.'

Many complained that the list was too narrowly prescribed and did not include the many common illnesses from which they suffered. Indeed, some men reflected that, once the presumptive list came into effect, it became harder to successfully claim illnesses not on the list. There was a period in the 1990s, Roy recounted, when things were looking up. Veterans' Affairs were accepting 'such conditions as ischemic heart conditions, prostate cancer', for test veterans applying for disablement pensions, 'and not just once or twice, but on numerous occasions'. However, Roy explained, after the presumptive list came into effect, they began to rule against such conditions.

By affording irrefutable causality to certain illnesses, such causality appeared more settled. The solidification of causation for certain cancers had the effect of making other illnesses seem, by contrast, even more tenuous. Many veterans feared the list was being misread to suggest that the association between illnesses beyond cancers and nuclear test service had been conclusively disproved. In reality, the links between test veterans' radiation exposure and illnesses beyond cancers had neither been proved nor disproved through medical studies. No such studies existed. Presumption and assumption spilled beyond the list and could appear relationally zero-sum. Gaining legitimacy for some illnesses came at the cost of others which, now in the shadow of the list, seemed fragile and unconvincing. To test veterans, this was more evidence that medico-legal thresholds of causation could shift and were relative to opaque rules.

The presumptive list also failed to ease bureaucratic burdens by not bypassing the assessment of disability essential to war pension claims. Even for cancers on the presumptive list, a medical specialist awarded a percentage point signifying level of debility. As test veteran Tom explained, 'I always say that we have to fight for every percentage point we get. You may say, "well, it's on the presumptive list, it's easy enough to get". Well, it is and it isn't. You may get the disability, but they've got you on the percentage they've got you on.'

DISABILITY QUANTIFIED

Legislation governing military pension claims sought to precisely calculate the level of impairment caused by different disabilities (*War Pensions Act 1954* (NZ), schedule 9). Total blindness or deafness, 'incurable insanity', lower limb amputation without a 'useful stump' or elbow function, and 'very severe facial disfigurement', all resulted in a 100 per cent impairment. By contrast severe facial disfigurement constituted an 80 per cent impairment, the loss of one eye or four fingers a 50 per cent impairment, and the loss of two fingers a 25 per cent impairment. This list reflected not only the nature of injuries associated with traditional kinetic warfare and conventional weapons but also societal expectations regarding how such injuries would exclude a man from his social world and (the presumed manual labouring) employment on which he would depend post service (Uttley 1994b, Wool 2013a).

For medical specialists, the degree of disability that a cancer patient experienced was neither prescribed by the Act nor clear-cut within the impairment assessment tool used – the American Medical Association Guides to the Evaluation of Permanent Impairment (AMA manual). As Ellen Pryor argues (1990) of the Guides, the idea of impairment is always in relation to contestable societal norms regarding what 'normal' male and female bodies are expected to be able to perform. Impairments that are not localized, observable, or somatically measurable such as mental distress or chronic pain are both difficult to report for patients, and difficult for medical specialists to measure and categorize as impairment. Indeed, the Guides acknowledge that many conditions are 'subjective' and 'open to interpretation on the part of both patient and examiner' (119, in Pryor 1990: 975). As Saxton and Struesse (2018: 72) note, 'the workers' compensation system intensifies biomedicine's fragmentation of bodies into their component parts, each associated with a monetary or reimbursement value'.

Hugo reflected on the limits of the AMA manual's impairment score in helping him assess an injury or illness's impact on a veteran's life, and thus their level of disability. 'It was an impairment guide not a disability guide', he stressed. The former was ill suited to determine the latter. He acknowledged that what constituted disability was dependent on the varied context of a claimant's life. 'If a concert pianist lost the tip of a finger that is a 1% impairment but a 100% disability. . . . And those sorts of thing the guide didn't address.' What counted as the 'wider context' was not obvious in the guide. Hugo explained: 'In the psychological area of that guide it talked about "impact on life", "tasks of daily living", so if you happened to have a mental health issue, the guide was much more attuned to that sort of wider impact on the individual.'

As Beth pointed out, for test veterans, many of whom suffered from cancers, the AMA manual was not well suited for such an ongoing and shifting disease. 'With cancer it keeps changing', she said. 'And if you have had your cancer removed, then the [impairment] number is zero. Some had some difficulties with that', especially when debility persisted in recovery, remission, or reoccurrence. Hugo pointed out that a claimant could apply for a reassessment of their impairment score if their disability persisted or if the cancer returned. But many test veterans described the utter exhaustion of reengaging with the application process, especially when sick over years.

Test veterans were keenly aware of how a stretched public healthcare system affected the enumeration of disability scores. Test veteran Roger explained of the form: 'its thirteen pages long. So it's a bit of a paper warfare. A lot of personal detail, service, history. Then we start the medical bit. Can you imagine going to a GP with this form? And how much time has he got to do this?'

Other veterans recalled medical specialists working at speed and thus missing vital information. A test veteran, Bernie, recounted trying to get a spinal injury recognized as an impairment.

> I walked in and sat down, [the specialist] asked me a few questions, told me to stand up and do this and that. And then I was gone, 10 minutes later, and then his report said there was no deterioration. "I examined him and there is no deterioration." So I wrote a letter, it's a complaint, about that,

> that I wanted to go see someone else. Because I'm a keen bowler, and I couldn't bowl. I play championship bowls.

Implicit in Hugo's example of the concert pianist is the centrality of work and labour to the moral legitimacy of disability claims. By contrast, for older, retired men such as Bernie, disability was felt most acutely when it upended life-enhancing 'leisure' activities that gave life purpose, structure, and a much-valued social network.

The personal meaning of debility and a good life – being able to bowl – motivated Bernie to fight for support. A new surgeon eventually provided two x-rays spaced months apart. Bernie finally had evidence of deterioration proving impairment. But his case's success relied upon stubborn doggedness, a sympathetic doctor, and the right proof – organic abnormality rendered visible. As Hugo recounted, the scores for disabilities were often inconsistent, illogically apportioned by specialists. 'There was often a [score] number, and we were like, where the hell did that come from? We would often get them reassessed by people who did this as a regular thing.'

Veteran advocates strongly advised wives to accompany veterans to medical assessments. Women, they argued, help voice their husbands' suffering, discomfort, and debility. Perceived norms of masculine stoicism curtailed claimants from recognizing, admitting, and expressing the necessary pain and vulnerability upon which a good impairment score relied. As veteran advocate Bill explained:

> I make sure I see the wife and veteran. I make it abundantly clear that the wife should accompany the veteran into the meeting with the specialist, because I've found in my experience when I'm questioning the veteran on how long he's had this disability, how much it impinges on your freedom to get around, your leisure time ... he won't know nothing. But the wife will. [She'll say] 'This happened such-and-such, you jump from bed and fling your arms around'. All this type of thing, you see? You get it from the wife. We try, and [we] portray ourselves as being the tough people. 'Oh, you know, it may hurt a bit'.... And this is why I advise them to take the wife, take all the information you can, and put it before these people.

When claiming illnesses and disabilities outside of the presumptive list, veterans also needed to convince medical specialists to assert that their conditions were possibly caused by radiation. Their principal challenge amongst medical gatekeepers, many noted, was a lack of up-to-date medical information regarding the effects of radiation on human health. 'It doesn't help when the majority of them don't know much about radiation', Trevor explained. Learning that oncologists, for example, were not necessarily familiar with the latest radiobiological research, test veterans took to compiling studies and writing summaries of recent research for doctors. Specialists did not always respond well to patients assuming the expert role. Some dismissed such information as biased and unscientific. Indeed, the accompanying commentary that veterans added to the studies, with roughly cut and pasted and photocopied covers, and whole sentences in bold or upper-case letters, tended to obscure the peer-reviewed, scientific rigor of the studies inside.

Test veterans shared information within their networks about which specialists were open to considering radiation as a causal factor in health claims. Anthony recalled how,

> There is a certain specialist here, who seems to be "Nah, that could never happen through service", and he's anti the veteran. We've had an occasion, some occasions here where a veteran has come away and said, "Well that was a waste of time". And he waited, six, eight months to see this guy. And he didn't want to know about it. So then we say, "Okay, do not send out veterans to Mr. Bloggs". Because we know that he's not going to support the application. Or if he does, he'll give him 5%, and the guy really needs more than that.

As Nettleton (2006) notes, contestation over illness leads patients to morally categorize doctors into 'good' and 'bad', a process that offers some surety within the uncertain horizons of claim-making. And it reveals how, in the process of using medicine as a tool for legal redress, veterans' 'legal consciousness' (Chua and Engel 2019, Merry 1990) became more critically attuned, disillusioned with the ways in which the law generates contradiction, the promise of equal treatment and the experience of uneven justice (cf. Scott 2024).

THE OPACITY OF LAW

The narrative contrasts between the experiences of veterans applying for war disablement pensions and those assessing them were stark. Assessors felt that they drew every line they could, no matter how thinly sketched, between the experience of an illness and a tentative causal explanation, between a private story of suffering and a public debt of gratitude, or between a doctor's circumspect statement of support and a missing military medical file. Developing a practical model of benevolent reason, they strove to both embody legislation through legal rationality, and at the same time, work around its shifting stages of proof. In practice, benevolent reason translated into a reliance on the believability of stories. Such stories needed to sound fair-minded, coherent, familiar, and predictable, according to the assessors' own understandings of past social worlds, long-finished theatres of war, and the established workings of injury and disease. For assessors, stretching proof as thinly as possible without breaking it entailed a careful moral, as well as legal and medical, labour. It was part of the gifts of listening they sought to give back to veterans.

For test veterans the system validated the truth of some claims and denied the basic legitimacy of others, offering an incoherent standard of reasoning. Pension appeal meetings could feel transparent, open, and even warm in their moment of enactment. But outside of them, the men struggled to reconcile their diverse stories of success or failure according to a consistent, legible criteria of bodily disability and military risk. It remained confusing how the presumptive list, with its solidity of causation, could exist alongside widespread scepticism amongst medical professionals assessing these claims. For veterans, the claim-making system compounded their physical illnesses and disabilities with a sense of helplessness. The process felt injurious in the uneven way it meted out resources, the way it divided the community between those who had won and those who had lost its performances of rationality. The system felt neither wholly cruel nor wholly just, but rather arbitrary and thus unfair. Yet, for assessors it was precisely this flexibility, the multiple lines of reasoning they could utilize, that allowed them to best apportion benevolent care within the limits of law.

These encounters show how each side came to care about the enactment of this rationality. They revealed how they each worked at the complex performance of benevolent reason, managing or failing to line up veteran illness narratives with the norms of biomedical diagnosis, hypothetical plausibility, and impairment scales. Such alignments, when successful, but also even when they faltered, recognized veterans as categorical subjects deserving of special care. A sense of grievance resulted not because of a denial of state responsibility, but through its confirmation by the pension system.

When examined at close range, evidentiary burdens of proof and plausibility can dynamically shift, lowering or rising according to the flexibility and discretion allowed by legislation. Ironically, more flexible legal systems of proof-making designed to lessen the evidentiary burdens on claimants do not necessarily solve the problems of injustice that injury claimants rail against. Instead, flexibility and benevolence can reinscribe injustices and exclusions in a new guise: unfairness. It can fail to dislodge a process centred on calling into question the believability and credibility of claimants' narratives. Equally, it can fail to solve the persistent limitations of science to account for exposures. Despite assertions of care, dialogical models for justice, and many favourable outcomes for claimants, flexible proof still rested upon a system of authority and a set of rules that test veterans had no say over. It still delayed care and let their health deteriorate. And such a system of authority, through its very arbitrariness, left many feeling confused, disempowered, disrespected, and further aggrieved.

CHAPTER 6

The Legal Limits of Knowledge

THE LAW CAN BE TERRIFYING. THIS WAS THE FIRST MESSAGE Brenda conveyed to me. A British widow in her seventies, Brenda lived in a tidy bungalow on a quiet street. I struggled to navigate the public transport to reach her, and she and her daughter Angela fussed over me with care and concern. We sat in her garden under a pink evening sky drinking tea. Mother and daughter sat close together, Angela protectively checking on her mother throughout the interview.

Brenda's husband had witnessed five nuclear tests at Kiritimati Island. Two decades after his death from cancer, Brenda joined a group action against the Ministry of Defence.

The test veterans' lawyers 'nearly didn't put Mum on the stand', Angela recounted. 'Because we went to chambers and it was awful. Because Mum's, you know, she's in her seventies now. She's not used to public speaking and things.'

Trying to prepare Brenda, the legal team sat her down to practice answering some basic questions. Brenda recalled that she immediately 'clammed up'.

'They asked her a question and she's going "mmm"', Angela recalled. 'And I'm like, God, oh for God's sake, speak Mother, say something. It was awful. Mum came out and said, "I just feel so stupid".'

Angela turned and took her mother's hand.

> But you were scared. It was like she was in a criminal court. And afterwards [at home] she was crying, and I was thinking, oh God, literally, she's going to get up there, and she was just like a rabbit in headlights. . . . And it took

a bit, because this is the government ... and to me it's scary, and Mum's generation, you hold authority in a bit more esteem than what we do.

Yet Angela recounted with pride how her mother rose to the occasion. 'Well, they actually called you a star witness in the end, and she did brilliantly, thank goodness.'

Brenda linked her hands in her lap as she described being cross-examined. 'They just try and confuse you, and badger you.' Despite trying to control her emotions, she said, 'I got upset ... and the Judge said, "Stop it" [the questioning], and the usher came over to me and she gave me a drink, and then I carried on.'

When Brenda began to sob on the stand, Angela said, 'I burst out crying. And when Mum broke down, our legal team said, "Stay there, you'll make her worse".'

Brenda topped up my tea. When she joined the litigation of over a thousand claimants, she reflected, she had no idea she'd end up on the stand. Perhaps it had been better *not* knowing what lay ahead.

How much must an injured party know and understand of their injuries and the hardships that will stem from them in order to deserve redress? When is knowledge useful and when does it hinder justice? By centring questions of knowledge, anticipation, and action, this chapter turns to the performance of legal personhood as constituted through injury. I explore how, in enacting such performances, claimants experienced a series of unjust reversals and ironies at the heart of injury law. First, the actions and duties of claimants, rather than those accused of injuring them, can become the primary subject of moral and legal judgment. Second, claimants' long-running quests for knowledge and answers about their health can become the very legal rationale to deny them justice. And third, such legal processes impose strict time limits on claimants' actions. At the same time, claimants wait decades for justice and appeals stretch over years, failing to attend to the urgent needs of sick and elderly claimants and oftentimes even outliving them.

Injury claims must establish three truths: *how* and *when* one was injured, and *who* caused it. Addressing these questions reveals the temporal horizons of justice. How does one establish durable knowledge within time? Put another way, how and when does one *know with enough certainty* that one has been injured? How and when does one *determine with enough certainty* who is responsible for the injury?

This chapter traces a group litigation against the British Ministry of Defence first initiated in 2004. A total of 1,011 test veterans from the UK, New Zealand, and Fiji jointly claimed damages due to injuries resulting from radiation exposure. Some claimants had died and were represented by their dependents or executors, most commonly their widows. Their case was first heard in the High Court of England and Wales (*AB* v *Ministry of Defence* [2009] EWHC 1421 (QB)), then appealed to the Court of Appeal (*Ministry of Defence* v *AB* [2010] EWCA Civ 1317), and later the UK Supreme Court (*Ministry of Defence* v *AB* [2012] UKSC 9). The stages of this legal proceeding draw to light the ways in which law 'encodes dominant cultural understandings of the state's obligation to explain itself to citizens, as well as tacit views of what citizens are capable of knowing' (Jasanoff 2012: 19).[1]

In courtrooms, test veterans attempted to temporally stretch legal subjectivity beyond limited windows for redress (Boyle 1991: 522). Over the course of the case and appeals, claimants formed relationships with lawyers, sat together in courtrooms for hours listening to legal arguments, assumed the role of witness, experienced being cross-examined, and made moral sense of legal rulings. Through these moments veterans asserted claims that transgressed legal ideals of the 'reasonable' individual. They refused to separate virtuous 'states of mind' from wider relationships, dependencies, and webs of action.

[1] The British system of tort law can be placed within a wider cultural approach to law and injury that creates barriers for group injury claims. As Mather (2009) points out in distinguishing British and American litigation, Britain has both an ethos of personal responsibility for injury, and a public health system that provides care regardless of fault. Thus, 'the British traditionally balance [personal responsibility] with faith in the government to provide social welfare and support for their citizens'. Moreover, in contrast to decentralized, elected, and jury-driven system in the US, the centralized political and legal system in Britain entails 'judges representing authority in the more hierarchical British judiciary' (193). Furthermore, a high reliance on limited legal aid and the 'loser pays' rule, in which the losing party pays the successful party's legal costs, disincentivizes costly and complex group litigation (202). Moreover, a no win–no fee basis for lawyers in Britain (in contrast to a percentage of winning costs fee for lawyers in the US) disincentivizes lawyers taking on such cases, although conditional fees are becoming common. And finally, there is a narrower set of rules that define 'multi-party actions' in Britain, in contrast to 'class actions' in the US (207).

This case reveals what legal scholars have amply demonstrated: how contentious political decisions and disputes are abridged and reduced into applications of law (Eckert et al. 2012: 5), to a 'politics by other means' (Abel 1995). Claimants attempt to transfigure political demands into legal arguments, and irrespective of the chances of success, trials become 'a stage for citizens to stand up for themselves against the government' (Baik 2023: 344). In the process, new legal subjectivities travel into claimant narratives (Eckert et al. 2012). Yet, as Harri Englund (2012) shows, claimants' alternative understandings of justice also travel out, brought to light within legal arenas. In such spaces, notions of subjectivity, agency, personhood, and reflection unmoor into objects of explicit debate (de Leeuw and van Wichelen 2020). They allow us to existentially 'call each other into question' in ways not normally available (Boyle 1991: 523).

LIMITATION PERIODS, KNOWLEDGE, AND BELIEF

Accessing legal restitution for injury establishes facts but denies knowledge. In response to the test veterans' claim the MoD's legal counsel focused on a technicality of law. They argued that the *Limitation Act* 1980 (UK) protected them from liability and legally prevented the case from going to full trial. The issue of limitation is a seemingly tangential and technical matter of law. Yet, as Riles (2005: 975) argues, technicalities of law are sites where central questions of socio-legal import play out. As Espinosa (2024: 246) argues, 'legal technicalities bridge the gap between the abstract legal framework and its practical application in the lived experiences of individuals and the social dynamics of power'.

Limitation law determines that a claimant must bring their legal claim within a limited time frame after the event in question (such as an injury) has occurred. The principle of limitation assumes that evidence will be less reliable and available the more time passes.[2] It speaks to an evidentiary distrust of memory, unofficial history, hearsay, and 'harmful

[2] The limitation principle is also premised upon an ideal of harm reduction, the idea that it iss in the interest of all parties for disputes to be resolved without significant delays, thus avoiding the negative impacts that the ongoing uncertainties of lingering legal action might create in people's lives. This acknowledges the double bind of injurious law that this book explores.

rumours' (Fukui 2024) unmoored from facts, how time is legally perceived to corrupts truth in nuclear claims.

The MoD argued 'that The Defendant has suffered irrevocable prejudice in particular because quite apart from the substantial global delay since the time of the tests, a large proportion of the Defendant's potential witnesses died during the periods of delay' (*AB* v *Ministry of Defence* [2009] EWHC 1421 (QB), [572]). These included 100 'core participants' of the nuclear testing programme, such as senior scientists, senior military personnel, policymakers, and even the prime minister at the time of the nuclear tests, Harold Macmillan. The passing of half a century, the MoD argued, 'fatally and irrevocably eroded the cogency of the evidence' (*Ministry of Defence* v *AB* [2010] EWCA Civ 1317, [39]).

Section 11 of the *Limitation Act* 1980 (UK) attends to 'Special time limit for actions in respect of personal injuries'. It states that 'any action for damages for negligence, nuisance or breach of duty (whether the duty exists by virtue of a contract or of provision made by or under a statute or independently of any contract or any such provision)' needs to be brought within three years. The Act states that the three-year time limit begins from '(a) the date on which the cause of action accrued; or (b) the date of knowledge (if later) of the person injured'. To timestamp knowledge requires two nested parameters of its content. What was the nature of their knowledge, and what is the nature of knowledge more broadly?

The Act offers some guidance.[3] The first point at which a person is considered to possess knowledge, after which the three-year clock begins, occurs 'when he first had knowledge of the following facts – (a) that the injury in question was significant; and (b) that the injury was attributable in whole or in part to the act or omission which is alleged to constitute negligence, nuisance or breach of duty; and (c) the identity of the defendant'.[4] The Act links knowledge to a clearly defined illness or

[3] Under section 14, 'Definition of date of knowledge for purposes of sections 11' (*Limitation Act* 1980 (UK).

[4] This also applies to veterans who have died, and the three-year time limit begins at the date of death or 'the date of the personal representative's knowledge; whichever is the later'. A personal representative includes descendants and will holders of deceased veterans, such as widows.

injury, a clearly defined causal agent, and a legally binding contract or law that defines appropriate levels of care, responsibility, and negligence.

As Boyle observes (1991: 254), 'contemporary legal and political argument can best be understood as a debate over the essential characteristics of the subjects whose actions those arguments describe and prescribe'. In limitation law, the acquisition of knowledge – the point at which a person becomes 'fixed with knowledge' – is based on the abstract principle of reasonableness: what an 'ordinary' and 'reasonable' person would be expected to know, observe, inquire about, and discover. The principle contains implicit and culturally normative assumptions about human intelligence, agency, and will, as well as ideal and typical behaviour (Engel and McCann 2009, Jeutner 2024).[5] The liberal legal subject is thus 'an ideal individual living in an ideal world' (Norrie 2011: 21), or, to quote de Leeuw and van Wichelen (2020: 3), 'in law persons are functional fictions with a real effect'.

Knowledge can also be provided and confirmed by scientific and medical authorities and experts. Thus, in the Act, 'A person's knowledge includes knowledge which he might reasonably have been expected to acquire (a) from facts observable or ascertainable by him; or (b) from facts ascertainable by him with the help of medical or other appropriate expert advice which it is reasonable for him to seek' (s 14(3)).

According to the Act, knowledge is divisible into two types: active and constructive. 'Actual knowledge refers to concrete and tangible knowledge of "actual" or "material" facts' while 'Constructive knowledge refers to the knowledge that one would be expected to pursue and acquire if one was prudent and exercised reasonable care' (Trundle 2020a: 85). The MoD argued that actual knowledge was evidenced in test veterans' engagements with prior medical investigations and legal claim-making. They also attempted to prove constructive knowledge. This was knowledge that claimants *should* have known. In the eyes of the law, injury contains a duty to know.

[5] As Engel and McCann (2009: 3) point out: 'All of these typical tort law practices rest on an assumption that judges, lawyers, and jurors are able to "read" their own culture to determine what is considered reasonable, outrageous, or valuable and that they can – and should – rely on such readings to inject cultural norms, values, and behaviors into the tort law system.'

With over a thousand claimants, the claimants' and the defendant's legal teams each chose five lead cases to test the issue of limitation, determining whether the claimants would be granted permission to launch damages, and the case could proceed to a full trial. During a two-week hearing in the High Court in London, the ten claimants were called to give evidence as witnesses. The legal teams sought to uncover and fix the exact date at which each claimant 'knew' about their own or their late husband's illnesses and its cause.

THE OBLIGATION TO KNOW AND TO ACT

In law, the choreography of facts, memory, and testimony establishes knowledge of injury. In the High Court, the MoD's QC quizzed test veteran widow Karen, gently probing and subtly rephrasing her own sentences back to her in order to draw to light test veterans' post service concerns about radiation exposure, and wives' collaboration in such fears.

QC: You read about fallout in the paper, you say in paragraph 48 [of your witness statement].
KAREN: Yes.
QC: And he [Tony] explained to you what fallout was?
KAREN: Yes.
QC What did he tell you about it?
KAREN: Well, he said that the fallout was debris from the bombs and it was in the atmosphere. That was what he said, debris from the bomb.
QC: And presumably it was dangerous?
KAREN: Dangerous in case he got hurt, yes . . . if it fell on him.
QC: Because of the radiation?
RC: No . . . he never mentioned radiation at all.

Through a combination of paraphrasing and questioning, the Defence's QC attempted to identify small quotidian moments in which talk between Karen and Tony permeated a minimal threshold of knowledge, talk that signified awareness and suspicion of radiation risk. Throughout her testimony Karen countered with contextual details that signified the absence of evaluative reflection. That her marital conversations lacked investigative curiosity reflected, she asserted, the innocence of youth, the rules of state secrecy, and the faith of a wife in her husband's assurances.

QC: He told you he was never examined by any medics or scientists [after the tests]?

KAREN: That's right.

QC: Was he saying he should have been examined?

KAREN: No, no just that – I mean ... and I never questioned him about being examined at the time, because I was a young girl at 17, I think, at the time when he came back from Christmas Island, and just said that I'd read in the paper and was he alright. Because of the bombs being exploded there. Because he couldn't write home about it, obviously. And he said, 'Yeah, fine, fine, I'm fine, nothing wrong with me.'

Many years later at the time of his cancer diagnosis, Tony did begin to raise concerns about the effects of radiation on his health and as a possible cause of his cancer. Navigating the difficult topic of death, the MoD's QC attempted to draw from Karen's testimony a narrative of Tony's growing certainty that radiation had caused his cancer. This involved, as MacLachlan notes (2024), avoiding the 'dirty work' of emotions expressively constrained within legal arenas.

QC: That's when you started discussing his recollections ... for example the fierce thunderstorm ... and what they were wearing [at the tests]?

KAREN: Yes, that's right, yes. That all came out again when he got in touch with the BNTVA [British Nuclear Test Veterans Association]. I don't know how he found out about them, but a representative came and sat down with my husband and they discussed what happened on Christmas Island, and that's when he told him to put down every illness he has since he was on Christmas Island ... and he was really, really ill at the time ... and very angry, because he know we was going to die and he was going to leave me and the three kids.

QC: Yes of course, let's move on from that.

...

QC: Presumably he told you that he had ... filled in the [BNTVA health questionnaire] form ... identifying the illnesses caused by radiation?

KAREN: No, he didn't mention radiation at all.

QC: What did he say: identifying the illnesses caused by the tests?

KAREN: No he just said that he filled in the form and he was asked to put down all the illness that he has had since Christmas Island.

...

QC: At the same time ... he made the [witness] statement ... what did he say about that, do you recall?

KAREN: He said that he wanted to put everything down because – for future reference, in case we need it in such a case like this.

Karen's testimony throws into relief the difference between knowledge and anticipation. Anticipation, as Adams et al. (2009) show, weds states of uncertainty and not knowing to an ethic of preparedness. Tony's desire to produce a witness statement 'just in case' speaks of prudence, Karen insisted, one that acknowledged the extraordinary limits of his agency. Tony was doing the only thing he could, while being deeply emotionally preoccupied by his terminal diagnosis. When the MoD's QC mentioned a letter that the BNTVA had written to Tony, Karen replied: 'I can't remember talking about it, because this was at a time when he was very, very down, very seriously ill.'

The MoD's QC pointed out that there were numerous newspaper articles and documentaries in the 1980s and 1990s and it would have been hard to miss seeing these and thus becoming concerned. Consequently, a reasonable person would have had constructive knowledge, that is, enough information to compel them to investigate further and seek legal advice. Yet, in her witness statement, Karen strongly disputed the class-based assumptions of this. 'He mainly worked night shifts, and hardly ever watched television and neither was he aware of the BNTVA until the details of this organization were given to him. ... Tony was a family man of simple tastes and he did not have much spare time for reading books or newspapers.'

The MoD's QC pointed out that BNTVA were active in the 1990s in collating and distributing newspaper clippings and any developments in their quest for recognition and compensation. Those receiving this information up to three decades before the litigation thus had the relevant knowledge of the *possibility* that illnesses were caused by the nuclear tests. Karen countered that she did not read any of the information sent by the BNTVA. 'I was more interested in caring for my husband and making sure he was properly supported.' Apart from one occasion in hospital, she explained, Tony 'never spoke to me about his thoughts on a possible link between his cancers and exposure to radiation. It is possible he kept any thoughts to himself so as not to worry us'. After his death, 'I myself have continued to receive BNTVA newsletters over the years but I barely looked at them.'

KAREN: I never read them, but my husband sort of glanced at them. But I couldn't tell you what was in them.

QC: So he looked at them ... 'Compensation for Victims of A-Bomb Tests' ... 'Pension Victories for A-Test Victims' and so on ... presumably in light of these you and your late husband were keen that you should be able to claim compensation as well?

KAREN: It didn't even come up about compensation. At this time, as I said, he was diagnosed in February, and you are talking a couple of weeks after that, and to be honest with you, I was just in a daze, so my husband was – I was not interested in any of that.

...

QC: So I appreciate you didn't read these documents in detail, but in the lead up to your own war pension application, presumably you familiarized yourself a little bit more with the documents?

KAREN: No, I didn't, to be honest ... and I only made the application because the BNTVA said to me I should ... but in my mind it wasn't going to bring my husband back ...

QC: You recall filling in a [pension application] form, giving your details, presumably?

KAREN: I remember doing it with an [BNTVA] area rep.

Legal reasoning on culpability often relies upon a genre of individual subjectivity and the 'apparently fixed world of free will' that such legal subjects embody (Boyle 1991: 522). The MoD's QC attempted to draw a smooth and inevitable link between diverse practices. The receipt of information led to an attention towards it, then to an understanding of it and its implications for legal redress, and then to a moral duty to seek redress. Karen's testimony, however, demonstrates that such links were far from obvious in the reality of a family life preoccupied with the shock and demands of illness. Karen insisted on describing herself as a loyal and dutiful wife, not an individual legal actor. She centred a relational account of personhood in the wake of illness (cf. Gardner and Warren 2019).

The Department of Social Security rejected Karen's application for a widow's pension, relying upon the assessment provided by the Atomic Weapons Establishment. Their report concluded that:

> From soundly-founded information currently available and reviewed, the following well substantiated facts are provided
>
> ...
>
> Brown was not exposed to any [radiation] levels sensibly different from ZERO in the areas in which he carried out his duties, either from initial ionising radiation or from radiations arising from early-local residual radioactive material (fall-out). ... The assessed maximum effective dose that might credibly have been received by Ex-Spr Brown consequent upon his participation in operations GRAPPLE Y and GRAPPLE Z was not distinguishable from ZERO
>
> ...
>
> that such zero levels of ionising radiations and other nuclear test effects in the Pacific area did not cause, or contributed significantly to, the lung cancer which he now has is beyond any doubt.

Official denials like these, with bold font certitude, made Karen think that legal action was a futile course. In her witness statement she explained: 'I come from a generation that has been conditioned to accept authority and I probably accepted in my own mind that Tony didn't have a case when my pension application was turned down.' She explained how, 'Having been told so definitely by the government that my husband did not have a case, I always thought there was nothing else

I could usefully do, other than wait to see what might turn up in the future in the way of evidence.' Financial constraints fused with a sense of political disempowerment.

> I never had any money to pay for lawyers, but the fundamental obstacle was the attitude of the government which I felt I had no choice but to accept. ... I have always thought that in order to bring a claim against the government more evidence would have been required ... and I was aware from my dealings with the BNTVA that further research and investigation into the subject was required.[6]

Knowing and acting were for Karen shaped by the need to make sense and meaning out of her husband's death, to make life liveable in the wake of loss. In her witness statement she argued: 'I wanted to keep an open mind but I think it was also probably easier for me to believe the MoD at that stage as a way of trying to move on.' Thoughts of a preventable death were deeply painful. 'I also preferred to think that Tony had died because it was his time to go rather than due to something that could have been prevented.' While the MoD's QC argued that in seeking legal advice in 2004, Karen had acquired the relevant knowledge to begin legal proceedings, Karen rejected this claim.

QC: This [legal advice] was in 2004. You brought your claim four years later in 2008 ... why did you wait?

KAREN: Well, I didn't think that any, well, I couldn't do it on my own and I was waiting for a group action. ... I got turned down by [the law firm], I thought, that's it. My husband's pension was turned down. My pension was turned down. It seemed as though I've got to get on with my life and – what with my [disabled grandchild] ... I had too much on my mind. As I say, it was only at that time, in 2008, that I thought, 'well, I should do this for my husband, because he would have wanted me to do it.'

[6] This claimant quote has previously been published in my chapter Translating Proof: Contested Illness, Radiation Exposure, and the Health Claims of Nuclear Test Veterans (Trundle 2020a: 85)

Throughout her testimony Karen challenged the notion of 'what a reasonable person would do'. Acting reasonably was, she insisted, acting morally as a person enmeshed in relationships of love and care. It involved, as Mittermaier (2012: 259) understands agency, 'acting and being acted upon' in ways that 'become indistinguishable'. Rather than a receptacle of knowledge, the mind was a space that became occupied, sometimes overburdened, with what mattered most. Pursuing an ethic of familial responsibility was at times incompatible with the claimants' legal responsibilities towards justice. Karen challenges assumptions regarding 'the exercise of the will-narrowly conceived to mean the capacity to make calculations of means-ends rationality' (Boyle 1991: 513) at the exclusion of life's competing demands upon her time, attention, and resources.

Exercising her will, Karen made clear, was never divorced from financial reality. In her witness statement she explained: 'I could not afford to pay for lawyers or take on the risk of suing the MoD, and legal aid would not have been available without strong evidence to support his claim.' Justice Foskett, who presided over the case, agreed with this argument. In his judgment he argued: 'I am of the view that going it alone against the Ministry of Defence by an individual claimant was, and always has been, at least since Legal Aid funding was unlikely to be forthcoming, an impossible task in this case, it seems to me that each individual claimant was entitled to wait until a group action was constituted' (*AB* v *Ministry of Defence* [2009] EWHC 1421 (QB), [557]).

According to the *Limitation Act* 1980 (UK) and its interpretation in the authorities (previous relevant case judgments), the MoD's QC argued that knowledge became 'fixed' in a claimant at a specifiable point in time. Knowledge acted as a cumulative, durable aspect of personhood. It did not ebb or flow, nor competed with other reflective concerns. But for Karen and other claimants, injury could not be known outside of the inequitable social relations that curtailed the possibilities for action. Knowledge was 'untimely' (McNeilly 2018) in refusing linear narratives of progression and accumulation.

JUST ASKING AS DURABLE KNOWLEDGE

When does asking for answers become knowledge? Barbara was also a lead case, and like Karen, her history of trying to understand her husband's illness and death was scrutinized on the witness stand. When asked by the MoD's QC about the period when her husband was diagnosed with cancer, she admitted that she did indeed ask him if he thought he'd been affected by his service on Christmas Island. He replied, adamantly, that he had been safe. Not wanting to cause any distress, she asked no further questions.

QC: But in your mind, the cancer had caused by –

BARBARA: No, no, I was just asking.

QC: So you weren't sure, but you knew it was capable of having been caused by radiation?

BARBARA: Well yes. But Glen had been protected. He understood that he had been protected totally. So it was just – it did not apply to him.

Widows like Barbara wanted to demonstrate how private questions about risk and harm were always truncated by a desire to care for their husbands, to protect their emotional well-being and avoid distress. Mary, a widow, reflected upon the idea inferred during the trial that being close to their husbands should have naturally resulted in deeper disclosure and discussion. Mary explained to me: 'Well, when you are close, say in a marriage for instance, there are times when you might maybe get a thought yourself, but you don't want to put it into words because you don't want to worry the other one. . . . Because sometimes you can't put things into words, can you, because of the worry.' 'His worry' in Mary's reflection slid into something bigger: 'the worry'. Avoiding the topic of radiation harm, its unspeakability, protected not just her husband but also herself from a permanent state of anxiety.

Staying quiet also underscored an obedience to military authority. Barbara explained: 'And I think Glen felt really, he should keep quiet, you know. He was a very loyal sort of person, the RAF was his life, he was so trusting and loyal.' She recounted, 'When he was diagnosed with cancer I said to him, do you think it might be the tests, Glen?' 'Oh no, Barbara, no, we were perfectly safe, they'd been told they were perfectly safe.' ... I think he died still thinking that he was perfectly, they had been perfectly safe, because that's what they had been told.'

During Barbara's marriage, loyalty to husband meant loyalty to the military. After Glen's death, she began posing questions to medical experts. She wrote to two doctors who had treated her husband's cancer. Her letter stated: 'I have always believed that Glen's cancers were caused by his RAF service in 1956/7, when he was flying through atomic clouds, collecting radiation samples.' The doctors responded equivocally that it was indeed a possibility that exposure to radiation increases risk of cancer, but that lifestyle factors were more strongly associated.

Barbara's letter and her phrase 'I have always believed' proved consequential. 'And I did make a mistake in the letters to the consultants, the oncologists', Barbara explained to me. 'Because I thought they're going to dismiss me as a batty old lady who's distraught because her husband's died and I didn't want them to think that, I wanted them to think of me as a rational thinking person. So I said I believe that Glen's cancer was caused. Now I didn't know at the time that it was, but I said that because I wanted to impress on them that I was not a batty old lady made desperate by grief, you know. I wanted them to take me seriously and to think about it. And of course [the MoD's QC] latched on that.'

As the later appeal judges argued, 'the word "always" is quite inconsistent with the notion that this was a recently acquired belief'. For Barbara, the phrase 'I have always believed' was tactical, expressing the moral urgency of her request for information. It was not literal. Indeed, the word 'always' can never be literal, for at what point in a life does the time of 'always' begin?

Barbara highlights the recontextualization of words into objects of judgement, practices that fail to distinguish between descriptive and performative statements (Latour 2004: 98). Words seek audiences, aim to persuade and incite a response. And they persuade, as Barabra understood, by speaking the values of the social arenas within which they are uttered.

The MoD's QC focused on the precise wording of Barabara's claim. He contended that a more accurate phrasing in her letter would have been that she believed that radiation was *capable of causing* her husband's cancers, as opposed to *actually caused.* The distinction felt unnecessary and irrelevant to the real issues at hand for Barbara and she responded reluctantly on the stand, 'Yes, I suppose.' From this admission the MoD's solicitors argue that, by the time she wrote the letter, she had acquired the lowest thresholds of knowledge necessary for the limitation clock to start running. Knowledge of injury needed only to amount to an understanding of causal potentiality.

For Barbara, this abstracted possibility too far from real-world concerns regarding probability. A year after sending the letter, she consulted a law firm considering a class action against the MoD on veterans' behalf. She'd need to wait, they advised her, until more medical evidence emerged to support her claim. When a second legal firm took up the class action, they requested a medico-legal report. This argued that it would be hard to prove radiation caused her husband's cancer. For Barbara, the state of her conviction regarding her husband's cause of death was far less important than the probable outcome of making such a legal claim. With a frustrated and confused look on her face, she asked me, 'how, honestly, was I meant to begin legal proceedings when I'd been told by lawyers I could not?'[7]

FOREGROUNDING WORLDS

Judges must make choices between various juridical understanding of time, and in doing so they have the capacity to make visible the workings of different practices of knowledge across claimants' lives (Chowdhury 2020). Justice Foskett ruled in his judgment that his 'preferred view' was that none of the claimants had acquired knowledge until the Cytogenetic Report from New Zealand (as discussed in Chapter 3, see Wahab et al. 2008), when substantiated facts were at last available regarding causation.[8] According to the precedent of the authorities, Karen and

[7] As Shriver and Bodenhamer (2018) document with miners' black lung claims in the US, the complexity and significant time frame and resources required to make such claims, as well as the common lack of financial resources claimants can offer towards the cost of tortious claims, means lawyers are reluctant to take on such complex claims, and as a consequence, few legal actors are willing to become dedicated litigators in this area, and few build up the skills and experience necessary to become expert in this work.

[8] Justice Foskett also argued that a factor in deciding discretion centred on whether 'the case was not a new one and could have been advanced before'. (*AB* v *Ministry of Defence* [2009] EWHC 1421 (QB), [620]). He argued that New Zealand cytogenetic study was

Barbara had indeed acquired knowledge once they first consulted solicitors. Yet he used his discretion under section 33 of the *Limitation Act* 1980 (UK) that allowed him to consider the broad merits of the case and reasons for delay.[9] He argued that the delay of four years did not significantly prejudice the defendant's case.[10] It was a victory for the veterans. Their case could proceed to a full trial.

In describing the broader merits of the case, Justice Foskett offered more than access to law. He honoured the veteran and affirmed military deservedness. Their service aiding nuclear proliferation was wiped clean of moral ambiguity and became venerable. The veterans deserved 'a day in court' and there is 'no other venue in which an independent assessment can take place', he contended (*AB* v *Ministry of Defence* [2009] EWHC 1421 (QB), [616]). He noted that this was a case

> where young servicemen, with no choice in the matter and who were in any event assured of safety, now claim to have suffered in consequence of serving in a cause designed to protect the security of their country ... a duty of care on the part of those organizing the tests exists. Indeed, on one view, what they all did served a world interest, not merely a national one ([617]).[11]

'crucial and pivotal' in the development of credible evidence. 'The emergence of the Rowland Report has changed the landscape significantly ... the fall-out case ... would have been unspecific and largely incapable of proof until the Rowland Report emerged' ([625]). Despite the court case centring on questions of limitation, both sides had presented evidence for and against causation, including medical expert statements, medical reports, and radiation records, and Justice Foskett took this into consideration when determining, under section 33, the case's 'prospects for success'.

9 In his ruling, Justice Foskett ruled that five cases were not statute barred by the *Limitation Act* 1980 (UK), and he used his discretion to accept the other five cases. One case was later withdrawn by the Appellant, and only nine cases proceeded to the appeal.

10 While many of chief architects of the tests had died, Foskett argued that a significant amount of documentary evidence was available, and that many of the key witnesses had given testimony at the Australia Royal Commission on Nuclear Testing in the 1980s, and this evidence could no doubt be used in other legal cases.

11 In this vein, Justice Foskett considered the public anxiety and public interest in the case, and the need to consider 'the overall justice of the situation ... and indeed the perception of what is just' in the eyes of the claimants and the public as a significant factor (*AB* v *Ministry of Defence* [2009] EWHC 1421 (QB), [618]).

Justice Foskett's approach to knowledge – his 'preferred view' – set a high threshold. Knowledge was separable from belief, conviction, and suspicion. Knowledge, when concerning complex medical issues, was based on confirmed facts and expert validation. Empirical proof externalized knowledge, left little room for subjective states of mind. In commenting on the defendant's claim, made through several expert witness statements by scientists, that there was no credible evidence for causation, Justice Foskett also pointed out a 'logical tension' in the defendant's case. The defence

> contended that each individual claimant should at the first sign of significant health effects have realized that link to the negligent acts or omissions concerning the tests such that the limitation clock started ticking, yet in the same breath it is contended that no reputable scientists then (or indeed now) could support any such link thus denying any chance of establishing liability ([519]).

When Justice Foskett's read out his ruling, veterans and widows crowded the courtroom in their test veteran blazers. Kim recounted the moment. 'We were ecstatic, finally. And we were hugging outside the court, and we popped a bottle of champagne in front of the cameras.' To a London reporter, she said: 'This is the beginning of the end. There's some light after years of darkness. I can barely believe it.' The lawyers for the test veterans tempered the euphoria, telling the media: 'We still have three years before the case can be brought to court for trial and, sadly, many of the veterans will have passed away. We hope that the MoD will recognize this and agree to settle the claims out of court, rewarding the veterans with the compensation they rightly deserve.' Legal claims are not always designed to ensure their full enactment. Threats of law can force extrajuridical modes of restitution.

SUBJECTIVE STATES OF MIND

Justice Foskett strongly urged the MoD to settle out of court. Instead, the MoD appealed, and won. A hearing in 2010 before three judges reversed Justice Foskett's ruling for all but one of the lead cases. The ruling argued: 'It is the knowledge of possibilities that matters; a claimant needs only enough knowledge for it to be reasonable to expect him to set about investigation. He can have knowledge even though there is no helpful evidence yet available to him' (*Ministry of Defence* v *AB* [2010] EWCA Civ 1317, [85]). The three judges concluded that in nine of the ten cases, there was sufficient evidence to show that claimants either stated to others or wrote that they held a firm belief, or demonstrated through actions, such as applying for a war pension, that radiation had caused their illnesses.

> We think what matters is the claimant's subjective state of mind. If a claimant comes to believe that there is a causal connection between his condition and the matters complained of, it will matter not from where he derived that belief, even if it were from an incompetent expert advisor or from a newspaper article, which was not based on sound research. If the belief were [*sic*] of such strength that it was reasonable to expect him to start investigating his claim, it would amount to knowledge' ([93]). 'It seems to us that . . . the judge has set too high a threshold for knowledge. He seems to require that the claimant should have a degree of conviction about the causal connection. That in our view is wrong. All that needs to be shown is that the claimant knew there was a real (as opposed to a fanciful) possibility that there might be a causal connection ([222]).[12]

[12] While in examining the board merits of the case Justice Foskett focused on the issues of justice for the veterans, the Court of Appeal's judgment instead raised the issue of cost as a factor worthy of consideration under section 33, and argued that for the MoD, 'if the appeals fail, face an extremely lengthy and expensive trial . . . the resource implications for the MOD and the impact of the Treasury Solicitors will be enormous.' Moreover, 'The trial will also impose a heavy drain on the resources of the court. It would be inappropriate for the court to allow an expensive and resource-consuming trial to take place if the prospects for the claimants' success are slight' (*Ministry of Defence* v *AB,* [2010] EWCA Civ 1317, [112]). The Court of Appeal judges also examined the question of causation (whether the veterans could prove that radiation caused their illnesses), as a vital consideration in reviewing the merits of allowing the cases to proceed, and concluded that in all but one of the cases 'the claimants cases on causation face very great difficulties, which are much more serious than they appeared to Foskett J' ([156]). And, 'Overall, the prospects for success are poor . . . it would not be equitable to allow this action to proceed' ([225]). Several weeks after the ruling I visited the test veterans' lawyer' offices in London. He explained that in the Appeal Court 'the MoD went first, and they spoke for two days about causation. They made causation important, and they made the judges think that causation was important. It was an ambush. We thought we were debating the issue of limitation'.

The claimants were devastated, but they levelled few rebukes at the legal system or judges. The MoD 'just don't care one hoot about us', Kim said as we reflected on the ruling in a pub. Her reaction revealed how her sense of culpability was neither distributed nor diluted through law's failure to address their claims. Blame had long crystallized into a single agent of harm: the MoD. Law still represented hope of justice, and their faith could not give way to cynicism quite yet. But an appeal to the Supreme Court would take between twelve and sixteen months. The veterans' lawyers described their clients to me as 'time challenged'. The protracted legal bid was harming them. 'This issue of limitation is a time waster', one of their QCs said to me when I visited him in his chamber. Perhaps the MoD were hoping that the test veterans' solicitors would run out of funds, he reflected, or that the veterans might end up all dying as they waited for justice, and the case would disappear. 'I have no evidence for this', he added. 'It's my cynical opinion, having seen this dragged out for so long, and no evidence that the MoD wants to settle.' Test veterans expressed the same view. 'It's a tactic', a British test veteran named Clive put it. 'They're just waiting for us all to die.'

Court One in the UK Supreme Court was modern and austere, with an opulently detailed ceiling, wooden panelling, and sandstone sculpture detailing. Upon entering, the veterans and widows immediately spoke in hushed tones. Barbara led us to the front row of the hard wooden bench seats behind the MoD legal team. She liked to sit there, she whispered, because she felt like their presence could be seen and felt by the MoD's legal team. She liked to remind their QC that the widows were indeed right there, listening to his words. 'How he goes home at the end of the day and sleeps, I don't know', she whispered to me. Test veterans regularly made this point to me: that they were engaged in, to borrow Laura Nader words, 'face-to-faceless disputes' (2002: 172). They made a point of showing up, while not once had anyone from the MoD ever come to court.

The veterans and widows filed in and filled the rows. Karen and her daughter sat in the front row behind their legal team. The veterans greeted each other warmly, the widows hugging and settling themselves with nervous anticipation. The courtroom was soon full. In front of three justices, the test veterans' QC argued that the Court of

Appeal judgment was wrong to equate belief with knowledge. The MoD has described the claimants as 'campaigners' who knew about the cause of their illnesses every time they went to an expert, he said. 'But every time they went to an expert they were laughed at; how did they have knowledge?' he asked, thumping his fist on the table lightly. When one of the justices, Lord Phillips, asked when factual knowledge entered the public domain, the test veterans' QC replied: 'The New Zealand Cytogenetic Report'.

The test veterans' QC continued. 'The question arises of when belief becomes knowledge. Many of the claimants have applied for pensions, where the burden of proof is more in their favour at a Pension Tribunal, and at these the MoD said, "No you've not been exposed". It's hopeless to say they had knowledge therefore.'[13] In response, one of the judges asked, 'Are you talking about a degree of certainty here? Knowledge doesn't mean total certainty; it means enough to investigate further.' The test veterans' QC explained that a belief had to be reasonable, and asked how an unreasonable belief amounted to knowledge, when the claimants were constantly being told that their beliefs were unreasonable. 'They went to people who were competent and were told to go away.'[14]

When the MoD's QC followed, he began by acknowledging, without looking behind at the veterans and widows, that this was a sensitive case for those present and he'd be dealing as much as possible with general

[13] This QC's quote, and his following quote, recorded through notetaking in my courtroom fieldwork, have previously been published in my chapter *Translating Proof: Contested Illness, Radiation Exposure, and the Health Claims of Nuclear Test Veterans* (Trundle 2020a: 85–86).

[14] The test veterans' QC also argued that that Court of Appeal judges had been wrong to elevate causation to a determining factor in the case, and to interfere with Justice Foskett's ruling. Judge Foskett in his ruling had said that no facts were actually determined definitely for the claimants or the MoD on causation. The experts had not given oral evidence or been cross-examined. The case had always been premised on the fact that further, more detailed evidence would be forthcoming on the question of causation. None of the claimants had yet gained medical certificates or mFISH tests, which could be useful in determining exposure. Nor did the MoD's scientific experts even examine the claimants. The MoD had proposed a defence based on the issue of limitation, he reminded the judges.

points rather than specific cases. Barbara rolled her eyes at me as he said this, then continued to stare at his back. He worked to build citational clout. Methodically working his way through the authorities, he established legal precedents set out in specific passages of limitation case law. He was in no hurry, leaving long pauses for the justices to find the correct sections in the large bundles of documents laid out before them. The material weight of precedent and the time needed to wade through it reinforced his assertions of settled law.

He argued that according to the authorities, firm belief constituted knowledge, and that firm belief did not require an expert opinion. 'If they are convinced in their own mind. That is enough.' A low level of factual knowledge was required about having suffered an injury. A claimant only needed to know there was a real possibility of attribution, he contended. He pointed out that under cross-examination many of the claimants when asked, 'Did you know that your cancer could have been caused by radiation?' had answered, 'Yes.' 'It's knowledge of the possibility that matters, you need to know enough only to set about investigating.' Furthermore, he claimed, one becomes fixed with knowledge. It can't be taken from a person, by an expert, for example. Lady Hale, however, appeared to disagree: 'Well, you can have knowledge, then it's proven wrong, and then you don't have knowledge.'

At other times, the MoD's QC seemed to undercut his own argument. He maintained that the evidence for causation could at most show that the low radiation dose alleged has increased genomic instability. Epidemiological research does not support more than a weak association. This, he asserted, was insufficient to prove causation. The Court of Appeal was right to conclude that the lead cases were in the end hopeless and too weak, he proposed, and thus should not proceed further, as they have no realistic prospect of success.

At lunch, I headed with the claimants to the Supreme Court's atrium café. We sat and ate our sandwiches, chewing over what we'd heard. They all agreed that the case was going well. The MoD's QC was 'making a bit of a pig's ear of it, in his low, dull voice', Barbara said. We laughed about his scruffy gown, which was coming apart at the back of his neck and 'looked tatty'. Mary noticed that the MoD legal team were having lunch catered in a private room. 'Don't want to face the widows in here', she said, 'and it's all on the taxpayer, while we have to buy our own sandwiches'. The widows nodded together solemnly.[15]

Back in the courtroom, after final rebuttal from the test veterans' QC, the judges retired, stating that they hoped to offer a decision today. The veterans chatted nervously, speculating that this was a good sign. After only three minutes the judges returned. 'We find in favour of the appellants, however we would like to caution that this does not mean they will succeed in appeal.' Against the conventions of the Court, the veterans and widows began to clap with delight.

We filed out onto the street by Parliament Square, the media cameras rolling, and TV journalists crowded around Barbara and Kim for comment. A test veteran, Harry, and I stood on the sidelines holding the handbags. He observed: 'They tend to interview the widows, more than the veterans. Perhaps it's better for public sympathy.'

Afterwards we all took a cab to the Royal Air Force Club in Piccadilly, where one of the widows was a member, to toast a glass at the Running Horse Pub. Kim was on the phone, calling the other veterans that she knew with the good news. Kim was certain they would win the appeal, she declared. She felt very positive about their prospects. But she reflected about what would happen when the case was over.

> It's alright for people with families, they have a lot to do, but it will be very difficult for those who don't have a lot of people in their lives. This has been a wonderful way to meet such good people, the other veterans and the widows. And with the lawyers, they are more than just lawyers to us. We've all come together over this, we're like family now.'

Fighting on through a slow appeals process was exhausting and stressful, Kim said, enough to make them all sick with nerves and worry and

[15] The full cost of the three court cases, as revealed in Parliamentary question time, was £4,786,939.48, for which the MoD recovered £4 million from the claimants' legal representation (UK Parliament 2021). The litigation was undertaken based on a no win, no fee arrangement. Even in such cases the economic impacts of injurious law should not be discounted. As noted, earlier attempts by British veterans to mount litigation were abandoned by some test veterans due to costs. For many test veterans, radiation injuries became economic injuries, generating harmful forms of financial precarity, as Kim's story starkly illustrates in Chapter 2.

anger, but the sociality it enabled, the rituals of coming together around the courtrooms in common cause made it possible to endure. It made meaning out of the uncertainty of law.

A DIVIDED DECISION

Legal judgments reveal what Werbner (2014) refers to as 'judicial morality', the place of morality within law. Law contains a certain flexibility and malleability for moral values to shape judgments, for morality and rationality to inhere in each other (Englund 2015). And legal judgments are a communicative act. 'In addressing their judgments to litigants and a lay audience, judges must appeal to moral values' (Werbner 2014: 503).

The full appeal was heard four months later before the seven justices of the Supreme Court. Once again, the veterans and widows gathered to sit through the trial. They felt their presence was important. Their bodies became evidentiary even when not on the stand. They hoped to remind the judges and the lawyers that behind debates over points of law were frail elderly people unable to wait much longer. Claims were coming to an end: the exhaustion of bodies dovetailed the final stage of legal appeal. Barabara explained that many claimants could not attend, 'because they're old and they're not well. So it's up to us who are fit to just keep battling on, you know'.

The legal teams presented their cases over four days, elaborating upon their arguments in the preliminary trial. On the second day, one of the lead claimants, a test veteran sitting beside me, quoted a Quaker proverb: 'What is morally wrong can never be made politically right.' No matter which way they argued it here, he explained, the truth of the matter was the MoD had wronged the veterans. 'They just want to drag this out, limitations is a smokescreen for what this is really about, their secrets and lies over the years.'

The justices of the Supreme Court released their ruling four months later. By a narrow margin of four votes to three, they ruled that the Court of Appeal's ruling would stand. Nine of the ten cases were to be struck out. Representing the majority position, Lord Wilson rejected the test veterans' QC's assertion that claimants did not have knowledge until the New Zealand cytogenetic study was published. The report was published in 2008, after all ten led claimants had begun their legal proceedings. He argued that it was a 'legal impossibility for a claimant to lack knowledge of attribution ... at a time after the date of issue of his claim. By that date he must in law had knowledge of it' (*Ministry of Defence* v *AB* [2012] UKSC 9, [3]). To argue otherwise would violate a core tenet of legal reason, that 'a "cause" should temporarily precede an "effect"' (Jasanoff 1992: 355). Belief became knowledge, the judge argued, when it was 'held with a degree of conviction (rather than to be little more than mere suspicion) and also to carry a degree of substance (rather than be the product of caprice)' (*Ministry of Defence* v *AB* [2012] UKSC 9, [7]). This threshold had indeed been crossed, he argued.

Yet three of the judges disagreed. Lord Phillips argued that 'Belief in attributability had to be founded on known fact if it was to amount to knowledge' ([55]). Lady Hale took aim at both the limitation law and the illogical decisions she saw it producing, asserting that the current law of limitation is complicated and incoherent' ([62]) and that

> the Court of Appeal has reached the position that a sufficiently strong subjective belief to send the claimant to a solicitor to investigate making a claim is "knowledge" of attributability for this purpose even though there is no reasonable basis in evidence or objective fact for that belief. This leads to unedifying inquiries, such as those which took place in these cases, into the strength of the various claimants' belief, however unreasonable – inquiries made on behalf of a defendant who has always maintained that there is no reasonable basis for their beliefs (and thus contributing to the strong sense of injustice they feel) ([64]).

At home in New Zealand, I watched online via a live feed as Lord Phillips announced the ruling in a short statement at the Supreme Court. On the screen there sat Barbara, in the front row. She had come up to London on her long train journey to sit in the court for the five-minute summary of judgment. Afterwards, I watched her rise with her cane with weary resignation, readying herself to take the train back home. She was shaking her head. Two days later, she called me.

'It was so close! The frustrating, silly thing is that the judges all expressed their sympathy, but they had to use the law. Hale said the law should be changed.' She reflected that two of her fellow claimants who she met in court had since died. 'They'll never see justice, the MoD are just waiting for the rest of us to die.'

I later spoke with the one widow claimant who had not been struck out and was allowed to proceed. 'I feel really guilty about it to be honest', she said. 'The others should have been allowed through, not just me.' The collectivisation of illness and identity built through a group claim was not, in claimants' minds, unevenly divisible.

Kim was disappointed but determined. 'We're taken setbacks, denials and delays for decades now. This won't stop us from carrying on the fight.'

Coutin and Yngvesson (2023: 8) argue that law can act 'as a fiction that creates and entangles impossible realities'. The ruling envisaged an impossible social reality, one in which claimants had never resided, where 'knowledge amounted to a decontextualized, depoliticized, and internal state of mind, regardless of the odds of success, one's resources, legal impediments, or more urgent familial commitments' (Trundle 2020a). Test veterans responded by showing the temporal shiftiness of knowledge as it ebbs and flows between servicemen and their families, and medical, bureaucratic, and scientific experts. In doing so veterans defined knowledge of military injury as unfinished and relational.

The MoD further bolstered their legal claims in the High Court by arguing that, beyond limitations, scientific plausibility mattered. The Court was required to weigh on the balance of probabilities whether the veterans had any real chance of successfully proving a conclusive link between radiation exposure, genomic instability and ill-health – the broad merits test. There existed no certain epidemiological, medical, or genetic proof of the state's culpability, they asserted. Placed alongside their limitation argument, knowledge amounted to delusion. The more firmly test veterans believed in something that was untrue, the more they were vested with knowledge.

The MoD's legal counsel used one form of legal reason to outmanoeuvre another. In setting up the case to be hinged upon and restricted to a legal technicality – the question of limitation – the MoD refused the claimants' counsel the time and space necessary to build a case of causation based on contestable science, all the while themselves alluding to a scientific conclusion that could not be robustly questioned in court. The veterans' solicitors protested that they did have sufficient proof, in the form of radiobiology experts and health studies, but were not able to present them. This tactic of 'allusive evidence' worked in the MoD's favour. The majority ruling by the Supreme Court argued that the court had a moral obligation not to let a 'hopeless' case such as this proceed to full trial. Here emergent genomic knowledge acted as a powerful legal spectre that became efficacious in negating test veterans' claims because of its unofficial, backgrounded, and undebated presence (cf. Kowal 2023).

There was a deep irony in such a ruling. As Justice Foskett stated in the High Court decision, by confining the case to the issue of limitation, the MoD had been able to withhold documents relevant to the claims of radiation injury. Justice Foskett thus wrote in his ruling: 'That there is a distinction between documents relevant to the substantive claim and to the issue of limitation is evidenced by a very lengthy letter from the Treasury Solicitor to [the test veterans legal counsel] ... in response to applications for specific disclosure made on behalf of the Claimants. ... It would seem, therefore, that more documents relevant to issues of breach of duty exist but have not (perfectly properly) been disclosed at the present stage of the proceedings' (*AB* v *Ministry of Defence* [2009] EWHC 1421 (QB), [582]). Limitation curtailed the MoD's responsibility to disclose all the evidence on causation that it possessed. All the while the broad merits test of the *Limitation Act* 1980 (UK) allowed the MoD to dismiss the available evidence of causation as incomplete.

KNOWING AND ITS INJURIOUS LIMITS

The law of limitation construes practices of knowledge as knowable and standardizable. Its temporality cannot contain the slow and unpredictable unfinishedness of many environmental exposure injuries (Cook and Trundle 2020, Loher 2020). Test veterans responded by adding the thickness of social context to legal norms. They rejected what Norrie

(2011: 21) calls 'juridical man', an 'abstraction from real people emphasizing one side of human life – the ability to reason and calculate – at the expense of every social circumstance that actually brings individuals to reason and calculate in particular ways'. Yet the issue of limitation was never the debate test veterans wished to have. The avoidance during litigation of their actual claim – the question of state responsibility for negligent injury – was for test veterans a bitter betrayal. Having to listen to hours of legal arguments testing how early test veterans knew about radiation harm and their lack of action inverted a core pillar of their claim: the state's early knowledge about the risks of radiation and *their* lack of action. This reversal added insult to injury and left test veterans feeling 'doubly betrayed' (Shriver and Waskul 2006: 476).

In asserting that the state was liable for their injuries, test veteran claimants found themselves held to account for imprudent delays in attending to their own injuries. Legal definitions of knowledge can penalise claimants for knowing too much, for reasoning in the wrong way, and for acting against their own legal interests. Such a legal tactic ultimately turned test veterans' very quest for justice against them. This was a particularly galling and egregious ruling for many given how, despite repeated efforts to act, they had felt blocked at every turn by state assurances of their safety, the withholding of potentially vital documentary evidence, the denial of pension claims, unsupportive doctors' assessments, and thwarted legal avenues. These denials, veterans experienced, compounded the impacts of their injuries by allowing their case to drag over five years, during which time many ageing and ill claimants died. For test veterans, this case represented the double face of the law, a system that expected them to know and act upon injury while simultaneously denying any injury upon which to know or act.

Coda

The Ends of Injury?

My digital recorder sat on the floor, its red dot of light pulsing. Tessa pointed at it and smiled. She recounted how her late husband Brian had battled the government for decades, seeking information about the nuclear tests, applying for a war disablement pension for illnesses he attributed to service at the nuclear tests, then appealing unsuccessful applications. Over time, he became deeply sceptical and suspicious. She recounted a moment when a doctor came to their house to assess his illnesses for his pension application.

'So he decided to put a tape recorder [hidden] in that drawer.' She pointed to a sideboard. 'So he borrowed one from a friend. And he only knew how to switch it on. Anyway, this doctor rang the doorbell . . . and it was all like a military operation.' Tessa chuckled, the memory playing out in front of her.

> So they were in here, tape recorder was on, and this tape only lasted for 20 minutes, and this doctor was here for longer than 20 minutes. It finished and the tape recorder started this high-pitched whining noise. And Brian pretended that he couldn't hear it.
>
> 'So this doctor said, "What's that noise?" and Brian said, "What noise? I can't hear any noise." So for the last twenty minutes of their consultation this high-pitched noise was going on. And the doctor said to him, "Right, I'd like you to close your eyes, because I just want to do a few things with your eyes first so I can test your balance".
>
> But Brian, being Brian, closed his eyes, half closed. And then he saw this doctor was walking around the lounge and trying to . . . establish where this high-pitched sound was coming from!'

This was so often how talking about death started – on the humorous surface of anecdotes that point inwards at a tragic core. Such stories nuanced narratives of a 'heroic death' (Seale 1995)[1] and a worthy life spent battling the state. These were stories of secret missions that didn't go according to plan. A trail of applications for care that eddied and led nowhere, but managed to stretch across the length of an adult life. These were encounters that clouded rather than clarified the past, and where the quest to find the government culpable for military harms multiplied rather than supplicated a sense of being aggrieved and injured.

'He was very driven, in his fight for justice.' Tessa explained. 'Very, very driven. To the point that I think it almost blighted his life. He was very bitter about it.'[2]

Towards the end of the interview, Tessa turned to her husband's death. She described a fraught interaction underpinned by intense grief. In the last stages of life, claimant families so often attempted to deal with, to borrow the words of poet Stanley Plumly, 'the heartsick feeling that none of it mattered' (2020: 21). Such moments witnessed the desire for claim-making work to have significance beyond the self. They point to the existential gravity of injurious claims and their continuity.

> Before he died, Brian said to me, the words he used, "Will you promise me you will carry on my fight for justice?" But, I said, "No I can't, Brian, I won't promise you that, because I don't know how I'm going to feel. And if I promise it you, then I will have to do it. If I don't promise it you, then it will be my choice." That's the difference. ... Because ... my life, a large proportion of my life has been listening to Brian talking about the injustice

[1] According to Clive Seale (1995), contemporary British society provides secular 'scripts for proclaiming heroic self-identity in the face of death ... [that involve] a struggle against external and internal enemies to gain knowledge, the opportunity to demonstrate courage and a beatific state of emotional accompaniment in which "carers" and dying people participate'. He also notes that 'People who provide accounts of others' dying ... also seek to place their own actions in an heroic narrative of care where themes of self-sacrifice produce what is often specifically female heroics' (597–8).

[2] This quote and portions of the following two quotes by Tessa have previously been published in my article *Tinkering Care, State Responsibility, and Abandonment: Nuclear Test Veterans and the Mismatched Temporalities of Justice in Claims for Health Care* (2020b: 208–209).

> at Christmas Island. It's not my battle. . . . And I've had enough. I've had enough.

Tessa paused and seemed all at once relieved to have navigated this memory and the space it opened for her own story. 'And I think, in addition to making him ill, in this part of his life, he was bitter, he was twisted, he was suspicious.' She added, 'All he wanted was for someone to say, "We got it wrong, and yes, we now know the effects." And so our lives were very, my life at times was almost unbearable, unbearable because of his fight for Christmas Island.'

Despite Tessa refusing to make a promise to her husband, after a period focused on her grief, she did decide to carry on her husband's case posthumously. 'The only thing I'm fighting for here, is for someone to accept responsibility and accountability.' She rejected any monetary motivation. 'I'm not interested in the money at all. I don't need it, I don't want it. I just want to be able to say, when I'm lying in bed, "Hey there, Brian, guess what? It's done." That's it. And that's all he wanted.' Afterwards, Tessa again stressed that, 'I *should* accept some element of responsibility' to see Brian's case through.[3]

Tessa helps us consider the shifts in legal consciousness involved in nuclear afterlives, the 'imaginative challenge of thinking about what will be created or produced' in the wake of nuclear injury (Harvey and Dominguez 2020: 954). After leaving Tessa's house I sat on the train, deeply affected by her story. I was struck by the harm caused to kin by what Atak (2022) calls the 'accumulated scepticism' that results from both a sense of legal estrangement and a resentful continued reliance on medico-legal processes. I was struck how injurious law became, as Goldblatt and Rai (2018: 672) frame it, a form of 'depletion' through care work, the 'intimate gendered and unremunerated work' that sustain families in the wake of injury.

For test veterans and their families, the ongoing enactment of injurious law always contained vivid imaginings of an end point. Of being able to say to a loved one – alive or dead – 'It's done.' By settling into the politico-legal temporality of an impasse (Civelek 2023), the state denied

[3] Tessa's claim took another six years and was unsuccessful.

test veterans any opportunity to explore what a good life *after* injurious law might entail, be it one of forgiveness, detachment, closure, or recovery. Injurious law, like the lingering afterlife of radiation, refused to unthread from test veterans' bodies and their social and moral worlds. Rather than offering solutions, law and medicine offered both promises and 'remedial vacuums' (Engel 2005: 502). Together, these created an inability to forget. As Nietzsche noted, being able to forget is a necessity for human flourishing, just as much as memory. 'Forgetfulness is a property of all action . . . life in any true sense is absolutely impossible without forgetfulness . . . there is a degree of sleeplessness, of rumination, of "historical sense," that injures and finally destroys the living thing, be it . . . a people or a system of culture' (1957: 6–7).

In the absence of an end point, many of my interlocutors were still pleased that the British government finally awarded test veterans a medal in 2022. Many cried with relief at the award ceremony in which the British prime minister described their medal as 'an enduring symbol of our country's gratitude' (Cabinet Office 2022). They saw value in the British government funding an oral history project in 2022 to record the memories of the dwindling numbers of test veterans who remained alive. But none of this was either an admission of moral guilt or the assignment of accountability for the harms of radiation and its varied forms of legal denial over the decades.

In a phone call with test veteran widow Kim, a year after the Supreme Court ruling, her anger had only calcified. 'I will never forgive them. And I will never forgive them for fighting this. [We] knew nothing and trusted implicitly in the fact that our country would look after us, our MoD would take care of us . . . And it's still going on. And they will still not say, "sorry" or "thank you and look, we are going to look after you".'

At the same time, engagements with injurious law were stitched through with life-affirming meaning. British widow Mary reflected, how she said to her lawyer, 'It's not the money we're after.' And he replied, 'What are we doing here? What have we put all that work in for?' She responded, 'No, it's the principle of the thing that, can't they just admit that they made mistakes?'. She went on to explain how she carried on the fight. 'Some people say, oh, you could do without all that, and I said, yes, but, well, it keeps my husband's name alive I suppose, and it's been something to focus on ... it's been something to get your teeth into really, and you want to beat them.' Seeking justice enmeshed claimants within a morally valued conflict. Through it they became indefatigable heroes and the victims of callous state negligence, identities that both soothed *and* aggravated the injuries that law produced. For test veterans and their families, the virtue of fighting the considerable resources of the state butted up against the psychological, social, and physical costs of such unending battles, costs that often inscribed the need to go on fighting even deeper into their identities.

The pages of this book have traced in detail the harms test veterans and their families have experienced seeking proof, redress, and recognition of harm. Rather than exploring these through psychological and medical lenses that foreground individual effects, I have foregrounded social, political, and ethical understandings of injury. Such approaches to injury necessitate acts of collective response. It is here, in the interaction of families, veteran communities, and legal institutions, that injuries manifest and are made visible in ways that blur the boundaries between biopsychosocial harm, political recognition, and deeply existential denials and demands. An exploration of the injurious nature of law is, I have argued, crucial for understanding both the political origins of injury, and the political responses possible for any meaningful redress.

While this book has not offered the definitive proof of state culpability for radiation exposure and harm that test veterans and their families so deeply desire, I have offered an account of *why* proof and legal recognition of radiation harm remains elusive, and, most importantly, *how* this leads to further harms. I have shown how uncertainties regarding proof of injury were socially and politically produced out of the secretive military nature of the tests, the inadequacy of the records taken and the records preserved, and the circumscribed thresholds and inequitable forms of proof required in legal and medical arenas. Put another way, such uncertainties are produced from and help to produce regimes of injurious law. Equally, I have shown how through law the veterans experienced and expressed a tension. They desired genuine justice and restitution, what McAlinden (2022a: 470) calls a 'sincere apology' that accepts harm and responsibility for repair. At the same time, by trying to force justice through law, redress could not by its very adversarial nature be sincere. In other words, injurious law did harm not only to test veterans' well-being but also to the very possibilities of redress. New Zealand test veteran Anthony summed up such a tension in gaining entitlements through the military pension system. 'It took 40 years, and we fought tooth and nail. They didn't just give it to us out of the goodness of their hearts.'

As I have shown across the chapters of this book, both claimants and the legal systems with which they engaged attempted to grapple with the myriad practices of risk, embodiment, counting, documenting, reasoning, and knowing that surrounded nuclear exposure and its damaging impacts. By focusing on the lived experiences of claimants engaging with law across decades, I hoped to lay bare the accumulating and intersecting harms that emerge through claim-making over time. It is only by attending to the cross-hatch of original, emergent, and ongoing injuries – be they physical, psychological, social, economic, or moral – that the scale of their combined harms become visible within the same frame.

All societies must find ways to 'accommodate their own moments of fracture, social suffering, and repair' (Goodale 2017: 77). How the law, in all its forms, aids or hinders this process is a vital question in the nuclear age. Nuclear exposure, and the harms that follow, stretch and challenge medico-legal definitions of injury and processes of redress. In their quest for justice, test veterans have revealed the necessity of reimagining injury in ways that can account for the historical, political, social, and institutional harms that accrue from our very systems of redress. That nuclear injuries have proven so very hard to respond to without doing further harm should inform our current approaches to nuclear risk, response, and disarmament. That the law has itself proven harmful to those affected by nuclear accidents, experiments, weaponry, and technology should also necessitate a reimagining of injury law. We would be wise to invite test veterans' critiques of medicine and of law to the table of debate, asking hard questions about the societal silences, the institutional control of exposure evidence, the narrative possibilities for storying harm, the temporal assumptions of medical proof, rights to information, and definitions of knowledge, all of which enable or thwart redress. To do so, to reimagine both injury and the legal contexts that govern it, ultimately offers us possibilities to prioritize new modes of collective responsibility, care, and justice.

APPENDIX A

BRITISH NUCLEAR BOMB TESTS

Operation Hurricane	Monte Bello Islands	Yield
3 October 1952	Hurricane	Kiloton
Operation Mosaic	Monte Bello Islands	
16 May 1956	G1	Kiloton
19 June 1956	G2	Kiloton
Operation Totem	Emu Field	
15 October 1953	Totem 1	Kiloton
27 October 1953	Totem II	Kiloton
Operation Buffalo	Maralinga	
27 September 1956	One Tree	Kiloton
4 October 1956	Marcoo	Kiloton
11 October 1956	Kite	Kiloton
21 October 1956	Breakaway	Kiloton
Operation Antler	Maralinga	
14 September 1957	Tadje	ton
25 September 1975	Biak	Kiloton
9 October 1957	Taranaki	Kiloton
Operation Grapple	Malden Island	
15 May 1957	Grapple 1	Kiloton
31 May 1957	Grapple 2	Kiloton
19 June 1957	Grapple 3	Kiloton
Operation Grapple	Kiritimati (Christmas) Island	
8 November 1957	Grapple X	Megaton
28 April 1958	Grapple Y	Megaton
22 August 1958	Grapple Z1	Kiloton
2 September 1958	Grapple Z2	Megaton
11 September 1958	Grapple Z3	Kiloton
23 September 1958	Grapple Z4	Kiloton
Minor Trials	Maralinga and Emu Field	
1953–1963	Kittens, Tims, Rats, Vixen A, and Vixen B, and others.	Varied

APPENDIX B

TIMELINE OF NUCLEAR CLAIM-MAKING

1958–1967: As Historian Fiona Bowler documents (2025), nine British test veterans or their surviving family members made early claims of radiation exposure and resulting illness and death due to the British nuclear testing programme. This included three men who died from leukaemia, one who died from Aplastic anaemia, two with skin conditions, one who suffered a mental breakdown and subsequent suicide, one who died on Kiritimati Island and was diagnosed with sudden onset diabetes, and another from unspecified organ disease. The men and their families raised their concerns through the media and largely unsuccessfully sought military disablement compensation and widow's pensions.

1970: In debate regarding the Radiological Protection Bill in the British House of Commons, Mr Tim Fortescue (MP for Liverpool) mentioned high rates of blood cancer amongst the nuclear tests on Kiritimati Island, noting that 'four or five [veterans] have already died of leukaemia' (Hansard 1970).

1979: The Republic of Kiribati became independent on 12 July.

1983: Establishment of the British Nuclear Test Veterans Association.

1984: The New Zealand Prime Minister David Lange barred nuclear-powered and nuclear-armed vessels from entering New Zealand ports. Three years later his government passed the *Nuclear Free Zone, Disarmament, and Arms Control Act* (1987), making all New Zealand waters, airspace, and land nuclear free.

1985: The *Royal Commission into British Nuclear Tests in Australia* (Mr Justice JR McClelland) released its report, finding that nuclear test safety procedures in Australia were not adequate, that safety advisors were not independent, that Indigenous communities were exposed to dangerous levels of radiation, that test veterans were exposed to unknown levels of radiation, and that concerning plutonium contamination remained at the test sites (Royal Commission 1985a, 1985b, 1985c).

1987: The repeal of the *Crown Proceedings Act* 1947 (UK) section 10 allowed armed forces personnel to sue the British government in civil courts for the first time.

1988: The first NRPB epidemiological study of mortality and cancer amongst British nuclear test veterans concluded that they had suffered from increased risk of multiple myeloma and leukaemia (except chronic lymphatic leukaemia) (Darby et al. 1988).

1990: The NZ Department of Defence commissioned an epidemiological study, *Mortality and Cancer Incidences in New Zealand Participants in United Kingdom Nuclear Weapons Tests in the Pacific* (Pearce et al. 1990). It found higher rates of leukaemia and other hematologic cancers amongst New Zealand test veterans.

1990: The New Zealand government instituted a policy change making test veterans with haematological cancers eligible for war pensions.

1993: The British government paid £20 million to the Australian government to decontaminate Maralinga and Emu Field.

1993: The follow-up second NRPB study (Darby et al. 1993) concluded that an increased risk of multiple myeloma found in the first report was a chance finding. An increased risk of leukaemia (other than chronic lymphatic leukaemia) as found in the first study was confirmed.

1994: The Australian government paid $13.5 million in compensation to the Maralinga Tjarutja for the effects of Maralinga on their lands and well-being.

1995: Formation of the New Zealand Nuclear Test Veterans' Association.

1996: Pearce et al. (1997) conducted a follow-up epidemiological study on New Zealand test veterans which confirmed the first study's finding (1990) that test veterans had suffered from elevated rates of leukaemia and other hematologic cancers.

1997: A New Zealand-registered nurse and test veteran widow, Ruth Mackenzie, distributed 380 questionnaires to test veterans surveying their health, and the health of their descendants. The 235 responses showed significant rates of cancers and miscarriages, but the self-selected sample was critiqued by government agencies.

1997: Two British test veterans lodged a claim with the European Court of Human Rights claiming that the non-disclosure of medical records breached their human rights (*McGinley* v *United Kingdom* (1998). In 1998, the ECtHR ruled that the UK had not violated the applicants rights under the *European Convention on Human Rights.*

1997: The New Zealand War Pensions Medical Research Trust Board commissions a review *Mortality and Health Effects in Participants of Atmospheric Nuclear Weapons Test* (MacDonald 1997). It recommended no shifts in the war pensions approach to test veterans' claims. The review was robustly critiqued by Professor Neil Pearce for misunderstanding core epidemiological principles (Pearce 1997).

1998: The Deputy Prime Minister of New Zealand Winston Peters reclassified Operation Grapple from 'routine service' to 'emergency' service, allowing nuclear test veterans or their widows to apply for war pensions and war disablement pensions.

1999: The Prime Minster of New Zealand commissioned the Reeves Report, an *Inquiry into the Health Status of Children of Vietnam and Operation Grapple Veterans* (Advisory Committee on the Health of Veterans Children 1999).

It concluded that a link between radiation exposure and children's health was 'limited/suggestive of no association' but could not be categorically ruled out, and recommended a range of supports for test veterans' children.

1999: Three hundred Fijian test veterans and family members established the Nuclear Veterans Association.

2000: The NZNTVA used a grant from the War Pensions Medical Research Trust Fund Board to commission University of Dundee scholars to conduct a *Family History Protocol Study* (Roff et al. 2000). Test veteran widow Ruth Mackenzie managed data collection: self-reported questionnaires via telephone interviews with 110 veterans. It recommended the New Zealand government to adopt a presumptive list for cancers.

2000: The New Zealand government awarded the NZNTVA a $200,000 grant, to support the aims and objectives of its charitable mission. The NZNTVA uses $100,000 to support funding the Massey University psychological study (Podd et al. 2005) and cytogenetic study (Wahab et al. 2008).

2001: In response to the Reeves Report (Advisory Committee on the Health of Veterans Children (1999), special government assistance for children of Operation Grapple veterans was introduced. Children suffering from conditions that had either sufficient or limited/suggestive evidence of an association to radiation received case management, family and genetic counselling, and reimbursement for healthcare for spina bifida and cleft lip/palate (New Zealand Cabinet 2001).

2001: Three scholars from the General Practice Department of the Wellington School of Medicine and Health Sciences (Otago University) released the McLeod Report, *The Health Needs of the Children of Operation Grapple and Vietnam Veterans: A Critical Appraisal Undertaken for Veterans' Affairs New Zealand Defence Force.* It concluded that there was not sufficient evidence that exposure to radiation had harmed test veterans' children's health (McLeod et al. 2001).

2002: New Zealand nuclear test veterans received medallic recognition (New Zealand Special Service Medal) on 24 July. Many test veterans complained that the medal did not contain their engraved rank and service number, that veterans had to apply for them, and that, with medals arriving in the post, the government failed to offer test veterans an appropriate awarding ceremony.

2003: The third NRPB study confirmed the results of the second study (Kendall et al. 2004, Muirhead et al. 2003).

2003: The British Secretary of State released a *Policy Statement on Claims for Ionizing Radiation-Related Conditions* for the armed forces. Test veterans suffering from leukaemia (except for chronic lymphatic leukaemia) and primary polycythemia rubra, where the onset had occurred within twenty-five years of the nuclear tests, were entitled to claim war pensions. They only needed to prove presence at the tests. Surviving widows could also claim. Twenty other cancers were also recognized, but test veterans would in these cases need to prove sufficient exposure to ironing radiation through dosimeter records (Secretary of State 2003).

2005: After initial resistance from the New Zealand Navy, test veterans gained permission to place a memorial plaque in the Naval Memorial Chapel of St Christopher at HMNZS Philomel (Auckland). Officials told test veterans the wording of the plaque could not mention nuclear deaths or harms to test veterans. The plaque reads, 'To the memory of veterans who served at the nuclear weapon test sites.' It was dedicated with a wreath and service on 15 May.

2005: *The New Zealand Nuclear Test Veteran Study – A Pilot Project (Psychological Impact)* (Podd et al. 2005) concluded that

New Zealand test veterans were suffering from chronic stress caused by uncertainties associated with the impacts of radiation exposure as well as increasingly strong beliefs that they had been harmed by radiation exposure. This had led to depression, long-term health problems, and impaired memory (see also Jourdain 2009).

2006: An Australian Department of Veterans' Affairs-sponsored epidemiological study, *Australian participants in British nuclear tests in Australia* (Gun et al. 2008), was released. It found that incidence rates and mortality from a wide range of cancers were significantly increased. However, based on the acceptance of the MoD's records of safe exposure, it found no association between radiation exposure and cancer incidence or mortality. The elevated rates were attributed to demographics and exposure during the tests to cigarette smoke and asbestos.

2006: The first British Nuclear Test Veterans Association memorial is unveiled at the National Memorial Arboretum, in Alrewas, Staffordshire. The memorial was upgrade in 2012 and extended in 2016. The BNTVA designated the 3rd of October as National Atomic Veterans Awareness Day. The date marks the first British Atomic bomb detonated in 1952 as part of Operation Hurricane. There are seventeen other smaller BNTVA memorials or standards dotted in cities and churches across the UK.

2006: 300 I-Kiribati from Kiritimati Island submitted a petition to the European Parliament. They demanded action for the British government 'breaking the law by failing to protect [their] health' (Edwards 2006).

2007: The *Rowland Report* (Wahab et al. 2008) was released (often referred to as the Massey Study). This cytogenetic study found New Zealand test veterans had three times the rate of chromosomal translocations (abnormalities) compared with controls, and such rates were associated with ionizing radiation.

2007: The British Nuclear Test Veterans Association commissioned a *Child Health Questionnaire Study* amongst its members (n = 280) (Busby and de Messieres 2007). Its results showed elevated rates of stillbirths, congenital conditions, and cancer rates amongst test veterans' offspring. The study was criticized for a self-selected and self-reporting sample, and controls chosen by the sample participants.

2007: Veterans' Affairs New Zealand introduced a *Presumptive List* for war pension claims. Twenty-five different types of cancer were now attributed to radiation exposure during service, and test veterans no longer need to prove exposure.

2008: Stephen Maire lodged a claim with the Waitangi Tribunal Registrar, on behalf of the children of New Zealand nuclear test veterans, and 'the hapū of Māori servicemen who served': *Wai 2036 Māori Navy Serviceman Nuclear Exposure Claim.* The claim listed forty-three Māori veterans of the nuclear tests and argues they suffered from radiation exposure and subsequent ill health. The year 2008 was the cut-off date for all historical claims to be lodged with the Waitangi Tribunal. The Treaty of Waitangi was signed between the British Crown and Māori chiefs in 1840 and is regarded as one of the nation's founding documents. The Waitangi Tribunal hears claims about breaches to the Treaty and makes non-binding rulings and recommendations to the government.

2009: A group of 1,011 nuclear test veterans brought a group claim against the MoD before the British High Court. The judge ruled that the claimants were not statue barred from proceeding with litigation based on the *Limitation Act* 1980 (*AB* v *Ministry of Defence* [2009] EWHC 1421 (QB)). Notices of claims in negligence were first issued against the Ministry of Defence in 2004, and a group litigation order lodged in 2006.

2010: A *Ministerial Veterans Health Advisory Group* (expert panel) reviewed the Rowland Report. They requested six external scientists to review the Massey studies. Based on the reviews they assessed that the study did show radiation exposure and genetic effects, but the effects of this on health were unknown. In their report to the Minister of Veterans Affairs, they did not recommend any new healthcare entitlements. They did recommend that 'the Government should acknowledge that nuclear test veterans were put at risk through exposure to nuclear radiation, and that [it has] been slow to address the concerns of veterans' (Ministerial Advisory Group on Veterans' Health 2010). The minster rejected this recommendation.

2010: The Court of Appeal reversed the High Court judgement in *AB* v *MoD* 2009 (*Ministry of Defence* v *AB* [2010] EWCA Civ 1317).

2011: The UK Supreme Court upheld the Court of Appeal judgement *MoD* v *AB* 2010 (*Ministry of Defence* v *AB* [2012] UKSC 9). All but one of the ten lead cases was statue barred from proceeding.

2011: The UK Ministry of Defence commissioned Miles and Green Associates (2011) to conduct a *British Nuclear Test Veterans Health Needs Audit* via a questionnaire ($n = 633$) and focus groups ($n = 84$). It recommended improving access to healthcare, improving services specific to test veterans, and creating accessible lay information for test veterans.

2013: Veterans' Affairs New Zealand commissioned and released the *New Zealand Nuclear Test Veterans Summary of Expert Reviews*, an assessment of the Massey studies based on the 2010 reviews commissioned by the Veterans Health Advisory Group. The summary critiqued the 'poor choice of exposed and control groups' in the Massey Studies (Veterans' Affairs New Zealand 2014).

2014: The Waitangi Tribunal announced it would join 109 claims lodged by Māori military veterans from diverse theatres of service into a single inquiry, Wai 2500. This included Wai 2036 on behalf of nuclear test veterans.

2015: British Chancellor of the Exchequer, George Osborne, announced a £25 million health fund for veterans over sixty (UK Government 2015). Nuclear test veterans criticized the fund for not ring-fencing an amount for nuclear test veterans.

2015: The Fijian government awards twenty-four surviving Fijian nuclear test veterans with around $9,000 FJD as compensation for their service on Kiritimati Island.

2016: The Waitangi Tribunal *Wai 2500 Military Veterans Kaupapa Inquiry* heard oral evidence from three nuclear test veterans.

2016: In 2009, nine nuclear test veterans and widows brought a joint appeal for rejected war pensions before the First-Tier Tribunal, War Pensions and Armed Forces Compensation Chamber (*Abdale* v *Secretary of State for Defence* (WPAFCC, 16 December 2016)). The case was significantly delayed by periods waiting for the MoD to search for and deliver relevant documents. It was then further delayed when a judge set aside an initial ruling due to a material error of law and instructed the case to be re-determined through a new hearing. In 2016, a final judgment found against the claimants, except for one deceased veteran's claim for cataracts.

2017: The MoD released an updated *Policy Statement on Claims for Ionising Radiation-Related Conditions.* While it upheld the presumption that leukaemia (except chronic lymphatic leukaemia) is linked to service if diagnosed within twenty-five years of service, it removed Polycythaemia Rubra Vera from presumption policy, and reduced the numbers of cancers for which test veterans could claim from twenty to fourteen (provided they prove sufficient exposure to ironing radiation) (MoD 2017).

2018: The NZNTVA and lead author of the Rowland Report met with Veterans Minister Hon Ron Mark. They requested that *New Zealand Nuclear Test Veterans Summary of Expert Reviews* (2013) be annulled. Geneticist Al Rowland argued that the expert reviewers critical of the Massey study were not genetic specialists and had fundamentally misunderstood the construction of the sample, mischaracterizing it as self-selected, when it was in fact randomly selected.

2021: Photographer Denise Baynham's exhibited portraits of New Zealand Nuclear test veterans at the Navy Museum in Auckland.

2022: The UK MoD awarded medallic recognition of service to veterans of the nuclear tests in November.

2022: A fourth MoD-funded study of the mortality and cancer incidence of UK test veterans was published (Gilles and Haylock 2022). It revealed overall elevated mortality compared with controls, higher rates of cerebrovascular diseases (e.g. strokes and aneurysms), elevated rates of some blood cancers, as well as stomach cancer, cancers of the respiratory system, prostate cancer, and bladder cancer. Like previous NRPB studies, it suggested that, due to assumed low radiation exposure levels, these were likely due to non-radiation-related factors, such as 'background characteristics' differentiating controls from the study cohort (e.g. diet and smoking).

2022: A study at Brunel University found no evidence of elevated genetic mutations amongst the descendants of British nuclear test veterans (Moorehouse et al. 2022). A smaller study of genetic risk reported an elevated rate of congenital abnormalities amongst test veterans' offspring (Rake et al. 2022). Yet the study authors cautioned that the small, self-reporting sample weakened the results.

2023: On 31 July, Ambassador Teburoro Tito (former president of Kiribati) delivered a statement to the UN Non-Proliferation Treaty Preparatory Committee. He asked that Britain award compensation to Kiribati for the effects of nuclear tests, including for physical health impacts, trauma and stress, environmental damage, and disruption of cultural practices (Tito 2023).

2023: The Treaty of Waitangi *Wai 2500 Military Veterans Kaupapa Inquiry* held hearings and testimony from claimants.

2023: In 2021, Veterans Affairs New Zealand commissioned a consultancy firm, Allen and Clarke, to conduct a *Literature review on the health impacts of exposure to ionising radiation* (Hooper et al. 2023). The report concluded there was strong evidence for links between radiation and cancer, mixed evidence for radiation's genetic effects, and weak evidence for hereditary effects. Consequently, the Veterans' Health Advisory Panel recommended to the government that no new illnesses be added to the Presumptive List and that a new review of evidence be repeated every seven to ten years.

2023: The British Office of Veterans Affairs launched a two-year *Nuclear Test Veteran Community Fund* to support the 'development of memorialisation and educational activity, as well as providing direct support'. The fund awarded \$172,530 to three charity groups to deliver the programmes (Office of Veterans Affairs 2024).

2023: The British Office of Veterans Affairs awarded £249,154 of funding for a two-year *Oral History of British Nuclear Test Veterans*, delivered by the University of South Wales, to record the life stories of forty nuclear veterans (Office of Veterans Affairs 2024).

2024: A group of British test veterans sent a 'letter before action' to the MoD and handed a petition into Downing Street. They demanded access to blood and urine data collected during the tests. They offered to settle in a special tribunal. The MoD denied they held such records.

References

AB v Ministry of Defence [2009] EWHC 1421 (QB) TLQ/08/0023.

Abdale v Secretary of State for the Defence (WPAFCC, 16 December 2016) ENT/00203/2015.

Abel, R. L. (1995). *Politics by Other Means: Law in the Struggle against Apartheid, 1980–1994*. New York: Routledge.

Access to Health Records Act 1990 (UK) www.legislation.gov.uk/ukpga/1990/23/contents.

Accident Compensation Amendment Act 1974 (NZ) www.nzlii.org/nz/legis/hist_act/acaa19741974n71311/.

Açiksöz, S. C. (2012). Sacrificial Limbs of Sovereignty: Disabled Veterans, Masculinity, and Nationalist Politics in Turkey. *Medical Anthropology Quarterly*, 26(1), 4–25.

Açıksöz, S. C. (2020). *Sacrificial Limbs: Masculinity, Disability and Political Violence in Turkey*. Oakland: University of California Press.

Adam, B. (1998). *Timescapes of Modernity: The Environment and Invisible Hazards*. London: Routledge.

Adams, V., M. Murphy, and A. E. Clarke (2009). Anticipation: Technoscience, Life, Affect, Temporality. *Subjectivity*, 28, 246–265.

Advisory Committee on the Health of Veterans' Children (1999). *Inquiry into the Health Status of Children of Vietnam and Operation Grapple Veterans (The Reeves Report)*. Wellington: Department of the Prime Minster and Cabinet. www.veteransaffairs.mil.nz/assets/Research/3c289fd60c/Inquiry-into-health-of-children-of-Vietnam-and-Operation-Grapple-veterans.pdf.

Alexis-Martin, B., M. B. Bolton, D. Hawkins, S. Tisch, and T. L. Mangioni (2021). Addressing the Humanitarian and Environmental Consequences of Atmospheric Nuclear Weapon Tests: A Case Study of UK and US Test Programs at Kiritimati (Christmas) and Malden Islands, Republic of Kiribati. *Global Policy*, 12(1), 106–121.

Anderson, B. (2020). Scenes of Emergency: Dis/re-assembling the Promise of the UK Emergency State. *Environment and Planning C*, 39(7), 1356–1374.

Armstrong, K. (2000). Ambiguity and Remembrance: Individual and Collective Memory in Finland. *American Ethnologist*, 27, 591–608.

Arnold, L. (1992). Lord Penney (24 June 1909–3 March 1991). *Proceedings of the American Philosophical Society*, 136(3), 445–448.

Arnold, L. and M. Smith (2006). *Britain and the Bomb: The Nuclear Tests and Their Aftermath.* Basingstoke: Palgrave Macmillan.

Atak, K. (2022). Racist Victimization, Legal Estrangement and Resentful Reliance on the Police in Sweden. *Social and Legal Studies,* 31(2), 238–260.

Atomic Energy Act of 1946. 60 Stat 755. www.govinfo.gov/content/pkg/STATUTE-60/pdf/STATUTE-60-Pg755.pdf#page=1.

Atomic Weapons Establishment (AWE) (1958). *Grapple 'Z'* [Film, online video]. Imperial War Museum. www.iwm.org.uk/collections/item/object/1060035427.

Auyero, J. (2012). *Patients of the State: The Politics of Waiting in Argentina.* Durham: Duke University Press.

Bagelman, J. and S. M. Wiebe (2017). Intimacies of Global Toxins: Exposure and Resistance in 'Chemical Valley'. *Political Geography,* 60, 76–85.

Baik, J. (2023). Speaking Up: Why People Dare to Sue the Government in China. *Journal of Law and Society,* 50, 344–368.

Barnes, T. (1948). The Crown Proceedings Act, 1947. *Canadian Bar Review,* 26, 387–398.

Barr, B., D. Taylor-Robinson, D. Stuckler, et al. (2016). 'First, Do No Harm': Are Disability Assessments Associated with Adverse Trends in Mental Health? A Longitudinal Ecological Study. *Journal of Epidemiology and Community Health,* 70, 339–345.

Barry, C., C. Westaby, M. Coen, and N. Howlin (2023). The Emotional Labour of Judges in Jury Trials. *Journal of Law and Society,* 50, 477–499.

Bear, L. (2007). *Lines of the Nation: Indian Railway Workers, Bureaucracy, and the Intimate Historical Self.* New York: Columbia University Press.

Bergman Blix, S. and A. Minissale (2022). (Dis)passionate Law Stories: The Emotional Processes of Encoding Narratives in Court. *Journal of Law and Society,* 49, 245–262.

Berlant, L. (2011). *Cruel Optimism.* Durham: Duke University Press.

Beyea, J. and F. N. von Hippel (2019). History of Dose, Risk, and Compensation Assessments for US Veterans of the 1966 Plutonium Cleanup in Palomares, Spain. *Health Physics,* 117(6), 625–636.

Billias, N., E. MacEachen, and S. Sherifali (2023). 'I Grabbed My Stuff and Walked Out': Precarious Workers' Responses and Next Steps When Faced with Procedural Unfairness During Work Injury and Claims Processes. *Journal of Occupational Rehabilitation,* 33(1), 160–169.

Birkinshaw, P. (2010). Freedom of Information and Its Impact in the United Kingdom. *Government Information Quarterly,* 27(4), 312–321.

Boggs, C. L. (1977). Marxism, Prefigurative Communism, and the Problem of Workers' Control. *Radical America,* 11(6), 99–122.

Boholm, Å. (2003). The Cultural Nature of Risk: Can There Be an Anthropology of Uncertainty? *Ethnos,* 68(2), 159–178.

Boldt, R. C. and J. B. Singer (2006). Juristocracy in the Trenches: Problem-Solving Judges and Therapeutic Jurisprudence in Drug Treatment Courts and Unified Family Courts. *Maryland Law Review,* 651, 82–99.

Bornstein, A., A. Marcus, R. Curtis, S. Rivera, and R. Swaner (2016). Tell It to the Judge: Procedural Justice and a Community Court in Brooklyn. *PoLAR: Political and Legal Anthropology Review*, 39(2), 206–225.

Borrelli, L. M. and S. Andreetta (2019). Introduction: Governing Migration through Paperwork. *Journal of Legal Anthropology*, 3(2), 1–9.

Bowler, F. (2025). 'Sacrificed on the Altar of Progress and Science': Early Cases of Disputed Disease among British Nuclear Test Veterans. *Contemporary British History*, 39(3), 1–22.

Bowler, F. J. (2022). The British Nuclear Test Veteran: Radiation, Activism, and the Soldier's Body, 1952–2002. Doctoral Thesis. University of Southampton.

Boyle, J. (1991). Is Subjectivity Possible? The Post-modern Subject in Legal Theory. *University of Colorado Law Review*, 62, 489–524.

Braverman, E. R., K. Blum, B. Loeffke, et al. (2014). Managing Terrorism or Accidental Nuclear Errors, Preparing for Iodine-131 Emergencies: A Comprehensive Review. *International Journal of Environmental Research and Public Health*, 11(4), 4158–4200.

Brenner, D. J., R. Doll, D. T. Goodhead, et al. (2003). Cancer Risks Attributable to Low Doses of Ionizing Radiation: Assessing What We Really Know. *Proceedings of the National Academy of the Sciences USA*, 100, 13761–13766.

Bromell, D. (2014). 'A Fair Go' in Public Policy. *Policy Quarterly*, 10(2), 12–21.

Brown, K. (2013). *Plutopia: Nuclear Families, Atomic Cities, and the Great Soviet and American Plutonium Disasters*. Oxford: Oxford University Press.

Brown, P. (2007). *Toxic Exposure: Contested Illnesses and the Environmental Health Movement*. New York: Columbia University Press.

Brown, P., S. Kroll-Smith, and V. J. Gunter (2000). Knowledge, Citizens, and Organizations: An Overview of Environments, Diseases and Social Conflicts. In *Illness and the Environment: A Reader in Contested Medicine*, edited by S. Kroll-Smith, P. Brown, and V. J. Gunter, 9–25. New York: New York University Press.

Brown, P. and E. J. Mikkelsen (1997). *No Safe Place: Toxic Waste, Leukemia, and Community Action*. Berkeley: University of California Press.

Brown, P., R. Morello-Fosch, and S. Zavestoski (eds.) (2011). *Contested Illnesses: Citizens, Science, and Health Social Movements*. Berkeley: University of California Press.

Brown, W. (1993). Wounded Attachments. *Political Theory*, 21(3), 390–410.

Bryers-Brown, T. and C. Trundle (2017). Indigenizing Military Citizenship: Remaking State Responsibility and Care towards Māori Veterans' Health Through the Treaty of Waitangi. *AlterNative: An International Journal of Indigenous Peoples*, 13(1), 43–50.

Burkett, J. (2012). The Campaign for Nuclear Disarmament and Changing Attitudes towards the Earth in the Nuclear Age. *The British Journal for the History of Science*, 45(4), 625–639.

Busby, C. (2013). Aspects of DNA Damage from Internal Radionuclides. In *New Research Directions in DNA Repair*, edited by C. Chen, London: Intech Open Limited.

Busby, C. (2022). Ionizing Radiation and Cancer: The Failure of the Risk Model. *Cancer Treatment and Research Communications*, 31, 100565.

Busby, C. and M. de Messieres (2007). Child Health Study: Preliminary Analysis. Aberystwyth: Green Audit

Cabinet Office (2022). Press Release: Nuclear Test Veterans to Receive Medal as Event Remembers Their Service 70 Years On. 21 November. www.gov.uk/government/news/nuclear-test-veterans-to-receive-medal-as-event-remembers-their-service-70-years-on.

Cable, S., T. E. Shriver, and T. L. Mix (2008). Risk Society and Contested Illness: The Case of Nuclear Weapons Workers. *American Sociological Review*, 73, 380–401.

Calabrese, E. J., P. B. Selby, and J. Giordano (2022). Ethical Challenges of the Linear Non-threshold (LNT) Cancer Risk Assessment Revolution: History, Insights, and Lessons to be Learned. *Science of the Total Environment*, 832, 155054.

Cameron, C. M., D. M. Purdie, E. V. Kliewer, and R. J. McClure (2006). Mental Health: A Cause or Consequence of Injury? A Population-Based Matched Cohort Study. *BMC Public Health*, 6, 1–9.

Campbell, J. (2010). *Correspondence to Hon Judith Collins Minister of Veterans Affairs*, 23 December. www.veteransaffairs.mil.nz/docs/documents/letter-chairman-of-advisory-group-to-minister-re-nuclear-test-veterans-231210.pdf.

Candea, M., J. Cook, C. Trundle, and T. Yarrow (2015). *Detachment: Essays on the Limits of Relational Thinking*. Manchester: Manchester University Press.

Carswell, G., and G. De Neve (2020). Paperwork, Patronage, and Citizenship: The Materiality of Everyday Interactions with Bureaucracy in Tamil Nadu, India. *Journal of the Royal Anthropological Institute*, 26(3), 495–514.

Case, P. (2004). Secondary Iatrogenic Harm: Claims for Psychiatric Damage Following a Death Caused by Medical Error. *The Modern Law Review*, 67(4), 561–587.

Castillejo-Cuellar, A. (2013). On the Question of Historical Injuries: Transitional Justice, Anthropology and the Vicissitudes of Listening. *Anthropology Today*, 29, 17–20.

Chalmers, H., and Colvin, J. (2005). Addressing Environmental Inequalities in UK Policy: An Action Research Perspective. *Local Environment*, 10(4), 333–360.

Chowdhury, R., D. Shah, and A. R. Payal (2017). Healthy Worker Effect Phenomenon: Revisited with Emphasis on Statistical Methods – A Review. *Indian Journal of Occupational and Environmental Medicine*, 21(1), 2–8.

Chowdhury, T. (2020). *Time, Temporality and Legal Judgment*. New York: Taylor and Francis Group.

Chua, L., and D. M. Engel (2019). Legal Consciousness Reconsidered. *Annual Review of Law and Social Science*, 15(1), 335–353.

Civelek, C. (2023). Beyond Lawfare: An Analysis of Law's Temporality through Russian-doll Urbanization from Turkey. *PoLAR: Political and Legal Anthropology Review*, 46(2), 241–263.

Clapp, R. W., M. M. Jacobs, and E. L. Loechler (2008). Environmental and Occupational Causes of Cancer: New Evidence 2005–2007. *Reviews on Environmental Health*, 23(1), 1–37.

Clark, R. W. 1961. *The Birth of the Bomb. The Untold Story of Britain's Part in the Weapon that Changed the World*. London: Phoenix House Limited.

Cohen, A. J., and Morgan, B. (2023). Prefigurative Legality. *Law & Social Inquiry,* 48(3), 1053–1082.

Collett, G., W. R. Young, W. Martin, and R. M. Anderson (2021). Exposure Worry: The Psychological Impact of Perceived Ionizing Radiation Exposure in British Nuclear Test Veterans. *International Journal of Environmental Research and Public Health,* 18(22), 12188.

Collie, A., L. Sheehan, A. McAllister, and G. Grant (2021). The Learning, Compliance, and Psychological Costs of Applying for the Disability Support Pension. *Australian Journal of Public Administration,* 80(4), 873–890.

Colonial Office Print (COP) (1957). *Region by Region Survey of Dependencies,* GEN 174/012, May. CAB 134/1551. The National Archives, Kew.

Commonwealth, *The Report of the Royal Commission into British Nuclear Tests in Australia (Mr. Justice JR McClelland).* Volume One. 482 (1985a). https://parlinfo.aph.gov.au/parlInfo/search/display/display.w3p;query=Id%3A%22publications%2Ftabledpapers%2FHPP032016010928%22.

Commonwealth, *The Report of the Royal Commission into British Nuclear Tests in Australia* (Mr. Justice JR McClelland) Volume Two. 483 (1985b). https://parlinfo.aph.gov.au/parlInfo/search/display/display.w3p;query=Id%3A%22publications%2Ftabledpapers%2FHPP032016010929%22;src1=sm1.

Commonwealth, *The Report of the Royal Commission into British Nuclear Tests in Australia* (Mr. Justice JR McClelland) Conclusions and Recommendations. 484. (1985c). www.austlii.edu.au/au/other/cth/AURoyalC/1985/19.pdf.

Conley, J., and W. O'Barr (1990). *Rules versus Relationships: The Ethnography of Legal Discourse.* Chicago: Chicago University Press.

Cook, J., and C. Trundle (2020). Unsettled Care: Temporality, Subjectivity, and the Uneasy Ethics of Care. *Anthropology and Humanism,* 45(2), 178–183.

Cooper, D. (2020). Towards an Adventurous Institutional Politics: The Prefigurative 'as if' and the Reposing of What's Real. *The Sociological Review,* 68(5), 893–916.

Coutin, S. B. (2020). Opportunities and Double Binds. Legal Craft in an Era of Uncertainty. In *Paper Trails: Migrants, Documents, and Legal Insecurity,* edited by S. B. Horton and J. Heyman, 130–152. Durham: Duke University Press.

Coutin, S. B., and B. Yngvesson (2023). *Documenting Impossible Realities: Ethnography, Memory, and the as If.* Ithaca: Cornell University Press.

Cox, A. M. (2015). *Shapeshifters: Black Girls and the Choreography of Citizenship.* Durham: Duke University Press.

Cram, S. (2015). Becoming Jane: The Making and Unmaking of Hanford's Nuclear Body. *Environment and Planning D,* 33(5), 796–812.

Cram, S. (2016). Living in Dose: Nuclear Work and the Politics of Permissible Exposure. *Public Culture,* 28(3), 519–539.

Crawford, J. (1989a). *The Involvement of the Royal New Zealand Navy in the British Nuclear Testing Programmes of 1957 and 1958.* Wellington: Ministry of Defence Report.

Crawford, J. (1998b). 'A Political H-bomb': New Zealand and the British Thermonuclear Weapon Tests of 1957–1958. *Journal of Imperial and Commonwealth History,* 26, 127–150.

Crawford, J. (2001). *New Zealand Observers and Indoctrinees at Nuclear Weapons Tests: 1956–1958.* Wellington: Ministry of Defence Report.

Crotty, M., N. J. Diamant, and M. Edele (2020). *The Politics of Veteran Benefits in the Twentieth Century: A Comparative History*. Ithaca: Cornell University Press.

Crown Proceedings Act 1947 (UK). www.legislation.gov.uk/ukpga/Geo6/10-11/44/contents.

Csordas, T. J. (1993). Somatic Modes of Attention. *Cultural Anthropology*, 8(2), 135–156.

Csordas, T. J. (2002). *Body/Meaning/Healing*. New York: Palgrave Macmillan.

Daiute, C., and F. Di Donato (2023). Tensions between Norms of Everyday Narrating and Legal Narrating. *International Journal of Law in Context*, 19(2), 177–196.

Dancig-Rosenberg, H., and T. Gal (2024). Many Shades of Success: Bottom-Up Indicators of Individual Success in Community Courts. *Law and Social Inquiry*, 49(1), 42–67.

Darby, S. C., G. M. Kendall, T. P. Fell, et al. (1988). Mortality and Cancer Incidence in UK Participants in UK Atmospheric Nuclear Weapon Tests and Experimental Programmes. Chilton, *National Radiological Protection Board (NRPB) Report R214*. London: Her Majesty's Stationery Office.

Darby, S. C., G. M. Kendall, T. P. Fell, et al. (1993). Mortality and Cancer Incidence 1952–1990 in UK Participants in the UK Atmospheric Nuclear Weapon Tests and Experimental Programmes. Chilton, *National Radiological Protection Board (NRPB) Report R266*. London: Her Majesty's Stationery Office.

Dauer, L. T., A. L. Brooks, D. G. Hoel, et al. (2010). Review and Evaluation of Updated Research on the Health Effects Associated with Low-Dose Ionising Radiation. *Radiation Protection Dosimetry*, 140(2), 103–136.

de Jong, M. (2023). 'Our Pacific through Native Eyes': Māori Activism in the Nuclear Free and Independent Pacific Movement, 1980–5. *The Journal of Pacific History*, 59(1), 60–82.

de Leeuw, M., and S. van Wichelen (2020). Brave New Law: Personhood in the Age of Biolegality. In *Personhood in the Age of Biolegality: Brave New Law*, edited by M. de Leeuw and S. van Wichelen, 1–17. New York: Springer.

DiGiacomo, S. M. (1999). Can There Be a 'Cultural Epidemiology'? *Medical Anthropology Quarterly*, 13(4), 436–457.

Dixon, P., P. Firchow, and F. Vera-Adrianzén (2024). The Paradox of Justice: From Transitional to Everyday Justice. *Law and Social Inquiry*, 49(1), 26–41.

Douglas-Jones, R. (2015). A 'Good' Ethical Review: Audit and Professionalism in Research Ethics. *Social Anthropology/Anthropologie Sociale*, 23(1), 53–67.

Douglas-Jones, R., M. H. Bruun, and D. B. Kristensen (2022). Ethics, Values, and Morality: Introduction. In *The Palgrave Handbook of the Anthropology of Technology*, edited by M. H. Bruun, A. Wahlberg, R. Douglas-Jones, et al., 509–527. Singapore: Springer Nature Singapore.

du Gay, P. (2005). The Values of Bureaucracy: An Introduction. In *The Values of Bureaucracy*, edited by P. du Gay, 1–15. Oxford: Oxford University Press.

Dumes, A. (2020). *Divided Bodies: Lymes Disease, Contested Illness and Evidence-Based Medicine*. Durham: Duke University Press.

Dumit, J. (2006). Illnesses You Have to Fight to Get: Facts as Forces in Uncertain, Emergent Illnesses. *Social Science and Medicine*, 62(3), 577–590.

Eckert, J., Z. Ö. Biner, B. Donahoe, and C. Strümpell (2012). Introduction: Law's Travels and Transformations In. *Law against the State: Ethnographic Forays into Law's Transformations*, edited by J. Eckert, Z. Ö. Biner, B. Donahoe, and C. Strümpell, 1–22. Cambridge: Cambridge University Press.

Edwards, R. (1996). Written out of history – Britain's nuclear test veterans may lose their long battle for compensation because the government is threatening to axe a database containing their medical records. *New Scientist.* 18 May. www.newscientist.com/article/mg15020302-200/.

Edwards, R. (2006). 300 Islanders Accuse UK Government of Exposing Them to A-bomb Fallout. *Sunday Herald.* www.robedwards.com/2006/10/300_islanders_a.html.

Elander, M., and R. Hughes (2024). Pressing Evidence: Activating Khmer Rouge Archives. *Social and Legal Studies*, 33(6), 839–862.

Elisha, O. (2011). *Moral Ambition: Mobilization and Social Outreach in Evangelical Megachurches.* Berkeley: University of California Press.

Emergency Powers Act 1920 (UK) www.legislation.gov.uk/ukpga/1920/55/pdfs/ukpga_19200055_en.pdf.

Emergency Powers Act 1964 (UK). www.legislation.gov.uk/ukpga/1964/38/enacted.

Engel, D. M. (2005). Globalization and the Decline of Legal Consciousness: Torts, Ghosts, and Karma in Thailand. *Law and Social Inquiry*, 30(3), 469–514.

Engel, D. M. (2009). Discourses of Causation in Injury Cases: Exploring Thai and American Legal Cultures. In *Fault Lines: Tort Law as Cultural Practice*, edited by D. M. Engel and M. McCann, 251–306. Stanford: Stanford University Press.

Engel, D. M., and M. McCann (2009). Introduction: Tort Law as Cultural Practice. In *Fault Lines: Tort Law as Cultural Practice*, edited by D. M. Engel and M. McCann, 1–17. Stanford: Stanford University Press.

Engelmann, S. (2022). Elemental Memory: The Solid Fluidity of the Elements in the Nuclear Era. *Theory, Culture and Society*, 39(2), 153–175.

Englund, H. (2012). Human Rights and Village Headmen in Malawi: Translation beyond Vernacularisation. In *Law against the State: Ethnographic Forays into Law's Transformations*, edited by J. Eckert, Z. Ö. Biner, B. Donahoe, and C. Strümpell, 70–93. Cambridge: Cambridge University Press.

Englund, H. (2015). Law, Law Everywhere. *HAU: Journal of Ethnographic Theory*, 5(3), 267–271.

Environmental Protection Agency (EPA) (n.d.) *EPA Facts about Strontium-90.* https://semspub.epa.gov/work/HQ/175430.pdf.

Epstein, S. (1996). *Impure Science: AIDS, Activism, and the Politics of Knowledge.* Berkeley: University of California Press.

Espinosa, I. R. (2024). 'There Is Just Nothing to Hold on to in This Case': Legal Technicalities and the Use of Psychological Reports in Chilean Domestic Violence Procedures. *Journal of Law and Society*, 51, 239–262.

European Committee on Radiation Risk (2009). Lesvos Declaration. www.researchgate.net/publication/358307695_European_Committee_on_Radiation_Risk_Lesvos-declaration.

Ewick, P., and S. S. Silbey (1998). *The Common Place of Law: Stories from Everyday Life.* Chicago: University of Chicago Press.

Fassin, D. (2015). Introduction: Governing Precarity. In *At the Heart of the State: The Moral Worlds of Institutions,* edited by D. Fassin, 1–10. London: Pluto Press.

Feldman, E. A., and Bayer, R. (1999). Introduction: Understanding the Blood Feuds. In *Blood feuds: AIDS, Blood, and the Politics of Medical Disaster,* edited by E. A. Feldman and R. Bayer, 1–16. Oxford: Oxford University Press.

Felstiner, W., and R. Dingwall (1988). *Asbestos Litigation in the U.K.* Oxford: Centre for Socio-Legal Studies.

Fenton, S., and Charsley, K. (2000). Epidemiology and Sociology as Incommensurate Games: Accounts from the Study of Health and Ethnicity. *Health,* 4(4), 403–425.

Fisher, J., M. Mostafanezhad, A. Nading, and S. M. Wiebe (2021). Introduction: Pollution and Toxicity: Cultivating Ecological Practices for Troubled Times. *Environment and Society,* 12(1), 1–4.

Floyd, H. H., and S. Kroll-Smith (1997). *Bodies in Protest.* New York: New York University Press.

Freedom of Information Act 2000 (UK). www.legislation.gov.uk/ukpga/2000/36/contents.

Ford, P. (2023). *Maralinga.* Australian Museum. https://australian.museum/learn/first-nations/unfinished-business/unfinished-business-maralinga.

Fortun, K. (2001). *Advocacy after Bhopal: Environmentalism, Disaster, New Global Orders.* Chicago: University of Chicago Press.

Frank, A. (1995). *The Wounded Storyteller: Body, Illness and Ethics.* Chicago: Chicago University Press.

Franklin, S. (2014). Rethinking Reproductive Politics in Time, and Time in UK Reproductive Politics: 1978–2008. *Journal of the Royal Anthropological Institute,* 20 (S1), 109–125.

Fukui, T. (2024). *Exposed Life Runs Free: Gender, Labor, and Speculation in TEPCO's Fukushima Nuclear Disaster.* Dissertation. Columbia University.

Galison, P. (1997). *Image and Logic: A Material Culture of Microphysics.* Chicago: University of Chicago Press.

Gammeltoft, T. (2008). Figures of Transversality: State Power and Prenatal Screening in Contemporary Vietnam. *American Ethnologist,* 35(4), 570–587.

Gardner, J. G., and N. L. Warren (2019). Learning from Deep Brain Stimulation: The Fallacy of Techno-Solutionism and the Need for 'Regimes of Care'. *Medicine, Health Care and Philosophy,* 22(3), 363–374.

Gilles, M., and R. G. E. Haylock (2022). Mortality and Cancer Incidence 1952–2017 in United Kingdom Participants in the United Kingdom's Atmospheric Nuclear Weapons Tests and Experimental Programmes. *Journal of Radiological Protection,* 42, 021507.

Gluckman, M. (1973 [1955]). *The Judicial Process among the Barotse of Northern Rhodesia.* Manchester: Manchester University Press.

Goldblatt, B., and Rai, S. M. (2018). Recognizing the Full Costs of Care? Compensation for Families in South Africa's Silicosis Class Action. *Social and Legal Studies,* 27(6), 671–694.

Goldstein, D. M, and M. E Stawkowski (2015). James V. Neel and Yuri E. Dubrova: Cold War Debates and the Genetic Effects of Low-Dose Radiation. *Journal of the History of Biology,* 48(1), 67–98.

Goodale, M. (2017). *Anthropology and Law: A Critical Introduction.* New York: New York University Press.

Grant, G., and C. Parker (2020). Lawyers' Responsibility for Claimant Health in Injury Compensation Schemes: Developing an Ethical Response. In *Unexpected Consequences of Compensation Law,* edited by P. Vines and A. Akkermans, 255–273. London: Bloomsbury Academic.

Gray, E., S. Farrall, and P. Mike Jones (2022). The Long Arm of Welfare Retrenchment: How New Right Socio-economic Policies in the 1980s Affected Contact with the Criminal Justice System in Adulthood. *The British Journal of Criminology,* 62(5), 1175–1195.

Gray, S. (2002). Paper given at the Nuclear Veterans Test Conference in Paris, 18th to 22nd of January 2002. www.bntva.com/aboutbntva/03_02/paris_conference_speech.htm.

Green, S. (2017). Fairchild and the Single Agent Criterion: Heneghan v Manchester Dry Docks Ltd & Ors. *Law Quarterly Review,* 133(3), 25–31.

Greenberg, J. (2020). Law, Politics, and Efficacy at the European Court of Human Rights. *American Ethnologist,* 47(4), 417–431.

Greene, G. (1999). *The Woman Who Knew Too Much: Alice Stewart and the Secrets of Radiation.* Ann Arbor: University of Michigan Press.

Greene, G. (2011). Richard Doll and Alice Stewart: Reputation and the Shaping of Scientific 'Truth'. *Perspectives in Biology and Medicine,* 54(4), 504–531.

Guerrero, M. (2020). *Strategic Litigation in EU Gender Equality Law. European Network of Legal Experts in Gender Equality and Non-discrimination.* Luxembourg: European Commission Directorate-General for Justice and Consumers.

Gun, R. T., J. Parsons, P. Crouch, P. Ryan, and J. E. Hiller (2008). Mortality and Cancer Incidence of Australian Participants in the British Nuclear Tests in Australia. *Occupational and Environmental Medicine,* 65(12), 843–848.

Günel, G., S. Varma, and C. Watanabe (2020). A Manifesto for Patchwork Ethnography. *Member Voices, Fieldsights,* June 9. https://culanth.org/fieldsights/a-manifesto-for-patchwork-ethnography.

Gupta, A. (2012). *Red Tape: Bureaucracy, Structural Violence and Poverty in India.* Durham: Duke University Press.

Gusterson, H. (1998). *Nuclear Rites: A Weapons Laboratory at the End of the Cold War.* Berkeley: University of California Press.

Gutmann, M., and K. Lutz (2010). *Breaking Ranks: Iraq Veterans Speak Out against the War.* Berkeley: University of California Press.

Guyer, J. I. (2004). *Marginal Gains: Monetary Transactions in Atlantic Africa.* Chicago: University of Chicago Press.

Hack, K. (2009). The Malayan Emergency as Counter-Insurgency Paradigm. *Journal of Strategic Studies,* 32(3), 383–414.

Hahn, F. F., B. A. Muggenburg, M. G. Ménache, R. A. Guilmette, and B. B. Boecker (1999). Comparative Stochastic Effects of Inhaled Alpha- and Beta-Particle-Emitting Radionuclides in Beagle Dogs. *Radiation Research,* 152(6 Suppl), S19–S22.

Hande, M. P., T. V. Azizova, C. R. Geard, et al. (2003). Past Exposure to Densely Ionizing Radiation Leaves a Unique Permanent Signature in the Genome. *American Journal of Human Genetics,* 72, 1162–1170.

Handsley, E. (1995). Mental Injury Occasioned by Harm to Another: A Feminist Critique. *Law and Inequality*, 14, 391–487.

Hansard (1970). HC Deb 10 February 1970 vol 795 c1175 (Mr Tim Fortesque). https://hansard.parliament.uk/Commons/1970-02-10/debates/f7e63a9d-540f-40c2-b8e5-551883833576/OrdersOfTheDay.

Hansard (1987). *Crown Proceedings (Armed Forces) Bill.* Volume 110. 13 February. https://hansard.parliament.uk/Commons/1987-02-13/debates/e1be2f63-8c03-4326-8f77-0c981b214f7e/CrownProceedings(ArmedForces)Bill.

Hansard (2003). *War Pensions Amendment Bill no. 2 Second Reading.* 4 March. www.parliament.nz/en/pb/hansard-debates/rhr/document/47HansD_20030304_00001242/war-pensions-amendment-bill-no-2-second-reading.

Harvey, P. (2020). Radiation as Social Relation. *Anthropology Today*, 36(6), 13–16.

Harvey, P., and V. R. Dominguez (2020). Intersections of Climate Change and Nuclear Power: An Interview with Penelope Harvey by Virginia R. Dominguez. *American Anthropologist*, 122(4), 953–958.

Hastrup, K. (2004). Getting It Right: Knowledge and Evidence in Anthropology. *Anthropological Theory*, 4(4), 455–472.

Hecht, G. (2012). *Being Nuclear: Africans and the Global Uranium Trade.* Cambridge, MA: MIT Press.

Hecht, G. (2013). Nuclear Janitors: Contract Workers at the Fukushima Reactors and beyond ニュークリア用務員　福島原発他においての 契約作業員. *Asia-Pacific Journal: Japan Focus*, 11(1 no.2), 1–13.

Hecht, G. (2014). Radioactive Excess: Modernization as Spectacle and Betrayal in Postcolonial Gabon. In *Modernization as Spectacle in Africa*, edited by P. J. Bloom, S. F. Miescher, and T. Manuh, 205–226. Bloomington: Indiana University Press.

Heimer, C. (2006). Conceiving Children: How Documents Support Case versus Biographical Analysis. In *Documents: Artifacts of Modern Knowledge*, edited by A. Riles, 95–171. Ann Arbour: University of Michigan Press.

Hennessy, P. (2002). *The Secret State: Whitehall and the Cold War.* London: Allen Lane.

Herremans, B., and T. Destrooper (2023). Moving beyond Formal Truth Practices and Forensic Truth in the Syrian Conflict: How Informal Truth Practices Contribute to Thicker Understandings of Truth. *Social and Legal Studies*, 32(4), 519–539.

Herzfeld, M. (1992). *The Social Production of Indifference: Exploring the Symbolic Roots of Western Bureaucracy.* Chicago: Chicago University Press.

Hikaka v Social Security Appeal Authority HC Wellington CIV-2007–485–330.

Hooper, C., K. Morrison, R. Manning, and E. Bohm (2023). *Literature Review on the Health Impacts of Exposure to Ionising Radiation.* Wellington: Allen + Clarke Consulting.

Horton, S. B. (2016). *They Leave Their Kidneys in the Fields: Illness, Injury, and Illegality among US Farmworkers.* Berkeley: University of California Press.

Horton, S. B. (2020). Paper Trails: Migrants, Bureaucratic Inscription, and Legal Recognition. In *Paper Trails: Migrants, Documents, and Legal Insecurity*, edited by S. B. Horton and J. Heyman, 1–26. Durham: Duke University Press.

House of Commons (UK). (2004). Public Accounts – Twentieth Report. www.publications.parliament.uk/pa/cm200304/cmselect/cmpubacc/551/55102.htm.

Howey, K. (2019). The Ranger Uranium Mine Agreement Revisited: Spacetimes of Indigenous Agreement-Making in Australia. *Transformations* 33, 96–115.

Hull, M. S. (2012a). *Government of Paper: The Materiality of Bureaucracy in Urban Pakistan.* Berkeley: University of California Press.

Hull, M. S. (2012b). Documents and Bureaucracy. *Annual Review of Anthropology,* 41, 251–267.

International Commission on Radiological Protection (ICRP) (2007). The 2007 Recommendations of the International Commission on Radiological Protection. Oxford: ICRP Publication, 103.

Ison, T. G. (1986). The Therapeutic Significance of Compensation Structures. *Canadian Bar Review,* 64, 605–637.

Jackson, M. (2002). *The politics of storytelling: Violence, transgression, and intersubjectivity.* Copenhagen: Museum Tusculanum Press.

Jackson, M. (2011). *Life within Limits: Well-Being in a World of Want.* Durham: Duke University Press.

Jacobs, R. (2013). Nuclear Conquistadors: Military Colonialism in Nuclear Test Site Selection during the Cold War. *Asian Journal of Peacebuilding,* 1(2), 157–177.

James, C. (2001). Aborigines Died in Test Site Bunker. *The Advertiser.* 10 July. http://web.archive.org/web/20050619225230/http://www.theadvertiser.news.com.au/common/story_page/0,5936,6407166%5E26839,00.html.

Jasanoff, S. (1992). What Judges Should Know about the Sociology of Science. *Jurimetrics,* 32(3), 345–359.

Jasanoff, S. (2012). *Science and Public Reason.* London: Taylor and Francis Group.

Jeffrey, C. (2008). Waiting. *Environment and Planning D: Society and Space,* 26, 954–958.

Jeutner, V. (2024). *The Reasonable Person: A Legal Biography.* Cambridge: Cambridge University Press.

Jobin, P. (2021a). Nuclear Labor, Its Invisibility, and the Dispute over Low-Dose Radiation. In *Legacies of Fukushima: 3.11 in Context,* edited by K. Cleveland, S. G. Knowles, and R. Shineha, 145–156. Philadelphia: University of Pennsylvania Press.

Jobin, P. (2021b). The Valuation of Contaminated Life: RCA in Taiwan and the Compensation of Toxic Exposure. [受污染的人命值多少: 台灣RCA案和毒物暴露的賠償] *East Asian Science, Technology and Society,* 17(4), 409–434.

Jobin, P., and Y.- H. Tseng (2014). Guinea Pigs Go to Court: Epidemiology and Class Actions in Taiwan. In *Powerless Science?: Science and Politics in a Toxic World,* edited by S. Boudia and N. Jas, 170–192. Oxford: Berghahn Books.

Johannesson, L. (2023). Silence and Voice in Oral Hearings: Spatial, Temporal, and Relational Conditions for Communication in Asylum and Compulsory Care Hearings. *Social and Legal Studies,* 32(3), 399–419.

Johnston, B. R., and H. M. Barker (2008). *Consequential Damages of Nuclear War: The Rongelap Report.* Walnut Creek: Left Coast Press.

Johnson, G. (2013). *Don't Ever Whisper: Darlene Keju, Pacific Health Pioneer, Champion for Nuclear Survivors.* Seattle: Createspace Independent Publishing Platform.

Johnston, P. N., P. A. Burns, S. B. Solomon, R. A. Tinker, and J. S. Lock (2010). Interpretation of Biological Dosimetry of New Zealand Sailors by Wahab et al. *Radiation Protection in Australasia,* 27(2), 4–11.

Jourdain, R. L. (2009). *'Psychological Fallout': The Effects of Nuclear Radiation Exposure.* Doctoral dissertation. Massey University.

Jung, M. (2024). A Scoping Review of Causal Associations between Occupation and Cancer Occurrence and Legal Burden of Proof. *Asian Pacific Journal of Cancer Prevention,* 25(6), 1875–1881.

Kalshoven, P. T. (2021). The Nuclear/Nuclear Family: Moralities of Intimacy under COVID-19. *Anthropology in Action,* 28(2), 44–50.

Kalshoven, P. T. (2022). The Fish in the Water and the Water in the Fish: Symbiosis in a Nuclear Whale Fall. *Cultural Anthropology,* 37, 349–378.

Kari, M. (2020). *First of Its Kind: Eurajoki as a Nuclear Community and Site for the Final Disposal of Spent Nuclear Fuel.* Doctoral dissertation. University of Jyväskylä, Finland.

Kendall, G. M., C. R. Muirhead, S. C. Darby, et al. (2004). Epidemiological Studies of UK Test Veterans: I. General Description. *Journal of Radiological Protection,* 24, 199–217.

Kendall-Tackett, K., and C. T. Beck (2022). Secondary Traumatic Stress and Moral Injury in Maternity Care Providers: A Narrative and Exploratory Review. *Frontiers in Global Women's Health,* 3, 835811.

Kilshaw, S. (2009). *Impotent Warriors: Gulf War Syndrome, Vulnerability and Masculinity.* Oxford: Berghahn Books.

Kim, J. (2013). Depression as a Psychosocial Consequence of Occupational Injury in the US Working Population: Findings from the Medical Expenditure Panel Survey. *BMC Public Health,* 13, 1–10.

Kimura, A. H. (2016). *Radiation Brain Moms and Citizen Scientists: The Gender Politics of Food Contamination after Fukushima.* Durham: Duke University Press.

King, T. J., J. D. Shaw, and L. Kennedy (2024). Documenting the Document: The Forensic Hospital Report and Its Knowledge Moves. *Social and Legal Studies,* 33(3), 309–327.

Kingfisher, C., and M. Goldsmith (2001). Reforming Women in the United States and Aotearoa/New Zealand: A Comparative Ethnography of Welfare Reform in Global Context. *American Anthropologist,* 103, 714–732.

Kinsella, W. J. (2001). Nuclear Boundaries: Material and Discursive Containment at the Hanford Nuclear Reservation. *Science as Culture,* 10(2), 163–194.

Kinsella, W. J. (2020). Extracting Uranium's Futures: Nuclear Wastes, Toxic Temporalities, and Uncertain Decisions. *Extractive Industries and Society,* 7, 524–534.

Kirsh, B., and P. McKee (2003). The Needs and Experiences of Injured Workers: A Participatory Research Study. *Work,* 21(3), 221–31.

Kleinman, A. (1988). *The Illness Narratives. Suffering, Healing and the Human Condition.* New York: Basic Books.

Kowal, E. (2015). Time, Indigeneity and White Anti-Racism in Australia. *The Australian Journal of Anthropology,* 6(1), 94–111.

Kowal, E. (2023). *Haunting Biology: Science and Indigeneity in Australia.* Durham: Duke University Press.

Krieger N. (2000). Epidemiology and Social Sciences: Towards a Critical Reengagement in the 21st Century. *Epidemiologic Reviews,* 22(1), 155–163.

Kuchinskaya, O. (2014). *The Politics of Invisibility: Public Knowledge about Radiation Health Effects after Chernobyl.* Cambridge, MA: MIT Press.

Kumaki, H. (2020). *Reasonably Exposed: Politics and Ethics of Living Fukushima.* Doctoral dissertation. University of Chicago.

Kumaki, H. (2022). Suspending Nuclearity: Ecologics of Planting Seeds after the Nuclear Fallout in Fukushima, Japan. *Cultural Anthropology*, 37(4), 707–737.

Laidlaw, J. (2023). Introduction. In *The Cambridge Handbook for the Anthropology of Ethics*, edited by J. Laidlaw, 1–32. Cambridge: Cambridge University Press.

Lange, D. (1985). *Are nuclear weapons morally indefensible?* Sound Archives/Nga Taonga Korero (File: Media Number 27995).

Latour, B. (2004). Scientific Objects and Legal Objectivity. In *Law, Anthropology, and the Constitution of the Social: Making Persons and Things*, edited by A. Pottage and M. Mundy, 73–114, Cambridge: Cambridge University Press.

Laucht, C. (2012). *Elemental Germans: Klaus Fuchs, Rudolf Peierls, and the Making of British Nuclear Culture, 1939–1959.* Basingstoke: Springer.

Laucht, C. (2016). Scientist, the Public, the State, and the Debate over the Environmental and Human Health Effects of Nuclear Testing in Britain, 1950–1958. *The Historical Journal*, 59(1), 221–251.

Law Commission (2008). *Towards a New Veterans' Entitlement Scheme: A Discussion Paper on the Review of the War Pensions Act 1954.* Wellington: Law Commission.

Law Commission (2010). *A New Support Scheme for Veterans: A Report on the Review of the War Pensions Act 1954.* Wellington: Law Commission.

Leung, H. H. S. (2009). *Undercurrents: Queer Culture and Postcolonial Hong Kong.* Vancouver: UBC Press.

Liboiron, M. (2021). *Pollution Is Colonialism.* Durham: Duke University Press.

Limitation Act 1980 (UK). www.legislation.gov.uk/ukpga/1980/58.

Lippel, K. (2007). Workers Describe the Effect of the Workers' Compensation Process on Their Health: A Quebec Study. *International Journal of Law and Psychiatry*, 30(4–5), 427–443.

Litz, B. T., N. Stein, E. Delaney, et al. (2009). Moral Injury and Moral Repair in War Veterans: A Preliminary Model and Intervention Strategy. *Clinical Psychology Review*, 29(8), 695–706.

Loher, D. (2020). Everyday Suffering and the Abstract Time-Reckoning of Law: Reflections on the Allocation of Responsibility for an Asbestos Disaster in Italy. *Journal of Legal Anthropology*, 4(2), 17–38.

Lowenkron, L., and Ferreira, L. (2014). Anthropological Perspectives on Documents: Ethnographic Dialogues on the Trail of Police Papers. *Vibrant: Virtual Brazilian Anthropology*, 11(2), 76–112.

Lunt, N. (2008). From Welfare State to Social Development: Winning the War of Words in New *Zealand. Social Policy and Society*, 7(4), 405–418.

Lutz, C. (2002). *Homefront: A Military City and the American Twentieth Century.* Boston: Beacon Press.

MacDonald, C. (1997). *Mortality and Health Effects in Participants of Atmospheric Nuclear Weapons Test: A Critical Review.* www.veteransaffairs.mil.nz/assets/Research/701c196a28/Critical-review-of-health-effects-in-participants-of-nuclear-weapon-tests.pdf.

MacEachen, E., Kosny, A., Ferrier, S., and Chambers, L. (2010). The 'Toxic Dose' of System Problems: Why Some Injured Workers Don't Return to Work as Expected. *Journal of Occupational Rehabilitation*, 20, 349–366.

MacLachlan, L. (2024). 'Circling the Drain': The Emotional 'Dirty' Work of Legal Aid Workers. *Social and Legal Studies*, 34(6), 918–940

MacLeish, K. (2018). On 'Moral Injury': Psychic Fringes and War Violence. *History of the Human Sciences*, 31(2), 128–146.

MacLeish, K. (2020). Damaged and Deserving: On Care in a Veteran Treatment Court. *Medical Anthropology*, 39(3), 239–254.

MacLeish, K. (2022). Moral Injury and the Psyche of Counterinsurgency. *Theory, Culture and Society*, 39(6), 63–86.

Maclellan, N. (2017). *Grappling with the Bomb: Britain's Pacific H-bomb Tests.* Canberra: ANU Press.

Maillochon, C. (2024). Customary Paths toward Denuclearization and Decolonization: Mā'ohi and Kanak Activists Passing through lo Larzac. *The Journal of Pacific History*, 59(1), 83–105.

Malone, W. S. (1956). Ruminations on Cause-in-Fact. *Stanford Law Review*, 9(1), 60–99.

Manderson, L., and C. Smith-Morris (2010). *Chronic Conditions, Fluid States. Chronicity and the Anthropology of Illness.* New Brunswick: Rutgers University Press.

Martin, N. (2007) Wounded Soldiers Betrayed by Delays. *The Telegraph.* 19 March. www.telegraph.co.uk/news/uknews/1545999/Wounded-soldiers-betrayed-by-delays.html.

Martin, P., L. Scullion, D. Young, et al. (2024). How Do Those Who Have Served Deserve to Be Treated? Military Veterans in the U.K. Social Security System. *Armed Forces & Society*, 0(0), 1–22.

Masco, J. (2004). Nuclear Technoaesthetics: Sensory Politics from Trinity to the Virtual Bomb in Los Alamos. *American Ethnologist*, 31, 349–373.

Masco, J. (2006). *The Nuclear Borderlands: The Manhattan Project in Post-Cold War New Mexico.* Princeton: Princeton University Press.

Masco, J. (2020). *The Future of Fallout, and Other Episodes in Radioactive World-Making.* Durham: Duke University Press.

Mason, K. A. (2021). Epidemiologizing Culture: Scaling Chineseness Through Narratives of Stigma in New York City. *Medical Anthropology Quarterly*, 35(1), 43–63.

Mather, L. (2009). Lawyers and Solicitors Separated by a Common Legal System: Anti-Tobacco Litigation in the United States and Britain. In *Fault Lines: Tort Law as Cultural Practice*, edited by D. M. Engel and M. McCann, 192–210. Stanford: Stanford University Press.

Mathis, E. (2024). Maralinga: 'Field of thunder' Australian Geographic. 3 April. www.australiangeographic.com.au/topics/history-culture/2024/04/maralinga-field-of-thunder/.

Mathur, N. (2014). The Reign of Terror of the Big Cat: Bureaucracy and the Mediation of Social Times in the Indian Himalaya. *Journal of the Royal Anthropological Institute*, 20(S1), 148–165.

Mathur, N. (2016). *Paper Tiger: Law, Bureaucracy, and the Developmental State in Himalayan India.* Cambridge: Cambridge University Press.

Mattingly, C. (1998). *Healing Dramas and Clinical Plots: The Narrative Structure of Experience.* Cambridge: Cambridge University Press.

Mattingley, C. (2016). *Maralinga's Long Shadow: Yvonne's Story*. Sydney: Allen and Unwin.

Mattingly, C. (2000). Emergent Narratives. In *Narrative and the Cultural Construction of Illness and Healing*, edited by C. Mattingly and L. C. Garro, 181–211. Berkeley: University of California Press.

Mattingly, C. (2014). *Moral Laboratories: Family Peril and the Struggle for a Good Life*. Berkeley: University of California Press.

McAlinden, A.-M. (2022a). From Shame to Guilt: Negotiating Moral and Legal Responsibility within Apologies for Historical Institutional Abuse. *Journal of Law and Society*, 49(3), 470–494.

McAlinden, A.-M. (2022b). Reconceptualising 'Risk': Towards a Humanistic Paradigm of Sexual Offending. *Social and Legal Studies*, 31(3), 389–408.

McCann, M., D. M. Engel, and A. Bloom (2018). Introduction. In *Injury and Injustice: The Cultural Politics of Harm and Redress*, edited by A. Bloom, D. M. Engel, and M. McCann, 1–24. Cambridge: Cambridge University Press.

McEwan, A. (2004). *Nuclear New Zealand: Sorting Fact from Fiction*. Christchurch: Hazard Press.

McGinley v United Kingdom [1998] EHCR 51. 794/995–996.

McIntyre, W. (2012). The Partition of the Gilbert and Ellice Islands. *Island Studies Journal*, 7(1), 135–146.

McKearney, P. (2018). The Weight of Living: Autonomy, Care, and Responsibility for the Self. *Journal of Disability and Religion*, 22(3), 266–282.

McLeod, D., D. Cormack, and T. Kake (2001) *The Health Needs of the Children of Operation Grapple and Vietnam Veterans*. General Practice Department Report No. 4. Wellington: Otago University. www.veteransaffairs.mil.nz/assets/Research/4e756b16f1/Critical-Appraisal-of-research-on-OP-Grapple-and-Vietnam-veterans-children.pdf.

McNeilly, K. (2018). Are Rights Out of Time? International Human Rights Law, Temporality, and Radical Social Change. *Social and Legal Studies*, 28(6), 817–838.

Merleau-Ponty, M. (2012[1945]). *Phenomenology of Perception*. Translated by D. Landes. London: Routledge.

Merry, S. E. (1990). *Getting Justice and Getting Even: Legal Consciousness among Working-Class Americans*. Chicago: University of Chicago Press.

Metzner, E. (2017). *Care beyond Justice: The Conflicted Ethics of Drug Treatment Courts*. Doctoral dissertation. University of Illinois at Urbana-Champaign.

Michel, D. (2003). Villains, Victims and Heroes: Contested Memory and the British Nuclear Tests in Australia. *Journal of Australian Studies*, 27(80), 221–228.

Miles and Green Associates (2011). *British Nuclear Test Veterans Health Needs Audit*. https://assets.publishing.service.gov.uk/media/5a798284ed915d0422069051/20111027NTVsMODHealthNeedsAuditFinal.pdf.

Ministerial Advisory Group on Veterans' Health (2010). *Ministerial Advisory Group on Veterans' Health to Hon Judith Collins, Minister of Veterans' Affairs*, 23 December. www.veteransaffairs.mil.nz/assets/Research/Ministerial-Advisory-Group-on-Veterans-Health-to-Minister-of-Veterans-Affairs.pdf.

Ministry of Defence v AB [2010] EWCA Civ 1405. TLQ/08/0023.

Ministry of Defence v AB [2012] UKSC 9. On appeal from [2010] EWCA Civ 1317.

Ministry of Defence (MoD) (2012). *UK Atmospheric Nuclear Weapons Tests Factsheet 5: UK Programme. Ministry of Defence.* The National Archives. Archived from the original (PDF) on 26 October 2012. https://webarchive.nationalarchives.gov.uk/ukgwa/20121026065214/http://www.mod.uk/NR/rdonlyres/D1BD228E-2E55-4254-8BB6-D083F50E7321/0/ntvfactsheet5.pdf.

Ministry of Defence (MoD) (2017). *Policy Statement on Claims for Ionising Radiation Related Conditions.* https://assets.publishing.service.gov.uk/media/5f44ecd28fa8f55de565f066/Policy_Statement_on_Claims_for_Ionising_Radiation_2017.pdf.

Mittermaier, A. (2012). Dreams from Elsewhere: Muslim Subjectivities beyond the Trope of Self-Cultivation. *Journal of the Royal Anthropological Institute*, 18(2), 247–265.

Mol, A. (2003). *The Body Multiple: Ontology in Medical Practice.* Durham: Duke University Press.

Moonie, L. (UK Under-Secretary of State for Defence) 2002 British House of Commons Parliamentary Debate: Nuclear Test Veterans (Compensation). *Hansard HC* Deb, 395 cc259-65WH. http://hansard.millbanksystems.com/westminster_hall/2002/dec/04/nuclear-test-veterans-compensation.

Moorehouse, A. J., M. Scholze, N. Sylvius, et al. (2022). No Evidence of Increased Mutations in the Germline of a Group of British Nuclear Test Veterans. *Scientific Reports*, 12, 10830.

Morgan, A., and Fortun, K. (2020). Toxic Soldiers, Flickering Knowledges, and Enlisted Care: Dispossession and Environmental Injustice. *Catalyst: Feminism, Theory, Technoscience*, 6(1), 1–26.

Morimoto, R. (2021). Home Otherwise: Living Archives and Half-Life Politics in Post-Fallout Coastal Fukushima. *Cultural Anthropology*, 36, 573–579.

Muirhead, C. R., D. Bingham, R. G. E. Haylock et al. (2003). *Mortality and Cancer Incidences 1952–1998 in UK Participants in the UK Atmospheric Nuclear Weapons Tests and Experimental Programmes.* Oxon: National Radiological Protection Board.

Nader, L. (2002). *The Life of the Law: Anthropological Projects.* Berkeley: University of California Press.

Natali, L. (2015). A Critical Gaze on Environmental Victimization. In *Green Harms and Crimes: Critical Criminology in a Changing World*, edited by R. A. Sollund, 63–78. London: Palgrave Macmillan.

National Archives of Australia (NAA). (n.d.) First British atomic bomb test on Montobello Islands – documentary. www.naa.gov.au/students-and-teachers/learning-resources/learning-resource-themes/war/defence-equipment-and-weapons/first-british-atomic-bomb-test-montobello-islands-documetnary.

Navaro-Yashin, Y. (2007). Make-Believe Papers, Legal Forms, and the Counterfeit: Affective Interactions between Documents and People in Britain and Cyprus. *Anthropological Theory*, 7(1), 79–96.

Neale, T., C. Addison, and T., Phan (eds.) (2022). Introduction. In *An Anthropogenic Table of Elements: Experiments in the Fundamental*, 1–21. Toronto: University of Toronto Press.

Nelson, D. M. (2015). *Who Counts? The Mathematics of Death and Life after Genocide.* Durham: Duke University Press.

Nettleton, S. (2006). 'I Just Want Permission to be Ill': Towards a Sociology of Medically Unexplained Symptoms. *Social Science and Medicine*, 62(5), 1167–1178.

New Zealand Cabinet (2001). *Cabinet Minute on Improved Services to Veterans* (CAB Min (01)12/9. www.veteransaffairs.mil.nz/assets/Research/2f1ec8df6a/Cabinet-minute-on-improvie-services-to-veterans.pdf.

New Zealand Defence Force (NZDF) (2017). *New Zealand Defence Doctrine (NZDDP- D)* (4th Ed). Wellington: New Zealand Government.

New Zealand Government (1998). *Peters Delivers on Promise to Nuclear Test Veterans.* Press Release. 31 March. www.beehive.govt.nz/release/peters-delivers-promise-nuclear-test-veterans.

Nietzsche, F. (1957). *The Use and Abuse of History*, translated by Adrian Collins. Indianapolis: Bobbs-Merrill.

Nixon R. (2011). *Slow Violence and the Environmentalism of the Poor.* Cambridge, MA: Harvard University Press.

Norrie, A. (2011). *Crime, Reason and History: A Critical Introduction to Criminal Law.* Cambridge: Cambridge University Press.

NRC–National Research Council, Division on Engineering, Physical Sciences, Commission on Engineering, Technical Systems, and Committee on Film Badge Dosimetry in Atmospheric Nuclear Tests. (1989). *Film Badge Dosimetry in Atmospheric Nuclear Tests.* National Academies Press.

Nuclear Free Zone, Disarmament, and Arms Control Act 1987 (NZ) www.legislation.govt.nz/act/public/1987/0086/latest/DLM115116.html.

O'Donnell, M. L., G. Grant, N. Alkemade, et al. (2015). Compensation Seeking and Disability after Injury: The Role of Compensation-Related Stress and Mental Health. *The Journal of Clinical Psychiatry*, 76(8), 3527.

Office of Veterans Affairs (2024). *Projects Funded by the Office for Veterans Affairs.* 17 July. www.gov.uk/government/publications/projects-funded-by-the-office-for-veterans-affairs/projects-funded-by-the-office-for-veterans-affairs.

Oliphant, K. (2024). Causal Uncertainty in Tort Law: The Special Case of Mesothelioma. In *Uncertainty in Comparative Law and Legal History: Known Unknowns*, edited by A. Bell and J. McCunn, 103–127. London: Routledge.

Orchard, C, N. Carnide, and P. H. Smith (2020). Does Perceived Fairness in the Workers' Compensation Claims Process Affect Mental Health Following a Workplace Injury? *Journal of Occupational Rehabilitation*, 30(1), 40–48.

Parsons, T. (2013[1951]). *The Social System.* London: Routledge.

Pearce, J., and S. Kingham (2008). Environmental Inequalities in New Zealand: A National Study of Air Pollution and Environmental Justice. *Geoforum*, 39(2), 980–993.

Pearce, N. (1997). *Letter to Gary Lewis, Secretary of War Pensions.* www.veteransaffairs.mil.nz/assets/Research/0f9f04969a/Neal-Pearce-response-to-critical-review.pdf.

Pearce, N., I. Prior, D. Methven, et al. (1990). *Mortality and Cancer Incidences in New Zealand Participants in United Kingdom Nuclear Weapons Tests in the Pacific.* Wellington: Wellington School of Medicine.

Pearce, N., R. Winkelmann, J. Kennedy, et al. (1997). Further Follow-up of New Zealand Participants in United Kingdom Atmospheric Nuclear Weapons Tests in the Pacific. *Cancer Causes and Control*, 8(2), 139–145.

Pearce v Secretary of State for Defence [1988] 2 WLR 1027.

Pennington, C. W., and J. A. Siegel (2019). The Linear No-Threshold Model of Low-Dose Radiogenic Cancer: A Failed Fiction. *Dose-Response: A Publication of International Hormesis Society*, 17(1), 1559325818824200.

Pensions Appeal Tribunal Act 1943 (UK). www.legislation.gov.uk/ukpga/Geo6/6-7/39/contents.

Petoukhov, K. (2023). 'They Just Let Us Rot to Death:' Anti-Colonialism, Contestation, and Resistance to Reparations for Indian Residential School Abuse. *Social and Legal Studies*, 32(5), 737–755.

Petryna, A. (2002). *Life Exposed: Biological Citizens after Chernobyl.* Princeton: Princeton University Press.

Petryna, A. (2012). Medicine. In *A Companion to Moral Anthropology*, edited by D. Fassin, 376–394. Hoboken: John Wiley and Sons.

Phillips, T. (2010). Debating the Legitimacy of a Contested Environmental Illness: A Case Study of Multiple Chemical Sensitivities (MCS). *Sociology of Health and Illness*, 32(7), 1026–1040.

Phillips, T. (2015). *Law, Environmental Illness and Medical Uncertainty: The Contested Governance of Health.* London: Routledge.

Phillips, T., and C. Trundle (2023). Contested Illness. In *Encyclopedia of Health Research in the Social Sciences*, edited by K. Dew and S. Donovan, 48–53. Cheltenham: Edward Elgar.

Pillayre, H. (2021). Compensation Funds, Trials and the Meaning of Claims: The Example of Asbestos-Related Illness Compensation in France. *Social and Legal Studies*, 30(2), 180–202.

Plumly, S. (2020). *Middle Distance.* New York: Norton.

Podd, J., J. Blakey, R. Jourdain, and R. Rowland (2005). *The New Zealand Nuclear Test Veteran Study – A Pilot Project (Psychological Impact)*. New Plymouth: Massey University. www.veteransaffairs.mil.nz/assets/Research/e164ed3941/NZ-Nuclear-Test-Veterans-Study-Psychological-Impact.pdf.

Polleri, M. (2020). Post-political Uncertainties: Governing Nuclear Controversies in Post-Fukushima Japan. *Social Studies of Science*, 50(4), 567–588.

Porter, T. M. (1992). Quantification and the Accounting Ideal in Science. *Social Studies of Science*, 22(4), 633–651.

Pottage, A. (2004). Introduction: The Fabrication of Persons and Things. In *Law, Anthropology, and the Constitution of the Social: Making Persons and Things*, edited by A. Pottage and M. Mundy, 1–39. Cambridge: Cambridge University Press.

Povinelli, E. (2011). *Economies of Abandonment: Social Belonging and Endurance in Late Liberalism.* Durham: Duke University Press.

Powaski, R. E. (1987). *March to Armageddon: The United States and the Nuclear Arms Race, 1939 to the Present.* Oxford: Oxford University Press.

Priestley, R. (2013). *Mad on Radium: New Zealand in the Atomic Age.* Auckland: Auckland University Press.

Pryor, E. S. (1990). Flawed Promises: A Critical Evaluation of the American Medical Association's 'Guides to the Evaluation of Permanent Impairment'. *Harvard Law Review*, 103(4), 964–976.

Quinlan, A. (2017). *The Technoscientific Witness of Rape: Contentious Histories of Law, Feminism, and Forensic Science.* Toronto: University of Toronto Press.

Raekstad, P., and S. S. Gradin (2020). *Prefigurative Politics: Building Tomorrow Today*. New York: Wiley & Sons.

Räikkä, J. (1998). Freedom and a Right (Not) to Know. *Bioethics*, 12(1), 49–63.

Rake, C., C. Gilha, M. Scholze, et al. (2022). British Nuclear Test Veteran Family Trios for the Study of Genetic Risk. *Journal of Radiological Protection*, 42, 021528.

Ralph, L. (2014). *Renegade Dreams: Living Through Injury in Gangland Chicago*. Chicago: Chicago University Press.

Reid, J., and L. Reynolds (1990). Requiem for RSI: the explanation and control of an occupational epidemic. *Medical Anthropology Quarterly*, 4(2), 162–190.

Reubi, D. (2020). Epidemiological Imaginaries of the Social: Epidemiologists and Pathologies of Modernization in Postcolonial Africa. *Medical Anthropology Quarterly*, 34(3), 438–455.

Reverby, S. M., and A. Moran-Thomas (2024). On the Appearance and Disappearance of Difficult Medical Histories: What Does It Take to Sustain Public Memory? *American Journal of Public Health*, 114(6), 564–568.

Richter, E., R. Laster, and C. Soskolne (2005). The Precautionary Principle, Epidemiology, and the Ethics of Delay. *Human and Ecological Risk Assessment*, 11, 17–27.

Ricoeur, P. (1992). *Oneself as Another*. Translated by K. Blamey. Chicago: The University of Chicago Press.

Riles, A. (2005). A New Agenda for the Cultural Study of Law: Taking on the Technicalities. *Buffalo Law Review*, 53, 973–1033.

Robbins, J. C. (2019). Expanding Personhood beyond Remembered Selves: The Sociality of Memory at an Alzheimer's Center in Poland. *Medical Anthropology Quarterly*, 33(4), 483–500.

Robbins-Rubszkowski, J. (2017). Responsibilities of the Third Age and the Intimate Politics of Sociality in Poland. In *Competing Responsibilities: The Ethics and Politics of Contemporary Life*, edited by S. Trnka and C. Trundle, 193–212. Durham: Duke University Press.

Roche v United Kingdom ([2005] ECHR 956, no. 32555/96.

Roff, S. R., P. Preece, R. McKenzie, and R. Sefton (2000). *Family History Protocol Study Report*. Dundee University Medical School. www.veteransaffairs.mil.nz/assets/Research/b4aa21a8b0/Family-History-Protocol-Study-Report.pdf.

Rusch, L., and F. Banner (2024). Homeless Group Representation in Detroit's Problem-Solving Court. *Law and Social Inquiry*, 49(1), 278–307.

Salmond, K. (1999). Setting Our Sights on Justice: Contaminated Sites and Socio-Economic Deprivation in New Zealand. *International Journal of Environmental Health Research*, 9(1), 19–29.

Sareen, J., J. Erickson, M. I. Medved, et al. (2013). Risk Factors for Post-injury Mental Health Problems. *Depression and Anxiety*, 30(4), 321–327.

Sawada, S. (2007). Cover-Up of the Effects of Internal Exposure by Residual Radiation from the Atomic Bombing of Hiroshima and Nagasaki. *Medicine, Conflict and Survival*, 23(1), 58–74.

Saxton, D. I. (2021). *The Devil's Fruit: Farmworkers, Health, and Environmental Justice*. New Jersey: Rutgers University Press.

Saxton, D. I., and A. Stuesse (2018). Workers' Decompensation: Engaged Research with Injured Im/migrant Workers. *Anthropology of Work Review*, 39(2), 65–78.

Schiller-Merkens, S. (2022). Social Transformation through Prefiguration? A Multi-Political Approach of Prefiguring Alternative Infrastructures. *Historical Social Research*, 47(4), 66–90.

Schuck, P. H. (1992). The Worst Should Go First: Deferral Registries in Asbestos Litigation. *Harvard Journal of Law & Public Policy*, 15(2), 541–594.

Schwelb, E. (1964). The Nuclear Test Ban Treaty and International Law. *American Journal of International Law*, 58(3), 642–670.

Scott, H. (2024). 'We Can't Help You – It Doesn't Concern Us': The Legal Consciousness of Young People Seeking Asylum in Sweden Who Report Violent Crime. *Journal of Law and Society*, 51, 36–56.

Scott, W. J. (1988). Competing Paradigms in the Assessment of Latent Disorders: The Case of Agent Orange. *Social Problems*, 35(2), 145–161.

Scott, W. J. (1992). PTSD and Agent Orange: Implications for a Sociology of Veterans' Issues. *Armed Forces & Society*, 18(4), 592–612.

Seale, C. (1995). Heroic Death. *Sociology*, 29(4), 597–613.

Secretary of State (2003). *Policy Statement on Claims for Ionizing Radiation Related Conditions.* https://assets.publishing.service.gov.uk/media/5f44ec7f8fa8f55de640f1ca/Policy_Statement_on_Claims_for_Ionising_Radiation_2003.pdf.

Shay, J. (2014). Moral Injury. *Psychoanalytic Psychology*, 31(2), 182.

Shore, C. (2008). Audit Culture and Illiberal Governance: Universities and the Politics of Accountability. *Anthropological Theory*, 8(3), 278–298.

Shostak, S. (2013). *Exposed Science: Genes, Environment, and the Politics of Population.* Berkeley: University of California Press.

Shriver, T. E. (2001). Environmental Hazards and Veterans' Framing of Gulf War Illness. *Sociological Inquiry*, 71(4), 403–420.

Shriver, T. E., and A. Bodenhamer (2018). The Enduring Legacy of Black Lung: Environmental Health and Contested Illness in Appalachia. *Sociology of Health and Illness*, 40(8), 1361–1375.

Shriver, T. E., and D. D. Waskul (2006). Managing the Uncertainties of Gulf War Illnesses. The Challenges of Living with Contested Illness. *Symbolic Interaction*, 29(4), 465–486.

Singleton, J., and P. L. Robertson (1997). Britain, Butter, and European Integration, 1957–1964. *The Economic History Review*, 50(2), 327–347.

Siwatibau, S., and B. D. Williams (1982). *A Call to a New Exodus: An Anti-Nuclear Primer for Pacific People.* Suva, Fiji: Pacific Council of Churches/Lotu Pasifika Productions.

Slynn, G. (2004). The Development of Human Rights in the United Kingdom. *Fordham International Law Journal*, 28(2), 477499.

Smart, S. (2024). Justice in Contention: The Dynamics of Legal Mobilisation in Caimanes' Environmental Struggle. *Social and Legal Studies*, 34(1), 43–66.

Social Security Act 1938 (NZ). www.nzlii.org/nz/legis/hist_act/ssa19382gv1938n7266/.

Stannard, J. N. (1973). Biomedical Aspects of Plutonium (Discovery, Development, Projections). In *Handbuch der Experimentellen Pharmakologie/Handbook of Experimental Pharmacology, vol 36*, edited by H. C. Hodge, J. B. Hursh, and J. N. Stannard, 309–320. Berlin, Heidelberg: Springer.

Stawkowski, M. E. (2016). 'I Am a Radioactive Mutant': Emergent Biological Subjectivities at Kazakhstan's Semipalatinsk Nuclear Test Site. *American Ethnologist*, 43(1), 144–157.

Steele, J., and N. Wikeley (1997). Dust on the Streets and Liability for Environmental Cancers. *The Modern Law Review*, 60(2), 265–276.

Stobbs, N. (2020). Therapeutic Jurisprudence in International and Comparative Perspective. *Oxford Research Encyclopedia of Criminology*. Oxford: Oxford University Press.

Stone, N. (2022). *Pinelandia: An Anthropology and Field Poetics of War and Empire*. Berkeley: University of California Press.

Strathern, M. (2000). Introduction: New Accountabilities. In *Audit Cultures: Anthropological Studies in Accountability, Ethics and the Academy*, edited by M. Strathern, 1–18. New York and London: Routledge.

Street, H. (1948). Crown Proceedings Act, 1947. *Modern Law Review*, 11, 129–142.

Struthers Montford, K. (2023). The Embodiment of Contempt: Ontario Provincial Prison Food. *Social and Legal Studies*, 32(2), 237–256.

Tanase, T. (2009). The Role of the Judiciary in Asbestos Injury: Compensation in Japan. In *Fault Lines: Tort Law as Cultural Practice*, edited by D. M. Engel and M. McCann, 233–248. Stanford: Stanford University Press.

Taubes, G., and C. C. Mann (1995). Epidemiology Faces Its Limits. *Science*, 269(5221), 164–169.

Taylor, I., and J. Kelly (2006). Professionals, Discretion and Public Sector Reform in the UK: Re-visiting Lipsky. *International Journal of Public Sector Management*, 19(7), 629–642.

Teaiwa, K. M. (2014). *Consuming Ocean Island: Stories of People and Phosphate from Banaba*. Bloomington: Indiana University Press.

Tito, T. (2023). *Joint Statement on Behalf of Kiribati and Kazakhstan 2023 NPT Preparatory Committee General Debate Delivered by H.E. Ambassador Teburoro Tito*. 31 July. https://docs-library.unoda.org/Treaty_on_the_Non-Proliferation_of_Nuclear_Weapons_-Preparatory_Committee_for_the_Eleventh_Review_ConferenceFirst_session_(2023)/Kiribati_and_Kazakhstan_Joint_Statement_General_Debate.pdf.

Trnka, S. (2017). *One Blue Child: Asthma, Responsibility and the Politics of Global Health*. Stanford: Stanford University Press.

Trundle, C. (2011). Biopolitical Endpoints: Diagnosing a Deserving British Nuclear Test Veteran. *Social Science & Medicine*, 73(6), 882–888.

Trundle, C. (2012). Military Citizenship: Emerging and Enduring Relationships between Soldiers and the State. PoLAR*: Political and Legal Anthropology Review*, 35, 358–366.

Trundle, C. (2013). Memorialising the Veteran Body: New Zealand Nuclear Test Veterans and the Search for Military Citizenship. In *War and the Body: Militarisation, Practice and Experience*, edited by K. McSorely, 194–209. London: Routledge.

Trundle, C. (2017). Genetic Bystanders: Familial Responsibility and the State's Accountability to Veterans of Nuclear Tests. In *Competing Responsibilities: The Ethics and Politics of Contemporary Life*, edited by S. Trnka and C. Trundle, 213–232. Durham: Duke University Press.

Trundle, C. (2020a). Translating Proof: Contested Illness, Radiation Exposure, and the Health Claims of Nuclear Test Veterans. In *Personhood in the Age of Biolegality: Brave New Law*, edited by M. de Leeuw and S. van Wichelen, 75–90. Cham: Palgrave Macmillan.

Trundle, C. (2020b). Tinkering Care, State Responsibility, and Abandonment: Nuclear Test Veterans and the Mismatched Temporalities of Justice in Claims for Health Care. *Anthropology and Humanism*, 45(2), 202–211.

Trundle, C. (2020c). Documentary Hinterlands. In *Flash Ethnography*, edited by C. McGranahan and N. Stone, *American Ethnologist* website, 26 October. https://americanethnologist.org/online-content/collections/flash-ethnography/documentary-hinterlands/.

Trundle, C., I. Singh, and C. Broer (2014). Fighting to be Heard: Contested Diagnoses. In *Social Issues in Diagnosis: An Introduction for Students and Clinicians*, edited by A. Jutel and K. Dew, 165–179. Baltimore: Johns Hopkins University Press.

Trundle, C., and T. Phillips (2023). Defining focused ethnography: Disciplinary boundary-work and the imagined divisions between 'focused' and 'traditional' ethnography in health research: A critical review. *Social Science and Medicine*, 116108.

Trundle, C., J. Gardner, and T. Phillips (2024). The Ethnographic Interview: An Interdisciplinary Guide for Developing an Ethnographic Disposition in Health Research. *Qualitative Health Research*. 10497323241241225.

Turner, E. (1997). There Are No Peripheries to Humanity: Northern Alaska Nuclear Dumping and the Iñupiat's Search for Redress. *Anthropology and Humanism*, 22, 95–109.

Tweedale, G. (2007). Hero or Villain? – Sir Richard Doll and Occupational Cancer. *International Journal of Occupational and Environmental Health*, 13(2), 233–235.

Tynan, E. (2016). *Atomic Thunder: The Maralinga Story*. Sydney: NewSouth.

Tynan, E. (2022). *The Secret of Emu Field: Britain's Forgotten Atomic Tests in Australia*. Sydney: NewSouth.

UK Government (2015). *Chancellor George Osborne's Budget 2015 Speech*. www.gov.uk/government/speeches/chancellor-george-osbornes-budget-2015-speech.

UK Government (2022). *Nuclear Weapons Test Participants Study: Information Sheet*. www.gov.uk/government/publications/nuclear-weapons-test-participants-study/nuclear-weapons-test-participants-study-information-sheet.

UK Parliament (2021). Written Questions, Answers, and Statement. Nuclear Weapons: Testing. Question for Ministry of Defence. Answer from Leo Docherty (Conservative) https://questions-statements.parliament.uk/written-questions/detail/2021-07-05/26987/.

Ureta, S., P. Flores, and L. Soneryd (2020). Victimization Devices: Exploring Challenges Facing Litigation-Based Transnational Environmental Justice. *Social and Legal Studies*, 29(2), 161–182.

Urwin, J. (2025). Contaminated Country: Nuclear Colonialism and Aboriginal Resistance in Australia. Seattle: University of Washington Press.

Uttley, S. (1994a). *An Enduring Obligation: A History of War Pensions*. Wellington: Victoria University Social Policy Department.

Uttley, S. (1994b). The Development of War Pensions Policy. *British Review of New Zealand Studies*, 7, 33–48.

Vanderlinden, L. K. (2011). Left in the Dust: Negotiating Environmental Illness in the Aftermath of 9/11. *Medical Anthropology*, 30(1), 30–55.

VANZ – Veterans' Affairs New Zealand. (2013). New Zealand Nuclear Test Veterans: A summary of expert reviews of three studies. www.veteransaffairs.mil.nz/assets/Research/00e7983c57/NZ-nuclear-tests-veterans-a-summary-of-expert-reviews-of-three-studies.pdf.

Veterans' Support Act 2014 (NZ) www.legislation.govt.nz/act/public/2014/0056/latest/whole.html.

Wahab, M. A., E. M. Nickless, R. Najar-M'Kacher, et al. (2008). Elevated Chromosome Translocation Frequencies in New Zealand Nuclear Test Veterans. *Cytogenetic and Genome Research*, 121(2), 79–87.

Walker, E. A. (2013). *'The Living Death': The Repatriation Experience of New Zealand's Disabled Great War Servicemen*. Dissertation, Te Herenga Waka-Victoria University of Wellington.

Wall, C. L., S. A. Morrissey, and J. R. Ogloff (2008). Personality Traits, Psychological Health, and the Workers' Compensation System. *The Australian Journal of Rehabilitation Counselling*, 14(2), 55–68.

Wardell, S. (2025). *Ethnography: The Basics*. London: Routledge.

War Pensions Act 1954 (UK). www.legislation.govt.nz/act/public/1954/0054/latest/DLM284375.html.

Weber, M. (2015 [1919]). Politics as a Vocation. In *Weber's Rationalism and Modern Society: New Translations on Politics, Bureaucracy, and Social Stratification*, edited by T. Waters and D. Waters, 129–198. New York: Palgrave Macmillan.

Weichselbraun, A. (2020). From Accountants to Detectives: How Nuclear Safeguards Inspectors Make Knowledge at the International Atomic Energy Agency. *PoLAR: Political and Legal Anthropology Review*, 43, 120–135.

Wellerstein, A. (2021). The Untold Story of the World's Biggest Nuclear Bomb. *The Bulletin of the Atomic Scientists*. https://thebulletin.org/2021/11/the-untold-story-of-the-worlds-biggest-nuclear-bomb/.

Welsh, L. (2023). Informality in Magistrates' Courts as a Barrier to Participation. *International Journal of Law, Crime and Justice*, 74, 100606.

Wemrell, M., J. Merlo, S. Mulinari, and A.-C. Hornborg (2016). Contemporary Epidemiology: A Review of Critical Discussions within the Discipline and a Call for Further Dialogue with Social Theory. *Sociology Compass*, 10(2), 153–171.

Werbner, P. (2014). 'The Duty to Act Fairly': Ethics, Legal Anthropology, and Labor Justicein the Manual Workers Union of Botswana. *Comparative Studies in Society and History*, 56(2), 479–507.

Wertsch, J. V. (2008). The Narrative Organization of Collective Memory. *Ethos*, 36(1), 120–135.

Wexler, D. B. (2008). Two Decades of Therapeutic Jurisprudence. *Touro Law Review*, 24, 17.

Wexler, D. B. (2020). The DNA of Therapeutic Jurisprudence. Arizona Legal Studies Discussion Paper No. 20–43, the Methodology and Practice of Therapeutic Jurisprudence. Carolina Academic Press. Edited by Nigel Stobbs, Lorana Bartels, and Michel Vols., https://ssrn.com/abstract=3731574.

Wexler, D. B., and B. J. Winick (2008). *Therapeutic Jurisprudence. Therapeutic Jurisprudence, in Principles of Addiction Medicine*, 4th Ed, https://ssrn.com/abstract=1101507.

Whiteside, N. (1996). Creating the Welfare State in Britain, 1945–1960. *Journal of Social Policy*, 25(1), 83–103.

Whitlock, J., E. Lloyd-Richardson, F. Fisseha, and T. Bates (2018). Parental Secondary Stress: The Often Hidden Consequences of Nonsuicidal Self-injury in Youth. *Journal of Clinical Psychology*, 74(1), 178–196.

Whittaker, A. (2022). Demodystopias: Narratives of Ultra-low Fertility in Asia. *Economy and Society*, 51(1), 116–137.

Wiebe, S. M. (2016). *Everyday Exposure: Indigenous Mobilization and Environmental Justice in Canada's Chemical Valley*. Victoria: University of British Columbia Press.

Williamson, V., D. Murphy, A. Phelps, D. Forbes, and N. Greenberg (2021). Moral Injury: The Effect on Mental Health and Implications for Treatment. *The Lancet Psychiatry*, 8(6), 453–455.

Wing, S. (1998). Whose Epidemiology, Whose Health? *International Journal of Health Services*, 28(2), 241–252.

Wing, S. (2000). Limits of Epidemiology. In *Illness and the Environment: A Reader in Contested Medicine*, edited by S. Kroll-Smith, P. Brown, and V. J. Gunter, 29–45. New York: New York University Press.

Wing, S., D. Richardson, and A. Stewart (1999). The Relevance of Occupational Epidemiology to Radiation Protection Standards. *New Solutions*, 9(2), 133–151.

Wool, Z. (2013a). War Sick: Meaningful Illness and Military Victimhood. *Focaal—Journal of Global and Historical Anthropology*, 66, 139–147.

Wool, Z. (2013b). *After War: The Weight of Life at Walter Reed*. Durham: Duke University Press.

Wool, Z. (2023). All That Is Solid Burns into Smoke: US Military Burn Pits, Petrochemical Toxicity, and the Racial Geopolitics of Displacement. *Catalyst: Feminism, Theory, Technoscience*, 9(1), 1–22.

Wright, G. C. (2007). *We Were There: Operation Grapple: The Story of New Zealand's Involvement in the British Nuclear Weapons Tests at Christmas Island 1957–58*. Auckland: Gerry Wright.

Yamaguchi, M., Y. Tatara, E. D. Nugraha, et al. (2022). Detection of Biological Responses to Low-Dose Radiation in Humans. *Free Radical Biology and Medicine*, 184, 196–207.

Yates-Doerr, E. (2012). The Opacity of Reduction: Nutritional Black-Boxing and the Meanings of Nourishment. *Food, Culture and Society*, 15(2), 293–313.

Yates-Doerr, E. (2020). Antihero Care: On Fieldwork and Anthropology. *Anthropology and Humanism*, 45(2), 233–244.

Young, K. (2007). A Most Special Relationship: The Origins of Anglo-American Nuclear Strike Planning. *Journal of Cold War Studies*, 9(2), 5–31.

Ziegler, C. A., and D. J. Chleck (1960). Latent-image Fading in Film Badge Dosimeters. *Health Physics*, 4(1), 32–34.

Zonabend, F. (1993[1989]). *The Nuclear Peninsula*. Translated by J. A. Underwood. Oxford: Oxford University Press.

Zussman, R. (1992). *Intensive Care: Medical Ethics and the Medical Profession*. Chicago: University of Chicago Press.

Zwart, H. (2007). Genomics and Self-knowledge: Implications for Societal Research and Debate. *New Genetics and Society*, 26(2), 181–202.

Index

Printed in the United Kingdom by TJ Clays Ltd.